Michael Bishop
and the Persistence
of Wonder

Recent Volumes in Critical Explorations
in Science Fiction and Fantasy
(a series edited by Donald E. Palumbo and C.W. Sullivan III)
**Earlier Works:** www.mcfarlandpub.com

52 *Michael Moorcock: Fiction, Fantasy and the World's Pain* (Mark Scroggins, 2016)

53 *The Last Midnight: Essays on Apocalyptic Narratives in Millennial Media* (ed. Leisa A. Clark, Amanda Firestone, Mary F. Pharr, 2016)

54 *The Science Fiction Mythmakers: Religion, Science and Philosophy in Wells, Clarke, Dick and Herbert* (Jennifer Simkins, 2016)

55 *Gender and the Quest in British Science Fiction Television: An Analysis of* Doctor Who, Blake's 7, Red Dwarf *and* Torchwood (Tom Powers, 2016)

56 *Saving the World Through Science Fiction: James Gunn, Writer, Teacher and Scholar* (Michael R. Page, 2017)

57 *Wells Meets Deleuze: The Scientific Romances Reconsidered* (Michael Starr, 2017)

58 *Science Fiction and Futurism: Their Terms and Ideas* (Ace G. Pilkington, 2017)

59 *Science Fiction in Classic Rock: Musical Explorations of Space, Technology and the Imagination, 1967–1982* (Robert McParland, 2017)

60 *Patricia A. McKillip and the Art of Fantasy World-Building* (Audrey Isabel Taylor, 2017)

61 *The Fabulous Journeys of Alice and Pinocchio: Exploring Their Parallel Worlds* (Laura Tosi with Peter Hunt, 2018)

62 *A* Dune *Companion: Characters, Places and Terms in Frank Herbert's Original Six Novels* (Donald E. Palumbo, 2018)

63 *Fantasy Literature and Christianity: A Study of the Mistborn, Coldfire, Fionavar Tapestry and Chronicles of Thomas Covenant Series* (Weronika Łaszkiewicz, 2018)

64 *The British Comic Invasion: Alan Moore, Warren Ellis, Grant Morrison and the Evolution of the American Style* (Jochen Ecke, 2019)

65 *The Archive Incarnate: The Embodiment and Transmission of Knowledge in Science Fiction* (Joseph Hurtgen, 2018)

66 *Women's Space: Essays on Female Characters in the 21st Century Science Fiction Western* (ed. Melanie A. Marotta, 2019)

67 *"Hailing frequencies open": Communication in* Star Trek: The Next Generation (Thomas D. Parham III, 2019)

68 *The Global Vampire: Essays on the Undead in Popular Culture Around the World* (ed. Cait Coker, 2019)

69 *Philip K. Dick: Essays of the Here and Now* (ed. David Sandner, 2019)

70 *Michael Bishop and the Persistence of Wonder: A Critical Study of the Writings* (Joe Sanders, 2020)

71 *Caitlín R. Kiernan: A Critical Study of Her Dark Fiction* (James Goho, 2020)

72 *In* Frankenstein's *Wake: Mary Shelley, Morality and Science Fiction* (Alison Bedford, 2020)

73 *The Fortean Influence on Science Fiction: Charles Fort and the Evolution of the Genre* (Tanner F. Boyle, 2020)

74 *Arab and Muslim Science Fiction* (Hosan Elzembely and Emad El-Din Aysha, 2020)

# Michael Bishop and the Persistence of Wonder

## A Critical Study of the Writings

### JOE SANDERS

*Foreword by* Paul Di Filippo

CRITICAL EXPLORATIONS IN SCIENCE
FICTION AND FANTASY, 70
*Series Editors* Donald E. Palumbo *and* C.W. Sullivan III

McFarland & Company, Inc., Publishers
*Jefferson, North Carolina*

**Also of Interest**

*The Heritage of Heinlein: A Critical Reading of the Fiction,*
Thomas D. Clareson *and* Joe Sanders (McFarland, 2014)

Library of Congress Cataloguing-in-Publication Data

Names: Sanders, Joseph L., author. |
Di Filippo, Paul, 1954– writer of foreword.
Title: Michael Bishop and the persistence of wonder : a critical
study of the writings / Joe Sanders ; foreword by Paul Di Filippo.
Description: Jefferson, North Carolina :
McFarland & Company, Inc., Publishers, 2021 |
Series: Critical explorations in science fiction and fantasy ; 70 |
Includes bibliographical references and index.
Identifiers: LCCN 2020041465 |
ISBN 9781476671512 (paperback : acid free paper) ∞
ISBN 9781476640570 (ebook)
Subjects: LCSH: Bishop, Michael, 1945– —Criticism and interpretation.
Classification: LCC PS3552.I772 Z87 2020 | DDC 813/.54—dc23
LC record available at https://lccn.loc.gov/2020041465

British Library cataloguing data are available
**ISBN (print) 978-1-4766-7151-2
ISBN (ebook) 978-1-4766-4057-0**

© 2021 Joe Sanders. All rights reserved

*No part of this book may be reproduced or transmitted in any form
or by any means, electronic or mechanical, including photocopying
or recording, or by any information storage and retrieval system,
without permission in writing from the publisher.*

Front cover image © 2021 Aranami/Shutterstock

Printed in the United States of America

*McFarland & Company, Inc., Publishers
Box 611, Jefferson, North Carolina 28640
www.mcfarlandpub.com*

To the Next Generation of the Sanders Family
Eleanor and Kaia
Andrew and Evan
Trevor, Cameron, and Sydney
And to the Memory of Elijah

# Table of Contents

*Foreword: The No-Showboatin' Sage of Pine Mountain, Gee-Ay*
   (PAUL DI FILIPPO)     1

*Preface*     5

**Part I—Exploring Strange Worlds**     9

1. The Perilous Discovery of Empathy: Short Fiction, 1970–1980     11
2. Outside/In & Inside/Out: Novels, 1975–1980     34

**Part II—Discovering Stranger Worlds Next Door**     71

3. Surreal Estates: Short Fiction, 1981–1994     72
4. Family Reunions: Novels, 1982–1994     87

**Part III—Settling In**     151

5. Later Fiction: Darkness, Wonder and Grace     152

*Other Works*     181
*A Final Q & A*     183
*Works Cited*     187
*Index*     191

# Foreword
## *The No-Showboatin' Sage of Pine Mountain, Gee-Ay*

### Paul Di Filippo

How does one date precisely the start of a long friendship?

Perhaps the moment when the seeds of my camaraderie with Michael Bishop were first sown occurred in the autumn of 1970. Sixteen years old, I had a subscription to *Galaxy* magazine, and when the October–November issue arrived, I was gobsmacked by a story titled "Piñon Fall" from an author I had never encountered, one Michael Bishop. I can still see in my mind's eye the haunting Jack Gaughan illustration that accompanied the tale, Bishop's professional debut. (I will not try to elucidate the virtues of this freshman effort, for Joe Sanders outdoes any efforts of mine along these lines in the comprehensive, informative and keenly perceptive study that you hold in your hands. But more on Sanders' accomplishments later.)

Hooked by that seminal reading experience, I eagerly devoured all subsequent work by Bishop, especially a series of brilliant tales in *The Magazine of Fantasy and Science Fiction*, the other digest magazine to which I subscribed. His writings earned him a place in my personal pantheon. But still our relationship remained one only of distant author and worshipful silent reader.

That changed when I discovered organized SF fandom in 1973. By 1974, I was contributing pieces to the fanzine *Mythologies*, the creation of writer and critic Don D'Ammassa. Don, a fine friend dating from that far-off year and to the present day, was also enamored of Bishop's work and sent him copies of the zine. Soon, Bishop was appearing in those pages, and I began to enjoy the kind of fannish give-and-take with one of my heroes for which the whole famously familial field is known.

*Mythologies* ceased publication in 1986. Somewhere in that

interval, Mike—I could call him "Mike" now—and I had established a good old-fashioned one-on-one epistolary correspondence (morphing to email contact when the Internet bloomed). And so when I did my own short-lived fanzine *Astral Avenue*, circa 1986, Mike was a generous correspondent.

But when did we first meet in the flesh? At some convention or other? At a book signing held also around 1986, at the Willimantic, Connecticut, premises of bookseller Mark Ziesing? I can no longer say with certainty, as neurons die off by the hundreds.

In any case, wherever the much-anticipated encounter occurred, I found a gentle fellow who fully lived up to the merits of his fiction—not a commonplace happening. Forever youthful, energetic, worldly yet homespun, self-abnegating yet forceful in his presentation, funny, sympathetic, quick-witted, warm-hearted, the man was as far-removed from any clichéd portrait of nerdy, oblivious sci-fi guy as possible. Our too-infrequent meatspace meetings in subsequent years would always be occasions of pure joy, including longer-than-usual hangout times whenever Mike attended my local convention, Readercon, bringing with him, of course, the indispensable and likewise charming Jeri Bishop.

Over these years I got to know also Mike's children, Jamie and Stephanie, and eventually even his grandkids. Shortly after the stunningly senseless murder of Jamie in 2007, my partner Deborah and I attended Jamie's memorial service in Pine Mountain, and we learned the truly infinite depths of Mike and Jeri's character and spirit, a nobility surfaced by this horror.

And throughout these years, we of course talked about our mutual trade—for I had begun to sell my own fiction in the eighties. Perhaps my frequent reviews of Mike's books also furthered our discourse. So when Michael found himself marooned in a creative Horse Latitudes after the success of his novel *Brittle Innings*, I felt at ease in suggesting that we work on a project together, to shake the shared dust off our boots. And so were born our two Will Keats mystery novels, the first published in 1998. And have I mentioned that whenever I needed a rural birthplace for one of my characters, I'd assign Pine Mountain as their origin spot, as an Easter egg reference to Mike's longstanding role in my life?

And here we are some twenty years after our big collaboration, after much additional personal and professional waters have flowed over some big dams, bruised, annealed, wiser, sadder, richer not in money but in the things that count. If I can indeed choose the year 1970 as the start of our relationship, one-sided as it was at the outset, then Michael Bishop and I are approaching fifty years of comradeship.

A few weeks ago I just hung up the phone from one of my regular conversations with the man, wherein we talk of things mundane and cosmic. I did not then tell him that my review of his latest publication, *The City and the Cygnets*, would soon appear online. I wanted the publication of the essay to be a pleasant surprise, because—well, just because that's what pals do, try to lay down little landmines of happiness in each other's path.

Mike's writings have certainly sent up innumerable joy explosions in my life and in the lives of thousands of other readers. Which brings me to *Michael Bishop and the Persistence of Wonder: A Critical Study of the Writings*, Joe Sanders' book-length critical survey of the Bishop canon.

I have not been so impressed by a career retrospective of this type in a long time. Sanders' knowledge of the Bishop oeuvre is extensive and deep. His organization of the material is pellucid and conducive to understanding and enjoyment. There is nothing of the fusty academician about this text, but neither is there any fanboy lack of discernment or standards. Sanders walks the perfect center of the road between theory and practicality. He is a lover of fiction first and a discerning critic second. Besides his knowledge of Bishop's works, he also draws on a capacious familiarity with other genre and naturalistic landmarks. This comes out most vividly in Sanders' long passionate discussion of *Brittle Innings*, which he forthrightly labels "Bishop's very best book." (Sanders is confident in his estimations of the fiction, knows precisely what he thinks, but he is not overbearing in his opinions, always open to other judgments and perspectives.) The role that Somerset Maugham's *Of Human Bondage* plays in *Brittle Innings* is masterfully illuminated. This section alone would make the purchase of this book a bargain, but there's so much more, from analyses of many short stories and other novels to a look at Bishop's poetry.

In 2003, I managed, with the help of my editor, Richard Bleiler, to smuggle an essay on Mike's work into a volume titled *Supernatural Fiction Writers* (Thomson Gale, second edition). Not the most intuitively appropriate place for a Bishopian disquisition, since Mike is hardly Stephen King or M.R. James. But Bleiler and I were eager to accord Mike some time in our spotlight, and so with a little judicious picking and choosing and hedging, I shoehorned Mike and his work into this category. I opened my essay thus:

> Michael Bishop has revealed a questing spiritual intelligence uniquely concerned with moral conundrums. While his works are often full of both the widescreen spectacles associated with science fiction and the subtle frissons typical of more earthbound fantasy, his focus remains on the engagement of characters with ethical quandries any reader might encounter in his or her daily life. Whether to succor

a dying relative at some personal expense; how to earn an honest living while being true to one's muse; how best to establish essential communication among strangers forced to rely on each other for survival: these issues and others equally vital form the core of Bishop's concerns. And his prescription for success most often involves not derring-do or superhuman efforts, but simply the maintenance of an honest, open heart and a charitable, brave soul. While only occasionally delving into explicitly religious themes, Bishop's personal Christian faith—wide enough to embrace references to Buddhism, Sufism and other creeds—shines through in every tale.

Joe Sanders takes this ball and runs it a hundred yards for a touchdown.

I concluded in 2003 with this statement, and will conclude likewise today, for it remains as true now as then (if you perhaps substitute "fiction" for "fantasies").

> In *Brittle Innings*, a dead ballplayer who has expired while giving his all in a game is eulogized thusly: "He wasn't no showboat. He had this easy stillness that spoke straight through everybody else's jive and moonshine." Such a capsule description applies admirably to both Michael Bishop the writer and his quietly magnificent fantasies.

---

*Paul Di Filippo is a writer of quirky short stories and novels that force readers to reexamine their certainties by new takes on familiar themes and genres. (What if, for example, Joseph Campbell, rather than John W. Campbell, had been editor of* Astounding Science Fiction...*). His short fiction has been collected in several volumes, including* The Steampunk Trilogy, *which William Gibson called "spooky, haunting, and hilarious."*

# Preface

I've been writing about Michael Bishop's fiction since the 1990s, struck by its subtlety and power. It's been puzzling, however, to see how reader awareness of Bishop has faded in recent years although his stories remain painfully relevant. Perhaps that's the problem. Bishop is a wonderful storyteller, but he asks a lot of his readers. In an essay about *Gulliver's Travels*, he describes how Swift "tickled, stretched, amused, and disquieted" readers. That's even more true of Michael Bishop, who quietly but persistently demands sympathy for the unsympathetic, tolerance for the intolerable. He does so movingly and memorably. He deserves careful reading and sympathetic discussion.

That's what this book hopes to encourage.

Usually, a critical study of an author can proceed chronologically. *The Heritage of Heinlein*, for example, my collaboration with Thomas D. Clareson that McFarland published in 2014, began by looking at an unpublished prentice-work novel by Heinlein, then examined each piece of his published fantastic fiction or sf-related writing in the order of publication. That won't work with Bishop. For instance, the short pieces that were turned into the fix-up novel *Catacomb Years* (1979) somehow add up to a *prequel* to the novel *A Little Knowledge* that had been published a year earlier. And then there's "Dogs' Lives," placed in *The Door Gunner and Other Perilous Flights of Fancy: A Michael Bishop Retrospective*, edited by Michael H. Hutchins (2011) according to its first publication in 1984 but actually written in the mid–1970s and accepted by Harlan Ellison for "The Last Dangerous Visions" but then withdrawn from that doomed project and examined here in its revised form. So "chronological order" does not always dictate the order of discussion; commentary on individual pieces should clarify what's going on.

Another complication is that, since Heinlein maintained (somewhat disingenuously) that he was just an average-guy writer who didn't believe in revising what he'd written, the chronological approach made sense in tracing his development. It's not quite that simple with Michael

Bishop, whose concerns remain consistent but whose actual *writing* is always subject to revision as a result of suggestions or of Bishop's own realization that there might be a different and better way to tell a story. Lewis Shiner, for example, describes how his disappointed reaction to a story Bishop had submitted to a proposed anthology led Bishop to respond by writing a much longer, stronger version: "I'm proud of Mike for not giving up on it. For doing the work the story demanded of him, without regard to the time and pain it cost him, without concern for the rewards it might—or might not—bring. If there's another way to write to the best of your ability, I don't know what it is." Bishop himself modestly reports his willingness to revise by "tightening and clarifying" his prose. This laudable devotion to the craft of writing results in readers frequently having a choice of different versions of one story. It obviously would be worthwhile to compare early and later versions in order to see how Bishop evolved as a writer, but that seems less important than examining the content of his successful works. It also seems churlish to spend much time on work that no longer fully satisfies its creator. Therefore, this study uneasily compromises by discussing Bishop's writing by using the latest, preferred versions of selected short fiction from *The Door Gunner*, a collection that contains Bishop's own selection of his best work, in their (currently) final form. Other pieces were found in the collections *Blooded on Arachne* (1982), *Blue Kansas Sky* (2000), *Other Arms Reach Out to Me* (2017), and *The Sacerdotal Owl* (2018). Even here, inconsistencies are unavoidable. Revised, shorter versions of two books were published in a one-volume edition as *The City and the Cygnets* in 2019, too late for consideration in this study. Scheduling also prevented consideration of Bishop's thorough, much-tightened revision of *Unicorn Mountain*, published in mid–2020.

Bishop's revision process will be discussed in relation to how the novel that was published as *A Funeral for the Eyes of Fire* (1975) was then massively reconceived as *Eyes of Fire* (1980). I also will consider briefly how Bishop's second novel *And Strange at Ecbatan the Trees* shrank to become simply one of the "longer tales" in *The Sacerdotal Owl*.

I've tried to offer a careful, close reading of what each text is saying. This is not a book about a writer but about his writing. Except for such outside intrusions into the texts as the Vietnam War—or personal crises such as the murder of Bishop's son Jamie—I've tried to concentrate on the world created by the piece of fiction.

Selection of *which* stories to examine was simplified by Bishop's own choice in *The Door Gunner*, with a few additional pieces as needed—stories that were too long to include in that omnibus collection or that were published after the book appeared.

Finally, I'm reluctant to overemphasize continuing themes in a writer's work, fearful of making each new item fit a preconceived pattern. Except possibly for this book's title, I've tried not to stress the religious faith that pervades Bishop's fiction. He is a devoutly religious man, a sincere Christian. Recognizing this, readers may wonder how much his faith influences his fiction. Some pieces, such as "Miriam," seem to explore the nature of faith. Others, such as *Count Geiger*, feature characters who look suspiciously like Christ figures. But Bishop does not ostentatiously display his Christianity by straining to make his work Inspirational by showing how Good characters succeed and Bad characters fail. He takes human beings as the God-forsaken messes we are, sometimes striving forward but frequently stumbling, uncertain of which way *is* forward. As with Tolstoy's "The Death of Ivan Illych," Bishop believes in examining each person, each situation, as honestly as he can, confident that respect for truth is the best way to express faith in a loving Creator. Thus, much of his fiction inspires questions rather than simple, "inspirational" answers. He is both a person of faith and an honest writer.

This study looks at the range of Bishop's fiction to consider how Bishop's great subject has been an exploration of what human beings need—not want, not even crave, but *need*—to satisfy their full potential. He sees that people sometimes convince themselves that they can settle for something different or less than that, but he sees the possible hope as well as the possible tragedy in human life. That he has devoted a lifetime of intelligent, sympathetic effort to examining that subject from different angles is remarkable; that he has been able to do so within the field of fantastic literature is truly, literally fantastic. In the real world, meanwhile, some powerful people simply dismiss anyone who disagrees with them as a "loser," while the slogan "I feel your pain" has become a tired cliché. So it is time now, especially now, to take a fresh, careful look at Michael Bishop.

\* \* \*

Readers with eidetic memories may note that several of the following pages echo essays that appeared in *The New York Review of Science Fiction*, beginning in 1994, following their presentation in shorter form as papers that were read at the annual International Conference for the Fantastic in the Arts. My thanks to editors Gordon Van Gelder, David Hartwell, and Kevin Maroney for their support. (And, yes, considering how much of Michael Bishop's recent publication has been in the form of revised fiction, it is mildly amusing that so much of this book consists of repolished/reconsidered criticism.)

Thanks also to my wife Mary for reminding me that I'd have to let go of the manuscript *sometime*. And, above all, deep thanks to Mike for his patient encouragement, willingness to answer endless questions, and putting up with my uncertain grammar, atrocious spelling, and worse typing.

PART I

# Exploring Strange Worlds

It would be useful to isolate separate periods in Michael Bishop's fiction to show how his interests have developed, but it's difficult to define borders. For instance, the label "anthropological science fiction" frequently has been stuck on Bishop's early stories and novels, and it's true that many of his characters act like anthropologists by setting out to observe and interpret alien (sometimes figuratively so, sometimes literally) societies. However, those inquirers seldom remain objective, academic observers. On the contrary, they tend to become passionately, inextricably involved in what they're studying. They may appear to be drawn to the mission of anthropology, but their own needs interfere with carrying out that disinterested pursuit of knowledge. We may also wonder exactly which stories belong in that group. The excellent Wikipedia entry on Bishop attempts to limit the "anthropological" period of his novels to those beginning with *A Funeral for the Eyes of Fire* (1975) and ending with *Under Heaven's Bridge* (1980), his collaboration with Ian Watson; thus two intervening novels, *A Little Knowledge* (1978) and *Catacomb Years* (1979), are placed in a separate little category, the UrNu Sequence, that shows what happens when some inhabitants of Earth try to withdraw into sealed domes. However, UrNu is part of *A Funeral for the Eyes of Fire*'s background, an oppressive regime that's part of Earth society that the protagonist is so desperate to escape that he is forced to decipher *two* alien societies.

Labels such as "anthropological" actually give only a rough idea of what Bishop is doing. In fact, these early novels focus on individuals' encounter with a closed system, either from the outside or the inside, whether it's on an alien planet or back home. Whether they come from the outside (like anthropologists looking for clues to interpret unfamiliar behaviors) or the inside (like captives struggling to get out of an airtight cell before they smother), Bishop's characters confront barriers that prove to be both external and internal. Insanely difficult as it proves to be, they must attack those barriers. They simply have no choice. His early short fiction also shows characters who suffer the effects of broken barriers. They are forced to confront the power of empathy—potential transcendence of personal barriers—in their lives, not because that inevitably makes them happier or more successful but because doing so is part of the human condition. Bishop's characters may have some choice about how they respond to that fact—whether or not they acknowledge the fact that interpersonal barriers *can* sometimes be broken—but they experience it too directly to ignore successfully.

That's where Bishop begins his career as a storyteller.

# 1

# The Perilous Discovery of Empathy
## *Short Fiction, 1970–1980*

As Michael Bishop tells it, his early attempts at writing fantastic fiction were spurred on by his office mate at the United States Air Force Academy Preparatory School. Since Bishop wasn't having success at selling stories to mainstream markets and since he admired Wells and Bradbury, why not try writing for science fiction magazines? And so he was delighted, in late 1969/early 1970, to receive a phone call in which *Galaxy* editor Ejler Jakobsson bought "Pinon Fall," calling the story "beautiful." It was published in *Galaxy*'s October/November 1970 issue, which bore Bishop's name on the cover.

It is, in fact, a gentle wisp of a story, as apparently uncomplicated as a Bradburyesque mood piece. Seven matter-of-fact scenes, separated by line spaces, present a matter-of-fact small-scale story without commentary, like a parable. One winter day while they are out gathering pinon nuts, three Chicano boys discover a naked insect-humanoid alien lying helpless in the snow. He says that they may call him Papilio, though it isn't his real name "or even an approximation." They revive him, feed him the nuts they've collected, and help him get back to their home neighborhood. At the same time, a bigoted old woman whose house is close to where the boys live looks out her window and sees a glistening mass in her yard. Assuming that the boys have trespassed and left litter on her property, she walks over to their house and berates their mother before borrowing a rusty axe and going back home to attack the alien object. The three boys return home, and their mother sends Jamie, the oldest, to retrieve the axe. He discovers the old woman crouched over the "gutted" remains of a giant cocoon, whereupon Papilio appears, declares, "'She has just killed the female of this region,'" and strangles her to death before Jamie can give him a fatal blow with a piece of *bric a brac*.

Although the immediate scope of this story is very limited, the implications are immense and ominous. If a set of male and female aliens was intended for *this* region, there must be other regions where other fertile pairs have been sent. In fact, the boys' mother shares with her nasty neighbor a dream she just had:

> Last night I dreamed about the snow, a very strange dream. Snow was falling over the whole world. It fell in Colorado and in Mexico. It fell even on the deserts of Africa. The camels were standing in the snow.... There were mariposas [butterflies]. All over the world, huge butterflies swam in the white storms, and moths, shaggy moths, dancing among the snowflakes, moths and butterflies of every color.

This message goes unheard, but it is confirmed when Papilio tells Jamie, Many others will come.... They're coming now.'" And Jamie sees and hears proof that the sky is full of winged shadows drifting downward, while the omniscient author calmly adds, that "Somewhere, miles and miles beyond the Sangre de Cristo Mountains, camels were standing in the snow."

Evidently some great change in the natural order is occurring. The question is what place, if any, humans will have in the new world. We don't appear to be very perceptive or adaptable. The story shows a series of incidents in which people fail to connect with each other or with the world around themselves. Sometimes this leads to violence, sometimes their verbal fumbling just subsides into futility, but a sense of wasted lives or potential hangs over the story. Thus the boys' generous impulses toward Papilio are genuine but ultimately useless. What is happening is far beyond the ability of Jamie and his brothers, let alone the short-sighted adults around them, to comprehend, manage, or correct. So, although the story stops short of saying so directly, humanity's prospects aren't good.

That's true of much of Bishop's early work. As a beginning writer, he was concerned that science fiction should be taken seriously, which meant that his early work tends to be mercilessly grim.

That's certainly true of "Cathadonian Odyssey" (*F&SF*, September 1974), which critiques the naive optimism of Stanley G. Weinbaum's "A Martian Odyssey" (*Wonder Stories*, July 1934), chosen by the Science Fiction Writers of America to lead off the landmark anthology *The Science Fiction Hall of Fame*. In Weinbaum's story, after a mechanical malfunction strands intrepid space explorer Jarvis in an unexplored region of Mars, he carefully figures out what he needs to do, shoulders his gear, and starts trudging back to the base where an ethnically-balanced crew from Earth is waiting. Soon, however, he begins traveling in the company of Tweel, a bird-like alien that Jarvis recognizes as intelligent, shown by how pronoun references in the narrative shift from "it"

## 1. The Perilous Discovery of Empathy

to "him." At the same time, the story shows how difficult communication would be with a truly alien intelligence. But understanding does prove to be possible, so that the two draw closer: At the story's climax the human exclaims, "'Thanks, Tweel. You're a man!'"

Jarvis adds that calling Tweel a man may not be "any compliment at all," but "A Cathadonian Odyssey" systematically dismantles the earlier story's assumptions about humanity's cheerful benevolence. In particular, Bishop's story questions human confidence that we are ready to extend ourselves intellectually and emotionally into new relationships. How far, in other words, can we trust our innate empathy to guide us?

Weinbaum's Mars, first of all, is a morally neutral setting, full of surprises that are sometimes dangerous but never anything that can't be mastered and exploited by human intelligence. However, humans have blithely tainted the setting of Bishop's story before protagonist Maria Jill Ian arrives there. "Cathadonia" is a compound of "Cathay" and "Caledonia," chosen by "a murderer with the sensitivity of a poet" to praise the planet's exotic beauty. He was aboard the merchant-ship *Golden* when it discovered the wonderful place on a rest stop during which the crew relaxed by killing as many of the strange "little tripodal natives as their laser pistols could dispatch." While doing this, the humans made it easier to butcher the creatures by calling them diminutive, dismissive names such as *Treefish*, *Fintails*, *Willowpusses*, or *Devil Apes*. For some reason, the *Golden*'s captain chooses not to mention these bloody activities when reporting the beautiful planet's coordinates to the authorities, so that the survey probeship *Nobel* has no idea what humans had done on Cathadonia before *it* arrives and launches a three-person descent craft toward the shore of the ocean that covers much of the planet's surface. However, "some odd, anomalous force" slams the craft down far from the ocean. Only Maria Jill Ian survives.

Weinbaum's Martian explorer knows that he needs to return to the rocket that will take him home, and he carefully evaluates what he needs to make the trek. Maria Jill Ian wonders why she survived the crash—and half-wishes that she hadn't. After the *Nobel* dropped them, it went on its programmed mission and won't be back for three months; she believes she will be dead by then. However, she dazedly goes on living. Somehow she buries the body of her husband Arthur and the other dead crewmember in one of the ponds that cover the landscape, after which she starts trudging west toward the ocean although "she didn't understand why the horizon drew her implacably toward the twilight baths of Ogre's Heart [the planet's sun]."

Weinbaum's hero rescues Tweel from a monstrous beast because the birdlike alien's possession of manufactured objects show that he is affiliated with a civilization. The alien whom Maria Jill Ian meets bears no artifacts and actually comes to *her* aid. She does not know anything about the Cathadonian natives or how the first human visitors treated them, so she is startled and frightened when one appears above her in the tree she is climbing to get a piece of the fruit she has learned to eat. After her desperate fear subsides, she describes the armless little creature in human terms—*"face: small, expressive, curious, and winning. The eyes are an old man's (sometimes), the mouth an infant's, the ears a young girl's."* She gives him the name Bracero because he *"swims like the much maligned 'wetbacks' of another time."* As she soon discovers, Bracero has telekinetic powers to compensate for his lack of arms, inviting readers to surmise how an intelligent race could advance without physical tools and also to guess what inexplicable force caused the descent craft to crash before the aliens could send a representative to verify that this human was not dangerous and in fact could write in her journal, *"We are friends, Bracero and I."*

And so Bracero accompanies Maria Jill Ian as she continues her plodding, compulsive journey west, toward the ocean. He considers her a friend too, unfortunately. Though she remarks on how effortlessly he can telekinetically pick fruit from the trees, compared to how much humans must strain to move small objects with their frail mental gifts, she accepts Bracero's generous gifts. She also verbalizes her grief about the loss of her husband Arthur, saying, "I miss him, Bracero, I wish he were here now." Sure enough, after Bracero falls into a coma as he exerts his telekinetic powers, Maria Jill Ian awakens from a nap to find her husband's rotting corpse beside her. Then the alien falls into a much deeper stupor, probably enlisting the telekinetic powers of his whole species, to satisfy one final need—her home:

> At last, far away to the west, a rounded shape rose over the horizon, looming up as if to intercept Ogre's Heart on its afternoon descent. The shape, a planet, cleared Cathadonia's edge and floated into the sky like a brown, crustily wrinkled balloon.
> It was Earth.
> She knew at once it was Earth. She knew despite the fact that its atmosphere had been heated up, boiled off, and ripped away in the psychokinetic furnace of Bracero's people's minds. It was a lifeless, battered shell that floated out there now, not an ocean upon it.

Filled with guilt, Maria Jill Ian believes that Bracero sacrificed himself out of love. The humans who come back to Cathadonia later see things differently. Perhaps they surmise that the casualties on Earth were revenge for that initial massacre by the crew of the *Golden*, or perhaps they simply fear an unpredictable, alien power. In any event, they wipe out all life on the planet. No trace of Maria Jill Ian or Bracero is

## 1. The Perilous Discovery of Empathy 15

left. Eventually, worldshapers turn the double planet into a lush paradise where human tourists pay to retrace the journey "of Maria and her Cathadonian sidekick," while listening to a recorded message from Arthur Ian: "'Men are hardy creatures. Men are the ultimate vermin, as indefatigable as cockroaches.'" Validating this message is the fact that the tourists are satisfied: "No one ever demanded a refund."

Although Maria Jill Ian is an empathetic and innocent character, overall "Cathadonian Odyssey" validates Arthur's statement. Humans are most comfortable when they can avoid feeling guilty about the damage they're doing. The story's conclusion resembles the cynical narrator of Jonathan Swift's "A Modest Proposal" in assuming that people, represented by the tourists who flock to Cathadonia, are selfish animals who can see an alien as at best a "sidekick." Maria Jill Ian is better than that, but even she is undone by the expression of careless, unguarded desires.

"Dogs' Lives" illustrates the uncertainty of studying a writer's work in chronological order of publication. Bishop explains that the story was written sometime around 1974 and accepted by Harlan Ellison for his gigantic anthology *The Last Dangerous Visions*, which never was published. Eventually, Bishop reclaimed "Dogs' Lives" so that he could submit it to a special issue of *The Missouri Review* (Spring 1984), after which it was selected for *The Best American Short Stories 1985*, *Nebula Awards Stories 20*, and other anthologies and collections.

Bishop comments that "during its writing, I believed I was accomplishing something until then unrealized in my work: the marshaling of many disparate notions and scenes in the service of a narrative bestowing on these elements a meaning greater than that implicit in its parts." Indeed, the story develops the technique of "Pinion Fall" by presenting a series of vignettes that readers recognize *do* cluster around the relationship between dogs and people, which in turn offers insight into the human condition. The story deliberately doesn't quite pull the fragments together chronologically, though it does offer enough information to assemble a fairly reliable chronology, nor does it aim toward a clear purpose. The pieces simply exist, equally significant, equally solid, permitting readers to play at relating them. The following commentary is one attempt to account for the story's considerable power.

Nicholas, the story's default narrator, is a 27-year-old college English teacher whose classroom is invaded one day by a wandering Great Dane. As he takes it by its collar and guides it out of the building, "the dog's power and aloofness coursed up my arm." Nicholas calls the animal "magnificent" and watches admiringly as it "loped gracefully" away; by contrast, he merely "slunk" back to work. Following this, his memory summons scenes of himself at different ages: at eight (wonderingly holding a newborn puppy), at five (being given a puppy himself that then runs away with older dogs), at 14 (watching his father's Labrador retriever Nick miraculously survive a terrible fall)—and at 46, 19 years into the future (using his imagination to project a time in which he has become a hyper-intelligent cyborg who first proves the existence of a planet revolving around Sirius, the dog star, then joins an exploratory mission sent there, a crew composed of cyborg humans and cyborg dogs). Nicholas is quite satisfied with his condition in this last cluster of scenes. As he sees it, his augmented brainpower was "the ultimate wish-fulfillment fantasy come true." In another section's "stream of history," he reports that he is a 38-year-old writer "projecting himself into that grandiose wish-fulfillment role." As the cyborg astronaut, he is paired with "Canicula, a.k.a. Threasie or 3C—short, you see for Cybernetic Canine Construct," a name from the past-perfect titled list of DOGS I HAVE KNOWN earlier in the story; as the writer, he talks to his current dog while pretending that the animal dreams "of canine heroics aboard a ship bound for Sirius."

Clearly, the narrator's consciousness/imagination is roaming freely through time and space in pursuit of—what? It must have something to do with how humans relate to dogs. We speak of them condescendingly, not just in the complaint that "it's a dog's life" but also in the pitying remark that "it shouldn't happen to a dog" or the criticism that a lazy worker is "dogging it." It is a serious insult to call someone "a son of a bitch." Yet we also hear that "a dog is man's best friend." Many of the episodes in Bishop's story demonstrate how the presence of a dog can let people express their brightest or darkest interests. Like the dog that appeared in the college classroom, a dog is Other, not necessarily a threat but still a distinctly alien presence, powerful and aloof.

That presence can be ominous. The dog in the classroom momentarily disrupts the routine business, and in a later section the narrator imagines facing a new class composed entirely of dogs who interrupt his role-taking, reject his authority, and finally devour him. In another episode, Nicholas projects himself into the mind of the ubiquitous Great Dane, 175 years in the past, when a pack of hounds is loosed on a naked eight-year-old Russian serf boy. They tear him apart. Nicholas ponders "how it must feel to be run down by a pack of predatory animals"—but he leaves the hound's consciousness only later, "after the dog boys return us slavering to the kennels."

Other scenes show how vulnerable dogs are. A carelessly driven cement truck can crush them, or, like the awesome Labrador Nick, they can be maimed and mutilated by thoughtless people, even killed for fun as in Stephen Crane's story "A Small Brown Dog."

Their uncontrollable, unknowable animal impulses discomfort us but also awe us. When his neighbor's mongrel bitch goes into heat, Nicholas tries to defend her from what he imagines is rape by a huge interloper—perhaps a Great Dane. Yet the result of their frantic copulation is a litter of newborn puppies that fascinate Nicholas' small son just as he himself was fascinated at the story's opening.

Dogs may be frightening, pitiable, and paradoxical vessels of our repulsion and attraction, but their most important role seems to be as the objects/sources of affection. Cyborg Nicholas reports that his family life suffered as his meat body was replaced by mechanisms. He credits his wife Katherine for staying with him even if she didn't understand his motives. Without conscious irony, he notes, "I was grateful, for I've always believed that human beings extract a major part of life's meaning from, in Pound's phrase, 'the quality of the affections.'" But the affection that really thrills Nicholas is that of Canicula-Threasie, as they trade affectionate quips on the way to Sirius. What they find on the Planet Elsinore is a race of intelligent, apparently immortal dogs who welcome humans as the Masters they have always waited for. These fragments of narration, remember, have been acknowledged already as a pure wish-fulfillment fantasy, probably too simplemindedly smug to be convincing. The story knows better.

And yet.... If this thread of the story shows the limits of human imagination, dogs nevertheless remain fascinating, tempting, in their alien, innocent warmth. On the ship bound for Sirius, Cyborg Nicholas listens approvingly to Threasie's story "of how dog and man first joined forced forces against the indifferent arrogance of a bestial environment." It would require arrogance to imagine that all human impulses, like all the threads of a story representing one tangle of fascination/dread, could be mastered easily. College teacher Nicholas is expressing more acceptance than arrogance at the end of the story when he imagines himself and his children in later years and realizes that "all a dad can do is live his life and, loving them, let his children—born and unborn—live theirs."

That doesn't mean that he doesn't still want to possess more than that finite "all." As the story ends, his infant son exclaims, "Dog! ... Dog!"

In "Blooded on Arachne" (*Epoch*, 1975), Bishop further considers how humans can become more aware of the diverse kinds of life around themselves. The story's plot is simple enough: Sixteen-year-old Ethan Dedicos, a cadet in the space corps, is sent to planet Arachne for "blooding"—i.e., his introduction to necessary behaviors; in this case, Ethan must undergo a challenging test of survival skills/attitudes. He is marooned in the desert but survives by clinging to a giant spider as it sails through the air back to its nest. What makes the story memorable is not just what happens to Ethan but how he—and readers who accept him as a sympathetic viewpoint character—makes sense of it.

Readers know nothing about Ethan Dedicos at the story's beginning except his name, just as he knows nothing about what lies before him except that he must be "blooded" if he is to become "a star-bearer, an officer" of the Martial Arm of Glaktik Komm. The high-tech jargon he uses to define himself collides with the convoluted, pseudo-archaic jargon of the "spidherds," the reclusive guild on Arachne that cares for a herd of giant spiders. Readers must assimilate both unfamiliar vocabularies so that they can absorb some of the information that sets up the particular situation, but just as that is happening—things change. One paragraph ends with Ethan safely asleep; the next begins with him awakening alone in the desert. There is no line break to indicate a transition; moreover, sentence fragments and missing punctuation indicate Ethan's disorientation as he looks around and sees "in every direction, whiteness whiteness whiteness whiteness."

After Ethan calms down a bit, he realizes that he must have been drugged and dumped here, so this must be a deliberate part of the blooding process. He recalls that when he tried to ask the spinherds about what he is supposed to do during his blooding, the answer was "'survive, of course.'" They even told him that sometime in future he would be dropped into the dry sea bed, emphasizing again that what he must come do is to "'come back to us, sweetling.'" The endearing way they address him may be sincere, even the words spoken to him as he sinks into drugged sleep just before being marooned, "'I love the boys I blood. Remember that, lamb's eyes,'" but that doesn't change the fact that he has been left to live or die on his own.

Readers must infer what Glaktik Komm intends this trial to bring out in boys who want to be officers in its service. One valued quality may be imagination. Ethan saw how the giant spiders extrude enough web to lift them off the ground in Arachne's strong wind, and the spidherds told him that this was the season for flocks to sail through the air for a time before returning to their nest. Trudging through the desert, a day or so into his blooding, he sees the sky thick with spiders and realizes that if he can climb aboard one he may be carried back to safety. Another quality that Glaktik Komm might find useful is ruthlessness. After some time aloft, Ethan realizes that his growing hunger and weakness may cause him to lose hold of the spider he is riding and fall to his death, so he must kill his mount and devour enough of its innards to sustain life before he transfers to another spider that is alive and capable of steering itself home. Perhaps Glaktik Komm needs to make sure its aspiring officers have both the ingenuity to see possibilities and the unscrupulous willingness to take advantage of them no matter what it costs. That callous practicality is consistent with the brutal way the test is set up. After all, Ethan's blooding is harrowing enough; some boys must fail to survive—but the ones who *do* survive must be considered fit and ready to serve the system.

However, Ethan's blooding reveals other qualities that may or may not be prized by Glaktik Komm. The spinherds love the spiders they tend and serve. They "'talk to them, croon to them, pipe to our spiderlings the homing call of Garden Home'"; in short, those humans see the spiders as "'the people who go eight-legged and wraithly in our hearts.'" When Ethan desperately mounts a spider drifting by in the air, he thinks of it as a "beast" but he also talks to it, calling it Bucephalus after Alexander the Great's warhorse, sometimes affectionately "Bucie." And when he realizes that he must kill it in order to survive, the choice bothers him: "'I'm sorry,' Ethan Dedicos said, meaning it. 'I'm sorry to have to do this.'" After he abandons Bucephalus' falling, gutted shell, Ethan does not give a name to his new mount, respecting its uniqueness and the fact that he is only nominally in control: "'I'm not going to name you,' he told his new pilot. 'I promise you that.'" When the spider does successfully follow the call that leads it home, Ethan is caught up in the spinherds' celebration of his successful blooding, literally as stained with spider's blood as they are. But his heart aches. "Lurching forward on his knees against the many friendly hands, he heaved up undigested bits of something saddening." Literally, he is vomiting the bits of Bucephalus that his human body couldn't digest. Figuratively, he is aware that his success was based on an action that may not have been exactly murder but that *felt* very much like it. "Just before passing out, Ethan whispered the word 'Bucephalus.' No one heard him. No one knew his hurt."

Just before this, realizing that he has won access to the realm of Glaktik Komm, Ethan looks up and sees "a thousand scornful stars" winking at him. Two dreams he has while riding spiderback further illustrate the uncertain mix of emotions in his final attitude. Close to the end of his voyage, he pictures splendid success, "dreaming of clip-on epaulets and probeship glory." Just after climbing aboard Bucephalus, however, when he dreamed of piloting a ship "through the surreal glooms of id-space," he felt like one "lost in a comforting nightmare of power." The trappings of glory certainly attract Ethan, and so does the illusion of mastery. But he ultimately has experienced how unsatisfying those things can turn out to be. This realization could also be Glaktik Komm's intent, to keep its officers from becoming too vainglorious. Even if this is true, though, this element of the blooding remains a part of Ethan's private education.

The conclusion of "Blooded on Arachne" feels like a positive evolution of "Cathedonian Odyssey," not because it necessarily is happier but because it is not so neatly pessimistic. Readers don't know what kind of man Ethan Dedicos will grow up to be, but at least he has some useful experience to digest—if he can, if he can remember his private grief in the midst of public celebration. In any case, winding up alive and uncertain is almost certainly better than being dead and obliterated.

Readers should hold that thought—living uncertainty vs. security in death—as they come to the end of "The Samurai and the Willows" (*F&SF*, February 1976), coming right after the suicide of one of the main characters. This is one of Bishop's stories set in or around the domed city of Atlanta which were assembled into the fixup novel *Catacomb Years* (1979), which will be discussed when that book gets its turn. The story itself gives all the background readers need to appreciate the characters' dilemmas: Major American cities have retreated inside massive, sealed domes, cut off from nature and the rest of humanity. All aspects of life inside the dome are mechanically regulated. That's how a two-person cubicle is assigned to such diverse and probably antipathetic people as Simon Kadaka Fowler, a subdued 38/9-year-old Nesei horticulturist and trainer of bonsai trees, and Georgia Cawthorn, brash African American 18-year-old speed-skating glissador. She calls him Basenji, for a quiet little dog; he calls her Queequeg, after the enigmatic harpooner in *Moby Dick*. They do not get along well. Still, Basenji is aware of Queequeg's female presence, especially her scent when she's looming over him; meanwhile, she is curious about the bonsai trees he grows and would buy one if she could afford it and if it could survive in their subterranean living unit—since the miniature willow is too expensive for her, she settles for decorating their living unit with reproductions of sentimental Norman Rockwell paintings. They are, in fact, lonely people who are ready for the sensual and emotional encounter they have near the story's end.

This development is so healthy and satisfying that it is disturbing at the story's very end to find Queequeg trying to work out why Basenji committed suicide by *seppuku*. But abundant hints have led up to that event. Basenji's private notebook—a combination of journal and confessional—shows him grappling with the distinction between honorable and praiseworthy *seppuku*—a ritual disembowelment formerly reserved for samurai warriors—and *hari-kari*, mere belly-cutting. In a recurring nightmare, he finds himself shrunk to a size commiserate with his bonsai trees, but when he tries to hang himself from a miniature willow the branch breaks off so that the attempt at suicide is a shameful failure. A poem in his notebook is addressed to someone who "gave" him the willow, but the last lines are heavily crossed out. He evidently is repressing full awareness of some personal failure, but he is able to articulate it only after he and Queequeg have affirmed their relationship by having sex. What he finally confesses to her is that he failed to help his mother when he came to visit her in the Geriatrics Hostel and found her calling for help but unable to recognize him and soaked in her own urine. Instead of honoring her for all she had been, including having instructed him in the art of bonsai shaping, he ran away. Now the only way he can see to vindicate his manly honor is by committing seppuku.

Readers may find the question more complex. For one thing, the characters themselves are aware that living under the city dome has shaped them just as Basenji's trees have been twisted into miniature versions of what they might have grown to be. Music and dance under the Dome are less animated, and art is less expressive. Everything has been warped to fit the available space. Nevertheless, it also is true that the characters' human desires and values survive in this cramped environment. Norman Rockwell's paintings may be facile, but they still express a desire for a shared community. Queequeg finds delight in gliding through the city's corridors. And she and Basenji do discover each other, however briefly. Looking forward, she speaks to Basenji of surviving bad times and raising children: "'I'm just like my mama.... She loves us all, I mean, but she ain't gonna fall over if bad shit happens to us. A quitting streak don't run in her. Or me neither.'" Basenji, in turn, leaves her materials and instructions so that she can start new bansai trees, carrying on his heritage. The process is a success. People living under the Dome may be shrunken, but they aren't ugly.

Still, as Queequeg observes in the story's last paragraph, Basenji couldn't develop quite far enough: "'He changed a lot. The blessed part is, he started asking himself questions 'bout who he was. He got a long way. But he just never asked the last question.'" That question isn't stated in the story, but it might be simply how one can admit personal failings, recognize limiting conditions, and still go on living. Basenji's conclusion may fit the question he was able to formulate, but it still feels incomplete.

Further developing an ambiguously grim conclusion that mixes hope and despair, Bishop's "The House of Compassionate Sharers" (*Cosmos*, May 1977) is distinctly uncomfortable to read because it pries open issues of personal selfhood/autonomy that most of us would rather not examine. The story works through a slow series of revelations that explore narrator Dorian Lorca's struggles with people whom he feels don't sufficiently appreciate his anguish. The first thing readers learn is that most of Lorca's mangled body has been replaced by artificial parts so that he now is repulsed by the moist, corruptible flesh of the humans around him. The only way he can imagine continuing to live is to become even more mechanical by merging his brain with the control system of a starship. In the story's opening, his disgust with the physical presence of his wife Rumai spoils a meeting that followed extensive therapy intended to help him desire her company. Because Rumai is first governor of the planet Miroste, however, she has the power to reach even farther for help, all of 46 light years to Earth. When Lorca meets her again, he is informed that he must return there with Wardress Kefa for one last attempt at therapy in the House of Compassionate Sharers.

Readers learn the House's nature only gradually. "'Is it a brothel?'" Lorca insultingly asks in that first interview. After an awkward silence, his wife replies that it is "a unique clinic for the treatment of unique emotional disorders," though Wardress Kefa admits that some call the House a brothel because economic necessity occasionally forces it to admit powerful people with what she calls "finicky" tastes. Lorca is unhappy to be told that revealing anything beyond a few basic facts would interfere with his therapeutic experience, but he accepts the command because Rumai tells him that if this treatment fails she will let him do as he wishes. When Lorca and Wardress Kefa arrive at the remote, chilly House after a largely silent journey, Lorca is told that he must spend that night with a Sharer. Lorca gropes through the dark room until he finds the Sharer waiting in the bed. At this point—remembering Lorca's initial question about the House and also his remark that the surgeon had informed him that his body was "still 'sexually viable'"—readers expect some kind of sexual encounter. But although Lorca's posture above the Sharer reminds him "of a lover or of one called to identify a mangled corpse," what he discovers when his fingers explore the recumbent, immobile body is that it is much like his own, a combination of artificial and organic. Lorca is upset that he has been paired with an elderly individual who evidently must have chosen to spend several years as man-machine. He takes this as a rebuke to his own urgent request to eliminate the "man" part of himself, so he leaves the bed to spend the rest of the night squatting on the floor and avoiding sleep that might bring nightmares. The following morning, however, Wardress Kefa calmly cuts through Lorca's hostility with the observation that the therapy has begun working since "'you talked to the Sharer. You addressed him, not once but several times. Many clients fail to get that far in their first session.'"

In Lorca's next session, moonlight illuminates the room. As he straddles the Sharer, his eyes can verify that the other looks "like a skull, oddly flattened and beveled, with the body of a man." Going farther this time, Lorca asks the Sharer to move; in fact, using devices that the Sharer gives him, Lorca puts the Sharer through a series of exercises, speculating that

> maybe the Sharer had surrendered control of his body to the man-machine Dorian Lorca, keeping for himself just those movements that persuade the manipulated of their autonomy. It was an awesome prostitution, even if Wardress Kefa would have frowned to hear me call it that. But I rejoiced. It freed me from the demands of an artificial eroticism, from any necessity to deduce what was expected of me. The Sharer would obey my least gesture, my briefest word. I just had to use the control he'd literally handed over.

Lorca's power is limited only by Wardress Kefa's request to "restrain [his] crueler impulses" and the Houses' fundamental rule: "'Don't kill the Sharer.'" Instead, he expresses his frustration by commanding the Sharer to kill the red-winged blackbird caged in the room, though the session ends before that can be done.

At this point, Lorca has given readers almost enough information to diagnose this not-quite-reliable narrator's disorder. "Artificial eroticism" aside, the story actually is about sex in the broader sense—i.e., intercourse between individuals. Sex can lead to shared release of tensions, emotional bonding, literally "making love." It also can be a display of power, an expression of control shown in physical or emotional manipulation. That is—and evidently has been—Lorca's mode of behavior, though he would insist that he has been forced into it. Considering the dreadful emotional pain he is in, however, readers recognize that he needs to learn a different, less destructive way to connect with other, separate individuals. His sessions with his Sharer have first made him curious about an obscure situation, then encouraged him to explore a place and another person, through both physical touch and verbal questioning. He now has discovered that the Sharer can show compassion for a patient like Lorca by giving up control temporarily and letting himself become physically as much a marionette as the patient feels himself figuratively to be.

From the beginning of the story, Lorca has pictured himself as manipulated by his doctor, his wife, his whole society. Trying to explain himself on a later evening, Lorca complains, "'Rumai *used* [emphasis added] me as an emissary, Sharer—a spy, a protocol officer, whatever state business required.'" He goes on to describe his "involvement" with a young, female bureaucrat whom he called only by her maternal surname. The relationship did not involve physical sex. Instead, Lorca gave the girl distinctive pieces of Rumai's jewelry before public events where his wife was certain to see them, then retrieved each item and returned it "'to my wife's sandalwood box before she could verify its 'theft.' I suppose I wanted to make my dishonesty conspicuous." His present condition—alienated, static, self-centered, and vindictive—simply continues the way he was behaving before the accident that ruined his meat body. Lorca now recognizes what giving up power to use the Sharer as "an external prosthesis" means not only freeing the other but himself also: "He was restored to himself. As was I to myself ... as was I."

Besides the influence of the Sharer's generous, accepting presence, Lorca benefits by confrontation with two other visitors, Cleva and Cleirach Orha, male and female clones whose usefulness in state business gives them power to use the House as a bordello; the woman requests "'the mouthless one ... preferably drugged.'" The revulsion the Orhas provoke also helps move Lorca out of his immobility, especially when he answers Wardress Kefa's cry for help and finds Cleirach choking the Wardress while Cleva plays with a stiletto, their eyes gleaming with too many drugs, liquor, "and the Orhas' own meanness." They have been torturing their assigned Sharer just short of killing him—as successful bureaucrats, the Orhas know how to obey the letter of the rules. After they leave, Lorca recognizes what he has been absorbing unconsciously: Wardress Kefa is also a Compassionate Sharer, like "the creature whose electrode-studded body and gleaming death's-head had mocked the efficient mechanical deadness in me: a deadness that, in turning away from Rumai, I had turned into a god"; he himself must find a new "mode of perception; a means of adapting" to escape from his isolation; and *that* finally means that he has the potential to become a Compassionate Sharer himself.

The story's conclusion is set many years later, after Lorca returned to Miroste and lived with Rumai for the rest of her life before entering the House as a novitiate. Although his mechanical body is still running smoothly, his brain cells are dying; he has strained his failing memory to share the stages of his awakening from narcissistic selfishness. This also, however, involves readers intensely in each stage of progress as he explores what is in front of him and tries to make sense of it. Following this process of discovery is difficult. Accepting its implications—the suggestion that one might willingly, lovingly submit to the whims of someone who is emotionally stunted, in hope that this will lead the other to self-examination and to healthy interaction—is almost unthinkable. Besides the surrender of one's ego, there's the practical/physical danger of becoming prey to "finicky" clients like the Orhas. But that self-discovery through self-sacrifice is what Lorca offers for readers' consideration.

"The House of Compassionate Sharers" does not show readers anything about Lorca's post–House relationship with Rumai. We can surmise only that it was based on truer understanding and sharing, within the limits of their social situation. There are enough clues, however, to show the nature of their society. We know, for example, that the surgical complex on Miroste was built to "patch up" mine workers enough to let them continue working after their bodies were damaged by their jobs; that, after Loca was catastrophically injured in a mining disaster, his wife's authority was the only thing that made him important enough to be put into a prosthetic body rather than discarded like the other accident victims; that society regards a Sharer as "an expensive commodity"; and that the Orhas are accepted and valued members of society before they damage a Sharer and that their only punishment for that atrocity is to be denied future access to the House. This is not, in other words, an environment that encourages compassion or sharing, any more than the readers' does. But Bishop's story shows how it is barely, barely possible for someone to discover—with much help and with painful self-examination—those personal values and to realize that wherever one is able to use them can be called "home."

Bishop's sf had begun to attract attention from his earliest publications, and "The House of Compassionate Sharers" was chosen for reprinting in three best-of-the-year anthologies. Most recently, it was included in Ann and Jeff Vandermeer's massive compendium *The Big Book of Science Fiction*. Turning to another branch of fantastic literature, he wrote "Within the Walls of Tyre" for Gerald W. Page's *The Year's Best Horror Stories* (though it was published first in *Weirdbook 13*, Spring 1978), and the story has been reprinted in other fantasy/horror anthologies since then. Actually, besides being different from the last three stories discussed above by being set in contemporary America, the story again shows how difficult it is to stick labels on Bishop's writing, for the reaction it evokes is much more complicated than simple "horror."

"Within the Walls of Tyre" is set in 1977, a few decades after the end of World War II. The protagonist Marilyn Odau is a successful 55-year-old manager of a woman's clothing store in a gigantic suburban shopping mall. Without making it feel grossly unpleasant, Bishop shows details that reveal how superficial and impersonal her existence has become; the only thing disturbing her businesslike composure early in the story are fragmented memories of her love affair with Jordan Burk, a young Marine who was killed during the war. But he is not part of her life now, and she seems to be satisfied with her routine of supervising retail staff, completing business paperwork—i.e., *managing* everything in her environment. When one of her salesgirls tells her that an exceptionally attractive salesman wants to see her, her professional aplomb is disturbed by how much he looks like her long-dead lover. The novelty product he is pushing—painted-on nylon stockings—has a retro-World War II vibe that disturbs Marilyn, but young Nicholas Anson develops a personal connection with her that leads to a sexual encounter that gives him access to her home and to her cherished, guilty secret: She unknowingly carried the young Marine's baby in her body for years as a *lithopedion*, a petrified fetus, before it was surgically removed; now she lovingly keeps it in a bassinet in her "nursery." Nicholas responds to this unsettling news with a revelation of his own: He is the son of Jordan Burk by the wife he abandoned for his affair with Marilyn. She is overwhelmed by this new information that could make her see her idealized lover as a heartless cad. Distraught, she throws out her not-quite-son and tries to reestablish her safe, mechanical equilibrium, even rationalizing away evidence later that Nicholas must have invaded her home to inspect the fossilized baby. Then, during the Christmas season, his phone call to her office summons her out into the mall, where she sees crowds of jolly holiday shoppers crowded in front of store windows filled with replicas of her stone child. At the story's end, Marilyn is totally out of control, screaming and shattering plate glass with her fists, while Nicholas "catching Marilyn's eye, smiled his boyish smile."

This certainly is an effectively disturbing story. It is worth noting, though, that its emotional impact lacks the supernatural element often present in a "horror" story to intensify the feeling of overwhelming menace and devastating shock. True, when Marilyn meets Nicholas, before most of her careful reserve is overcome by his physical likeness to Jordan Burk, she flashes on his resemblance to the angry motorist she cut off on her way to work; the story may be suggesting that Marilyn is the victim of an ominous, relentless pursuit. But probably not. Marilyn and Nicholas' interaction is unusually intense, but so is the burden of repressed emotion they carry because of their convoluted past. Even the *lithopedion* is a natural, though very rare, medical phenomenon. In *Supernatural Horror in Literature*, H.P. Lovecraft rather floridly explained that the source of horror in fiction was characters' discovery that the familiar rules by which they had been living were false, that the tiny circle of light in which we readers felt safe was surrounded by vast, impenetrable darkness—and that presences in that darkness could take an unkind interest in us—or, even worse, that superhuman powers could destroy us without even noticing, let alone caring. The horror in "Within the Walls of Tyre" doesn't spring from something beyond Marilyn's range of understanding, just knowledge she has chosen to repress: Society is based on commercial transactions, not generous sympathy. She had imagined that she could conceal the failings that made her vulnerable, that she somehow could escape having her dearest intimate secrets exploited. But she was wrong. Like the conclusion of "Cathadonian Odyssey," "Within the Walls of Tyre" shows that people will do absolutely anything for money or pure selfish fun. And that *is* a horrible reality for Marilyn to be left to live with.

Again, though, the story seems to be saying something rather more and different than this. Even while she is consciously reassuring herself early in the story, it's clear that Marilyn is at least semi-aware that she's trapped in meaningless commercialism. For example, she knows that it doesn't really matter whether she stays in her living unit in Brookmist or moves to Chateau Royale, Smoke Glade, Sussex Wood, or any one of the other elegant-sounding, faux-woodsy residential complexes. The place where she works, Summerstone, sounds equally posh and phony. And, after all, her job is just a matter of keeping one little shop in a huge mall running in competition with a host of other little shops, all selling much the same products to fickle consumers. Nothing in her life has much personal significance, and she believes that's how she likes it. However, her clinging to memories of her affair with Jordan Burk may actually be trying to hold on to a time when she was able to act on what she thought were genuine feelings, when she felt that her life had meaning. Thus, besides sexual yearning, her susceptibility to Nicholas' charm may be based on desire to do something real again and to break out of a protective shell that is becoming increasingly constrictive.

The story says as much in the scene when Marilyn finds Nicholas staring down into the bassinet:

> Instead of screaming and flying at him, she sank to the floor in the billows of her dressing gown, shamefully conscious of her restraint but too well satisfied by Nicholas's snooping to let it shock her. If she hadn't wanted this to happen, she would have never let him come. Or she'd have locked the door to her shrine. Or slain the young man in the numb sleep of his fulfillment—any number of things. But this prying, well, she might have even *willed* it.
> Confession and surcease.

What Marilyn truly wants is to reveal her disturbingly unnatural behavior and then to have it stopped. Unfortunately, Nicholas is unable to help her because his own unnatural compulsions have made him track down and seduce the woman who broke up his parents' marriage. Aghast at his behavior and her own, Marilyn feels she has no choice but to rebuild her awful but comfortingly familiar routine of concealment—until Nicholas shows her that her secret has been revealed in the most devastating way possible, not by singling her out as an example of unique strangeness but by making her private obsession a mere commercial novelty.

Horrible as the conclusion is for Marilyn at that moment, however, readers should ask whether it is much more awful than the thought of her continuing to live as she has been.

It may be valuable, here, to consider a story by Flannery O'Connor, one of Bishop's favorite writers. "Good Country People" is centered on supercilious Hulga, who looks down on her dull rural neighbors until she is seduced by a seemingly sincere Bible salesman who steals her artificial leg, taunts her, and leaves her helplessly frustrated. The horror of this conclusion is mitigated by the humor of Hulga's neighbors who watch the Bible salesman leave while commenting smugly that they can't understand how anyone could be as naïve as they assume *he* is. Readers have had trouble coping with this mix of tragedy and comedy, forcing O'Connor to write a letter to deflate one optimistic interpretation: "Nothing 'comes to flower' here except her realization in the end that she ain't so smart. It's not said that she has never had any faith but it is implied that her fine education has got rid of it, that purity has been overridden by pride of intellect through her fine education" (*Habit* 170). In other words, what Hulga "gains" is a confrontation with reality, an appreciation of her mortal weakness because her pretentions have been destroyed. Whether or not recognizing the fragility of her pride might turn her toward faith again is left uncertain, up to readers to decide. But unpredictably and dreadfully, Hulga has been offered a chance to see herself and to change her role in the world. This is called Grace, God's intervention in our self-centered, self-destructive lives. Not that Nicolas in "Within the Walls of Tyre" is in any way angelic— not even the score-settling, avenging variety of angel, but his actions could either shatter Marilyn or set her free. Bishop's story is not quite using "Good Country People" as a template, unlike how Joe R. Lansdale takes "A Good Man Is Hard to Find" as the basis for his bleakly nihilistic "The Night They Missed the Horror Show," but the protagonists of both stories are left in similar positions of despair and possibility. They must decide what to do next, and their choices are horribly difficult. However, as George Bernard Shaw observed in his preface to *Major Barbara*, speaking of the Salvation Army's efforts within an inhospitable society, "there is danger in such activity, and where there is danger there is hope."

Although it attracted little reader reaction when it was first published and received no award nominations, Bishop chose to include "Storming the Bijou, Mon Amour" (*Asimov's*, June 1979) in *The Door Gunner* because he has "an intractable fondness for it" due to its basis in devout film watching. And it is a very amusing story, showing the lighter side of eternal damnation.

"The world and its deep central valley were called Pit," the story begins, suggesting that the action could be set on an alien planet with different physical laws; in fact, there are just enough dabs of sci-fi flimflam throughout to disguise its surrealistic core. Readers also may catch an echo of William Ernest Henley's poem "Invictus," whose speaker mentions being sunk in the threatening darkness of "the Pit from pole to pole." In Bishop's story, however, the Pit's darkness is simply an appropriate setting in which to watch movies, and none of the characters can say, "I am the master of my fate/ I am the captain of my soul." Essentially, the all-powerful Count D—not Dracula but De Mille—has created the ultimate drive-in movie experience, a film-lover's nightmare. Pittites, the hoard of humans dwelling in the Pit, are permanently confined in little family viewing cabanas, on a diet of popcorn and soda pop, dressed in tattered costumes, and required to stare at an endless stream of movies seen through the windows of Count De Mille's Castle Bijou set high on a distant cliff. The title refers to an acclaimed foreign film, *Hiroshima mon amour* (1959), but there is no indication that films are selected by quality, origin, or any other imaginable criteria. They just pour out, one after another. Bands of "hushars" (hussars/ushers/hushers) ride through the audience to prevent sleeping or inattention, while the Pittites' emblematic family names—Seymour, Gazehard, etc.—show their role in life. Their first names are borrowed inappropriately from movie stars; however, despite not being naturally heroic, Gary Cooper Seymour recognizes their unbearable physical torment ("The Seymours were all thin and waxen-faced, with bad teeth and sore gums, and their eyeballs had such unhealthy glazes that they looked shellacked"), and he is fed up with having to watch movies forever, especially when they have to sit through *The Return of Dr. X*, one of Humphrey Bogart's worst films, for a second time. G.C. and his two sons, Oliver Hardy Seymour and Clint Eastwood Seymour, set out to scale the cliff, storm the castle, and set everyone free. When G.C. reaches the goal, the boys having fallen to their deaths during the climb, Count De Mille explains that he's not responsible for the lack of continuity between films, "'I'm here to keep things going, not to impose an impossible order on the whole. And what would you do if I didn't keep things going, please?'" When G.C. exclaims, "'We'd live,'" the Count obligingly shuts off the projector, so that there's no more film to watch, whereupon "there arose from the groundlings in Pit a gasp of dismay and terror so unlike anything G.C. had ever heard on a movie soundtrack that it took him a moment to hear it for what it was." The Count justifies himself as "'the alternately malign and kindly lackey of an impulse more human and powerful than any of your poor, put-upon Pittites.'" He does not reveal what that impulse might be, but G.C. finds himself whisked away by an invisible hand to another world, a Vast Wasteland, where "a voice that wasn't the Count's" commands "'*Lights!*'" and G.C. is exposed to endless reruns of TV shows such as *Love of Life* and *Hee Haw*. This is so awful that G.C. begs to be taken "home." And so he is:

> Five seconds or a dozen centuries later, he opened his eyes and found himself seated in his watching cabana beside Zsa Zsa [wife], Sissy [daughter], and his miraculously resurrected sons. High in the windows of the castle Bijou blazed the upright lie of Zinnemann's *High Noon*.

Readers will recognize the command "'Lights!'" as coming simultaneously from a film director and God ("Let there be light!"). Evidently, G.C. and the other passive receivers of mass diversion in the Pit have been placed in the best, freest, most satisfying existence they can handle, even if they're sometimes fretful. G. C.'s ultimate fate is more merciful than that of the unredeemable protagonist in William Golding's *Pincher Martin*, who finally is utterly dissolved "in a compassion that was timeless and without mercy." Or perhaps G.C. receives less mercy. Why is *High Noon* called an "upright lie"? Earlier in the story, when G.C. tries to trick a group of hushars, "he lied uprightly." Used as an adjective or as the root of an adverb, "upright" suggests on the one hand "trustworthy" but on the other "brazenly and effectively deceitful." In the movie, Gary Cooper plays a man who fights on heroically, alone, against impossible odds; the lie may be that such success is possible, making the Pittites more docile and contented. It's also true that the movie is built around a ticking clock, insisting that action has time limits, demanding that all things *must* stop sometime. In the Pit, however, the movies simply continue, one after another, reels without end.

Although good comedies have tragedies lurking inside them, it may seem unnecessary to spend so much time discussing such an inconsequential, amusing little story. After all, the situation is obviously contrived, and these characters are just simplified cartoonish figures with silly names. It would be different if *we* were like them, if *we* ever had any difficulty avoiding distractions and getting a purposeful grip on reality....

"The Yukio Mishima Cultural Association of Kudzu Valley, Georgia" (*Basilisk*, October 1980) is another funny/serious story full of characters with peculiar-sounding names, in this case people from the rural American South. Mr. Bernard Bligh Brumblelo, Ruby and Clarence Unfug, and Spurgeon Creed are leading citizens of the little Georgia town where the narrator, identified only as M., has gone to sulk.

According to the diary that begins on June 1, 1975, M. has just been fired by the state university, where he was "an instructor in the comparative literature section of the English department." His ego is bruised, but he doesn't appear to miss the actual teaching. He gives no indication of what courses he taught or of their content. The satisfaction of getting his job back would involve successfully bullying the Provost, receiving full back pay, and getting a private office in a more prestigious wing of the faculty office building. He received his M.A. degree with a thesis titled "'Mather Biles: His Role in the Introduction of the Heroic Couplet from England to the American Colonies'"; neither Biles nor the heroic couplet is ever mentioned again in the story. The official reason for M.'s firing is that, since he received his graduate degree from the same school, his continuing to teach there violates the academic taboo "against 'intellectual incest.'" More to the point, whether the state university noticed it or not, M. seems to have indulged himself in academic masturbation.

Exile from the halls of academia gives M. a chance to sneer at his old school *and* at the yokels among whom he is forced to live. He first plans to spend three months in splendid isolation; actually almost five months pass before he is invited to a social tea by Mrs. Bernard Bligh Brumbelo, "the foremost social lioness in town." M. lists the quaint names of the other guests, maintaining his superiority by explaining his field of expertise with a pedantic, dictionary definition: "'It's a discipline whose purpose is to discover significant relationships among different works of literature, across the barriers of both language and time.'" He is amused when another guest asks for an example, which gives him the excuse to drop a lump of esoteric lore on her: "'Well ... one of the graduate students in our section has just composed a paper detailing the similarities between the works of the French writer Proust and the Japanese novelist Yukio Mishima.'" Mrs. Brumblelo lives up to his expectations of glib ignorance by claiming to love Proust because "'he's so *soporific*,'" while her bookcase is full of Reader's Digest Condensed Books. But she and the others do appear to be really interested in Mishima and encourage M. to share everything he knows about the man (not much, since M.'s narrow scholarly interests were in Early American Literature) and his suicide. The gory details of *seppuku* especially fascinate them, and M. congratulates himself on fulfilling one of his original purposes: to "lead the local inhabitants out of their charming but dissolute provincialism."

As far as he is concerned, M. has been playing an amusing, ego-boosting game with the slow-witted provincials. As the sham poet Bunthorne explains, in Gilbert & Sullivan's *Patience*, "You must lie upon the daisies and discourse in novel phrases of your complicated state of mind,/ The meaning doesn't matter if it's only idle chatter of a transcendental kind./ The meaning doesn't matter if it's only idle chatter of a transcendental kind./ And everyone will say,/ As you walk your mystic way,/ 'If this young man expresses himself in terms too deep for *me,*/

Why, what a very singularly deep young man this deep young man must be." On the whole, M. is satisfied with his performance, though mildly uneasy about how intensely curious the people are.

Despite the "troubling foreboding" that M. feels at the end of the evening tea, he is surprised to receive a note from Mrs. Brumblelo two days later, informing him that *"Kudzu Valley is committing suicide by default ... and the old saviors of private pride, religion, community spirit, and free enterprise have failed us."* Consequently, she announces that the community leaders he met at her house are forming a Yukio Mishima Cultural Association *"to assist in drawing back from the abyss."* Although he wasn't present, the attendees unanimously appointed Mr. M chairman. Rather bemusedly, he cooperates by hanging posters of Mishima around town and by ordering copies of Mishima novels to be propped up in the show window of Unfug's Electric, "amid the propane space heaters, the air conditioners, the gas and electric water heaters, the portable fans, the toasters, the microwave ovens, and the automatic can openers"—a lengthy catalogue that M. probably intends to show that the books are out of place and will be ignored.

But they aren't. As M. sputters, "It has got out of hand, this business; it has got monstrously out of hand." People are buying Mishima's novels and absorbing their content. Elementary school children spend their recesses practicing combat with bamboo staves or meditating. A First Cosmic Nihilist church springs up and replaces the established Protestant congregations. In the evening, children and adults gather to present papers on weighty subjects such as "'The Influence of Lady Murasaki on Yukio Mishima'" and "'*Seppuku*: The Death of an Honorable Man.'" M. attends one paper reading but can't accept the participants' genuine commitment; instead he desperately critiques the surface of the proceedings, noting, "The children did not project their voices very well, and most of these papers, I feel certain, were improperly footnoted." And an overall-clad farmer stops M. on the street to say that he'd written directly to M.'s old department at the state university for "'any additional, you know, information you got on ol' Mishima.'" Things certainly have got out of hand, far beyond M.'s ability to control. How could he have imagined that people would actually involve themselves in things they read? That probably never happened with the bored students in his classrooms, or when he was dropping the names of unfamiliar authors at faculty parties. Seeing how far people are taking Mishima as an inspirational role model, M. records an especially shocking admission that he confides to his diary: "How am I going to tell these people that never in my life have I read an entire work by Yukio Mishima? How am I going to impress upon them that I don't intend to either?"

The story's humor comes from watching the smug, snooty M. being taken down a peg, floundering in bafflement. On the other hand, most humorous stories don't involve a townful of people committing mass suicide.

If M. had read Mishima and if he had paid attention to the people around him, he might have realized that Kudzu Valley is in an emotional crisis. When the nearby Cusseta Dam is completed, the town will disappear underwater. That is the doom Mrs. Brumblelo referred to in her note to M., proclaiming that the corrupt political process that ignores public welfare is a threat to the townspeople's core values. This apocalyptic interpretation actually is reinforced by the empty political jargon in a story in the *Atlanta Constitution* announcing that the legislature has voted to complete construction of the dam. At this moment, therefore, Mishima's devoted Kudzu Valley readers are ready to accept his notion of cosmic nihilism, to imagine that the only meaning in human existence is what they are willing to declare and enact. And that is why, a few months later, M. receives an invitation to lead the members of the Yukio Mishima Cultural Association of Kudzu Valley, Georgia, in committing *seppuku* on the post office lawn. He responds in the only way he can by belittling them: "The fools. The country simpletons. The redneck louts aspiring to be literary."

Then they actually follow through. The gory event itself isn't described, although a story in the *Atlanta Constitution* calls the ceremony "'lovely.'" But everyone in town is dead, "with the exception only of children under the age of six and a single responsible adult." M. is that adult, "the sole adult inhabitant of their anemic, tumbledown, backwater community," now somehow responsible for what happened but also for what might happen in the future. It would have been simpler for him to have committed *seppuku*. According to a newspaper clipping that Mrs. Brumblelo reads to M., even Mishima himself had no idea what *he* could do after completing the long tetralogy that was his final work: "'I'm afraid, and I really don't know why.'" Mishima's death, like the deaths of the Yukio Mishima Cultural Society of Kudzu Valley, Georgia, may be simply an expression of despair, a failure of imagination, and an admission of defeat. Or it could be a positive acceptance of cosmic nihilism. Or it could be a defiant commitment to traditional values that are being discarded. (But it almost certainly is *not*, as in "The Samurai and the Willows," a long-meditated, culturally-appropriate decision.) In any event, M. has no idea what has happened. He is left in frustrated bewilderment. All he can do is ask in a probably rhetorical prayer, "Dear, dear God, what am I supposed to do?"

# 2

# Outside/In & Inside/Out
## *Novels, 1975–1980*

At about the same time he was learning to write short fiction, Michael Bishop began his career as a novelist. As the following extended discussion of his first and possibly-seventh novel shows, Bishop immediately was attracted to extremely challenging subject material and was unable to leave well enough alone.

Very soon after his work began attracting attention from readers and reviewers, Bishop started getting hints of interest from publishers who were looking for a novel. According to his essay about the experience, the most recent version of which is included as an afterword to the 2015 revised edition of *A Funeral for the Eyes of Fire*, Betty Ballantine encouraged him to revise his preliminary version into "an interplanetary thriller with a strong anthropological dimension and a pervasive aura of neo-Shakespearean tragedy." Ballantine books published the novel under Bishop's preferred title in 1975. An extremely different version appeared in 1980 under the title *Eyes of Fire* as part of Pocket Books' Timescape line. And a somewhat revised form of the second text appeared under the original title in 2015. Examining the first two novels carefully will let us watch how Bishop learned to develop complex ideas convincingly as he thoroughly reconstructed a book that was good enough to be *published* but that didn't feel finished

In the following discussion, the title of the first novel is abbreviated simply to *Funeral*, the second to *Eyes*. To avoid confusion, a mention of "Gunnar" means that *Funeral* is being discussed; "Seth" indicates a reference to *Eyes*; "Gunnar/Seth" indicates things that are true of both of the first two characters/novels. For they really *are* two distinctly different novels. Ian Watson rightly describes the second novel as "a recreation, not a revision" of the first, and he adds accurately that "where another writer might simply have pruned excesses, Bishop hasn't merely reorchestrated the same source but has written an entirely different symphony based on the same themes; and on several new ones." Evidently, Bishop discovered that he was writing about something so important that he needed to return to the novel's raw materials and try again to get it right. So let's identify some of the major themes both novels share, to see how the second book develops harmonic variations of some themes from the first.

All the changes between *Funeral* and *Eyes* are too numerous to list here. To give some brief notion of their pervasiveness, note that the young central character is named Gunnar Balduin in *Funeral*, Seth Latimer in *Eyes*. His actions are described originally in the first person but later in the third. On a mission from planet Kier to planet Trope, he is physically attracted to a native who is a young male named Bassern in *Funeral*, a young female named Lijadu in *Eyes*. Throughout *Eyes*, moreover, Bishop frequently changes details of the characters' actions and of the actions' results.

It is easier to list the few things that don't change between novels. One is the fundamental theme announced in the title of both books. In *Funeral*, it is stated in one of the four long introductory epigrams, a quote from Theodore Roszak's *The Making of a Counter Culture*: "The Shaman ... is one who knows that there is more to be seen of reality than the waking eye sees. Besides our eyes of flesh, there are eyes of fire that burn through the ordinariness of the world and perceive the wonders and terrors beyond." Bishop chose not to use any of the epigrams themselves in *Eyes* because they struck him as "either overexplicit or pretentious," but in his "Author's Note" he praises Roszak's writing as "a trenchant essay on the conflict between the world views of the shaman and the technocrat." Obviously, then, Bishop is concerned with tension between flesh and fire, male and female, mechanical and prophetic. Since the action Bishop describes takes place in the realm of flesh, most of the characters insist on reducing the conflict to "reality versus fantasy, nothing more than that" (*Funeral*). In that context, as the word "funeral" in the first novel's title suggests, the physical power of the technocrat will succeed in suppressing the spiritual-emotional activities of the shaman in both books, an outcome that fits Bishop's original intent to give the story the feel of a tragedy.

This sense of tragedy, as it turns out, works with another consistent element in both novels: the role of the central character. Despite many changes in detail, including even his name, Gunnar/Seth occupies the same position in the action. Whether he is the narrator of *Funeral* or simply the viewpoint character in *Eyes*, readers can see only events that the young man is present to observe. In the same way, we are forced—though we do so with growing reluctance as the character's lack of perception becomes increasingly obvious—to interpret events by using his information. With his older, dominant brother, Gunnar/Seth is sent to planet Trope to persuade members of a religious sect to resettle on another world. Accompanied by representatives of the government that wants to get rid of the sect and by two representatives from the world trying to recruit the sect members as immigrants, the young man travels to the group's remote sanctuary. There, in apparently random outbreaks of violence, much destruction and many deaths occur, and through it all the main character awkwardly gropes about, trying to figure out what is happening and what role he should play.

To identify the particular Elizabethan tragedy Bishop has in mind, in *Funeral* Gunnar refers to the two ambassadors accompanying him as "Rosencrantz and Gildenstern." Direct echoes of *Hamlet* are fewer in *Eyes*, but there too Seth reflects that he "knew himself well enough to understand that hesitation rather than conscience frequently made a coward of him." Bishop does not intend to parallel *Hamlet*'s plot closely, but he does want readers to remember the frantic bafflement felt by Shakespeare's hero. In *Funeral*, for example, Gunnar must make major decisions even though "I wondered why I always seemed to be just missing connections with these aliens"; typically, *Eyes* describes how Seth "wasn't yet ready to confront the enigma of the prevailing situation" so that later "Seth gestured impotently at the ceiling, and made a moue of bewilderment." It sometimes appears, to paraphrase Gertrude's comment on the Player Queen, that Bishop's young man protests his innocent helplessness too much.

Or perhaps not. Like Hamlet, Bishop's character is forced to perform an important mission in a confusing setting with insufficient instructions. He also resembles Hamlet in that the immediate effects of many of his actions are disastrous. But Gunnar/Seth is even more isolated than Hamlet. Bishop's character has both been kept in the dark and also deliberately lied to by everyone he should be able to trust, including his brother. In particular, in both of these novels the central character eventually learns that he has been deceived about the true purpose of his mission, which actually is to lure the sect members to a barren area of their newly adopted planet where they will be treated essentially as slave laborers. So even if Gunnar/Seth could do without bloodshed what he has been told to, the achievement still would be sordid. As it is, the violent outcome makes the whole enterprise appear futile.

One final element that remains unaltered in Bishop's reworking of the story—along with the conflicting world views and the disastrously obtuse central character—is the insertion of three rather lengthy tales into the action. The first is a folk tale, the second a dream, the third a prophecy shared as part of a memory. Working together with the other constants in *Funeral* and *Eyes*, these interpolated visions clarify Bishop's purpose in writing and then rewriting his novel. One reason Bishop can delete the epigrams that introduced *Funeral* is that the stories do a more subtle but efficient job of focusing readers' attention; they also can influence the central character because he is the only person who hears all three.

The folktale is from the planet where the mission originates, the world that intends to trick and exploit the sect members. It is printed as a Prologue in *Funeral*, shared verbally with Seth in *Eyes*. In both versions, the main character is an immortal, playful vicious, utterly selfish "jongeleur-thief" who is finally trapped by the forces of Law and exiled to the Obsidian Wastes until he can find and submit to Conscience. He eventually discovers that Conscience is (1) his exact double, (2) sealed helplessly behind a wall of glass, and (3) doubly powerless because before the glass closed around him he bit off his own hands and had hawks distribute his fingers around the world wherever tribes were forming so that humans would feel a need to develop laws. In both versions of the novel, Conscience makes the same statement to the embodiment of chaotic selfishness: "'I am not your second self.... I am the half you [have—*Funeral*] denied.'" Conscience pleads that the halves they embody should be reunited, but the other denies this request. He will do as he pleases, leaving Conscience able only to protest and to "weep because he could not intervene."

The second tale, the dream, is related by the leader of the sect soon after Gunnar/Seth arrives in their valley refuge. In *Funeral*, the speaker is the Pledgeson; in *Eyes*, it is the Pledgechild, for in the second novel Bishop stresses that the androgynous natives who make up Trope's mainstream society represent male attitudes while the equally androgynous members or the sect are perceived as female. In both books, the human central character is accompanied by the two aliens who have come to invite sect members to their planet, the Magistrate (Trope's supreme ruler), and by the Magistrate's virulently anti-sect deputy. The sect leader tells them that in a recent dream she saw Seitabe Mwezahbe (the First Magistrate and founder of the mainstream society) confront Gaaidu (the founder of her sect). Mwezahbe—who stressed rationality and gave natives of Trope the ability to evolve deliberately into superior, masterful personalities—harangued Gaaidu, demanding submission because reason had already supplanted mysticism long before the messiah appeared: "'You came too late,'" he exclaims. This appears to be correct. The sect has been excluded from the mainstream and is about to be cast off the planet. Nevertheless, in dream Gaaidu "strangely ... senses that Mwezahbe longs for the rebuttal he fears." Analytic rhetoric is one of the societal founder's tools, so the sect founder never replies verbally to her opponent's tirade; however, she finally approaches the other and embraces him:

> [S]he steps forward into the body of Seitabe Mwezahbe. She allows herself to become one with the flesh dream of her inquisitor. For a brief moment the two are a unity, drinking in starlight through the same fiery eyes.... Together, they are whole and seamless.
> So is the world.
> But Mwezahbe begins to shake his head, discomfited by the surrender of his autonomy. When he can stand it no longer, he backs away from Gaaidu's all-encompassing embrace, thereby denying his nuclear union with her.

At the end of both versions of this tale, the Magistrate is disturbed by what he has heard. In the first novel, his venomous deputy explodes in outrage at the suggestion that his rational ideal could merge even briefly with its complement; in the second, the deputy has stalked out before the story begins.

The third and last tale is told to Gunnar/Seth alone. It is part of a memory shared by the Magistrate as they huddle together in a truck driving away from the sect's valley refuge. The Magistrate has been unable to restrain his subordinate in order to work out a peaceful solution. Several people have been killed, including the sect leader, and everyone is being driven back to a city. There, all surviving sect members will be transported to the orbiting starship where Gunnar/Seth's brother waits to take them into exile. While those around them in the truck sleep, the Magistrate tells Gunnar/Seth about something that happened when he himself was much younger, an army officer taking part in a brutal raid intended to terrorize the sect. In the confusion, separated from the other soldiers, he encountered Gaaidu alone. Knowing that the officer would kill her, the sect founder instructed him to preserve the dust of her crystalline eyes, a custom by which natives of Trope recognize and honor their dominant parent. The sect founder promised that if the young man did so the combination of his guile and her supernatural influence would help him rise to become Magistrate. After telling him that to prepare for supreme power he must "grow in wisdom, compassion, purpose," she explained how that change would take place: "I'll work for you in death as will my people, infusing you with wisdom, compassion, purpose." She also told the young man that it was fitting that her heir should be "hostile in his appointed position but sympathetic in his inmost self." This prophecy came exactly true. Now, though, the Magistrate realizes that he has failed to balance the two sides of humanity. He cannot remain in the role of Magistrate, even if that means that his (literally and figuratively) unbalanced deputy will take his place.

Listening to stories is a way to discover shapes that let us grasp our confusing, disturbing experience. We already have noted that Bishop's central character is extremely innocent, misled, and obtuse. Still, not even he can miss what this series of stories is saying as each interrupts (and interprets) his own confusing and disturbing experience: Human nature is torn by a conflict that can neither be resolved nor ignored. Shaman vs. technocrat, female vs. male, fire vs. flesh—each side craves yet fears intercourse/union with its opposite. They approach, retreat, approach, retreat, approach, retreat.... This movement cannot cease as long as we are both individual and social beings. When one of those complementary needs is repressed, people sink into disappointment, anger, and irrational violence.

Recognizing the desirability of balancing both sides of human nature, a person should strive to develop simultaneously as a distinct intellect and as a member of a larger community. Of course, successfully achieving this goal is difficult for a storyteller to imagine; it would be even more difficult to live out in the real world. Nevertheless, this is the task Bishop undertakes to show. The main character in both these novels gropes toward escape from isolated selfishness, impotent conscience, and bewildered hesitation. Uncertainly but persistently, he learns to become both realistic and morally responsible.

Truly listening to what the set of stories within these novels has to say and then applying the message is difficult. In *Funeral*, Gunnar briefly identifies himself with the active-destructive figure in the folk tale, then remind himself of his conscious role and protests, "I had not been separated from my conscience. I had not resolved to betray anyone." Nevertheless, he sees how the models of failure presented in the tales are echoed in the action around him. Even more explicitly, in *Eyes* Bishop refers to the same folk tale in a description of the high priests of Conscience who carry their identification with that self-mutilated ideal to a literal extreme by having both hands amputated as part of their elevation; nevertheless, they have trouble interpreting the role's significance, disdaining Conscience in shaping their current, deceitful policies. In both novels, the people who worship Conscience do dishonorable things in the name of their faith, as they try to entice sect members to emigrate from Trope to slavery in the Obsidian Wastes. The fanatically devout worshipers cannot see how much their actions actually resemble those of the jongeleur-thief who mocks Conscience. And they are assisted in their plotting by Gunnar/Seth's brother, whose schemes Bishop's central character caries out while energetically protesting his innocence.

Characters in both novels often fail because they cannot step back and look at themselves and at what they are doing. The stories Gunnar/Seth hears encourage him to notice analogs of himself and the people surrounding him.

He also has a chance to observe how and why people's actions don't get them what they want. In both novels, such failure has two aspects: Most obviously, characters feel disturbed when they are unable to subordinate someone they see as an opponent; in fact, they also are frustrated because they have been unable to express or carry out an impulse to surrender their isolation and unite with the other. At both levels, failure results from the initial conception of the other person as separate, radically different. And yet people insist that they *are* different. The androgynous natives of Trope, for example, insist on being considered male or female depending on their proclaimed ideological orientation.

The stories that interrupt the action of Bishop's novels illustrate this human desire to separate from others whether or not this behavior really suits the person, is appropriate to the immediate situation, or ultimately is likely to produce a desirable result. In both novels' interpolated tales, the characters actually are complementary but still insist to the point of destruction on their distinctly separate identities. The same is true of both novel's main action. On Trope, for example, "single-minded allegiance to reason" is insane. In fact, after hearing the Pledgechild's dream Seth realizes that the Magistrate and the Pledgechild are "afflicted with complementary varieties" of madness. Recognizing that separation produces frustration that can escalate into madness, Gunnar/Seth attempts to escape his own isolation—a painful, confusing process, both because his experience has not prepared him for the task and because he does not consciously realize what he is trying to do. The concepts embedded in the stories he hears do not make his growth easier, just more possible for it to begin.

How Gunnar/Seth begins his efforts is sometimes shockingly inept. One key scene occurs shortly after the visitors arrive in the sect's valley refuge. It also is interesting because it illustrates how Bishop literally revised (i.e., re*saw*) and improved the story, making his central character's development simultaneously more uncertain and more believable. This section in both novels describes the main character's attraction to a young-adolescent member of the sect—Bassern and Lijadu respectively. In *Funeral*, the scene in which Bassern invites Gunnar to share his sleeping room is extremely disturbing for Gunnar to understand because of its homoerotic and pedophilic overtones:

> I'm not ashamed to admit that I caught his body in my arms, pulled him unresistingly toward me, struggled to feel his strange heartbeat. Bassern was sinewy and frail then, and I rocked him against me as a father rocks his child, the father I've

never had the opportunity to become. It was easy to imagine Bassern a human child, maybe even a young daughter before puberty and adolescent willfulness have overthrown her dependence on her father. Bassern, a dependent child; Bassern, a daughter caught within her father's yearning. Despite what happened later, what happened in the Galleries then was too natural for shame. And I still am not ashamed of that terribly long, bitterly brief moment of communion.

This embrace occurs in the context of the Pledgeson's dream in which opposites merge physically. *Funeral* also prepares for it by Gunnar's first description of Bassern as physically uniting opposing halves:

Although his body was beautiful, his head was misshapen and brutish looking, entirely without symmetry. His eyes stared at us from different levels above his uneven cheek bones. His scalloped nostrils didn't match; whereas one flared the other was narrowly cupped. The ridge of flesh that marked the boy's vestigial mouth was a broken one. I could not help thinking that the boy's head had been violently halved early in his life and then ineptly put back together.

Gunnar has not yet worked out what this reunion of violently separated halves could represent. Dimly seeing the boy as a living symbol of joined opposites, though, Gunnar naturally is attracted to him and craves communion with him. Putting that desire in human terms is a mistake, the kind of oversimplification that Gunnar is prone to; however, the hazy but powerful desire for unity is nothing to be ashamed of, especially since Gunnar never attempts to go beyond emotional intercourse with Bassern to physical sex.

In *Eyes*, on the other hand, Seth tries to force himself physically on Lijadu, who promptly pins him face down on the ground and lectures him about his misunderstanding of intimacy. The revised scene is simultaneously less and more disturbing than the original. In one sense, the attempted rape is "normalized" because Seth sees the young native as female. At the same time, Bishop complicates the potential relationship considerably because all Seth's sexual experience until this moment has been homosexual. In particular, Seth has been forced into the submissive role by his brother, so he is at first unable to listen to Lijadu's instruction: "Fear, anger shame. Seth didn't know what she was talking about.... She had pinioned him as Abel had had often pinioned him, and what usually came next was acceptable or degrading according to his frame of mind."

This kind of sex isn't distasteful because of the character's gender identification but because it was forced on Seth so that all he could do was accept it. In truth, Seth is not especially homosexual. He and his brother are clones, and it was not affection but their isolation among aliens that brought them together sexually. Seth actually suspects that his brother "had introduced him to their unique variety of autoeroticism because Abel's self-love was so great that it had to have an object outside itself. Or, then again, perhaps Abel had merely been seeking to possess their common isosire in his, Seth's, person." In any event, Seth's experience has been as a sexual object, a reflection of self-love, or as a symbol of ownership; none of that prepares him to approach someone with whom he feels an urge to join.

Without downplaying Seth's lust, we may also suspect that he has been drawn to Lijadu because, like Bassern, she represents the joining of extremes. She explains, for example, why she returned to the valley after a sojourn in the city:

> "What made my reimmersion in my faith possible ... was that the polarity I'd insisted on seeing ... that between our Holy One and the First Magistrate—wasn't necessarily a polarity at all. J'gosfi and sh'gosfi [male or female self-images] are *orientations* toward the truth ... not embodiments or absolute negations of it. A sh'gosfi need not forfeit her identity if she learns to analyze her visions, nor j'gosfi surrender his rational orientation if he begins to perceive the world through sh'gaidu eyes of fire."

This is clearly stated in terms the novel has prepared readers to interpret, though Seth is still too confused to see it as more than a willingness to accept union in the mechanical terms he is used to.

The sexual amorphousness in this scene is due in part to the influence of Le Guin's *The Left Hand of Darkness*, which Bishop absorbed with admiration and delight before beginning his first novel. Describing the androgynous natives of planet Winter, Le Guin grappled with our language's refusal to let one person simultaneously be male/female/neuter ("Gender" 14–15). Bishop experiences the same problem, especially since his characters (and readers)—like Le Guin's are led to question familiar, comfortable categories of thinking and the language that describes them.

For example, readers must rethink the whole notion of "rape," based on the notion of absolute ideological polarities and isolated identities. The word "intercourse," used just a few paragraphs above, refers both to the accomplishment of physical sex and communication. Our language has no word for intercourse accomplished against the conscious will of another person but in genuine response to the other's needs. When the Magistrate sends telepathic messages to Seth, he perceives them in terms of the sex he is used to: "a kind of lovely violation. A windfall of microscopic seeds penetrating Seth's gray matter and instantly germinating. His own startled consciousness was briefly evicted in order to let this other burst through," and the same process is later referred to as "gentle, uncanny mind rape that made him feel warm and devastatingly petty at the same time." Though he can refer to it only in the language he already has, Seth clearly feels differently about this invasion of his solitariness than he did about the way his brother used him physically. This experience is "gentle," and it even can be "lovely" to feel the diminution of one's autonomy as part of making room to share the presence of another.

Actually, force could be the only way to open communication with people who believe that they are naturally, necessarily isolated from each other. In her dream, the Pledgechild would rather not listen to what the First Magistrate has to say, but the sect founder seizes her and "with the violence of a rape she opens me to the relentless arguments of First Magistrate Mwezahkbe." On the other hand, in his anger and shame, Seth rebukes Lijadu for entering his "mind unbidden.... That's a trespass as violent as anything I've done. It's a rape and a trespass." When she realizes how much her intrusion disturbs him and promises never to do it again, however, Seth is vaguely dissatisfied:

> They lay in the dark, facing each other. The shame in Seth had not completely subsided. He had found these people's cerebrations more fascinating than obtrusive or painful, and yet he had just extracted from Lijadu a promise never to send such pleasant messages to him again. Was this a clever vengeance for his self-inflicted shame? Perhaps it was. A clever vengeance upon himself.

What Seth is beginning to realize is that he himself is responsible for his shame and the "vengeance" it elicits, the curtailment of communication. He begins to understand that at a preconscious level he is afraid of communication and has been working to sabotage it.

"Rape," as we understand it and as Seth has experienced it, is based on one solitary personality dominating another. What looks like rape in these novels may sometimes be an effort to enter someone else's private space not to conquer it but to share it. Like Seth, readers can't rely on our preconceptions. We too must look again.

The theme of nakedness is similarly disturbing, similarly demanding fresh interpretation. *Eyes* especially stresses how unprotected/unconcealed a naked person is. Seth must remove his clothing to confer with the ruler of Kier before he leaves for Trope so that she can verify that he is trustworthy. On Trope, he finds that the Magistrate and his followers conceal their crystalline eyes behind slitted goggles, while the sect members expose theirs freely. When the Magistrate demands Seth's protective goggles as a sign of trust, in return giving into the young man's keeping the dust that actually is the residue of the sect founder, he leaves Seth open and vulnerable to experience. Consequently, he is unable to protect himself from what he sees, and he must reveal—even to himself—what he makes of it.

None of this growth in understanding is easy. In fact, the difficulties experienced by Bishop's character help make his ultimate development believable. From the beginning of *Eyes*, Seth (like Gunnar) has been manipulated into the role of diplomat, intermediary between alien groups. Events push him into a deeper understanding of that role. He is physically embraced by representatives of both sides on Trope. Furthermore, the Magistrate first declares that he and Seth are "*men of one mind*"; much later, after sharing his secret with Seth, the Magistrate declares that the young man is the avatar of the sect's Holy One, returned to save them in their present helplessness. The Magistrate himself, in expiation for his failure to control the catastrophic situation, reverses orientation and declares her intention to lurk in the wilderness, maintaining the sect's values and vowing "to range about this nation like their righteous, walking ghost." Like it or not, therefore, Seth (like Gunnar) has the responsibility of looking out for the helpless sect members, mediating between them and the mechanistic system that intends to exploit them.

The conclusions of both *Funeral* and *Eyes* show the main character taking up that task. He will accompany the sect members to the wastelands of Kier. There, he will do as much as he can to make their lives bearable. The second novel, however, has done a more thorough job of showing his preparation for this role and is more convincing in showing how he goes about it.

In *Funeral*, Gunnar and his brother are fugitives from the Urban Nucleus on Earth, so the last thing they want is to return there. It is practical as well as idealistic, thus, for them to make a lifelong commitment to service on another planet. The young sect member Bassern is forgotten, but to complete their family unit the brothers will welcome their sister from earth:

> *It now appears that Peter and I will die unwed and childless. Unwed, certainly—but Synnova will be our child. And the New Galapagos, arid as they are, sterile as they are, will afford us a brave furnace in which to test our love. Peter will have something to live for again, something other than accumulating riches by dint of Ouermartsee labor, and I will have the chance to shape the perceptions and participate in the discoveries of another of my kind.*

It appears to be taken for granted that the brothers will be given authority to run the colony in a humane fashion, toiling along with the immigrants from Trope in voluntary repentance. The situation sounds perfect for someone who wishes to assuage personal guilt while doing good. A life of noble suffering can be a very comforting conclusion if it validates one's tragic nobility. The only alternative is almost equally histrionic—suicide, as the Magistrate in the first novel chooses.

The situation at the end of *Eyes* is much less neatly resolved. For one thing, Seth and his brother are anxious to return to Earth. Seth has never felt at home among aliens, and he has just begun developing the empathy that readers realize he needs. He is finding fresh significance in the recurring line *"We are imperfect isohets of the same perfect progenitor."* The best he can manage at the moment is a temporary commitment to go to the Obsidian Wastes and help for a while, though the fact that he leaves his commitment open-ended is hopeful. Lijadu, meanwhile, is among the refugees aboard the starship, though Seth has no idea what he can say to her or what relationship they could have in the future. What he does know is that matters won't take care of themselves. He must assert himself immediately to keep people alive. That demands politicking rather than moral posturing, but Seth starts doing what he sees he must.

Both novels conclude with another variety of funeral. During the turmoil on Trope, one of the Kieran ambassadors accompanying Gunnar/Seth has been killed and his body lost. Even though this particular Hawk of Conscience is one whom Gunnar/Seth dislikes intensely, the young man insists that a symbolic burial in space be performed. As they launch an empty spacesuit into the void, Gunnar/Seth becomes disoriented and drifts aimlessly. When he then encounters the empty suit lacking its gloves, he remembers the folk tale of helpless, handless Conscience confronting the nimble jongleur-thief. And so Bishop's character is paralyzed by dread and by the shock of recognizing aspects of both legendary beings in himself.

Then Gunnar is guided back to the ship, feeling himself to be one who "would perhaps never have to be guided again, a man who had come out of emptiness and then back into it—in order to make himself whole." Earlier, Seth had doubted his ability to achieve certainty, although he felt that his experience had at least "given him freedom to discover the boundaries of his own autonomy as a moral agent. Perplexedly, he was still trying to stake those boundaries out." He draws a similar confidence from the funeral in space, letting himself be guided back to the ship by a murderer and reflecting that "through the ritual of a mock-funeral he had contrived to make himself whole, and if no one else understood either the mystery or the mechanics of such a feat, Seth no longer cared."

Recognizing both sides of himself, the man has to get to work. The last scene in *Eyes* shows Seth and Lijadu moving refugees to slightly healthier quarters aboard the starship "which stank now with the natural effluvia of living bodies pent together for long, uninterrupted stretches"—as real, living bodies naturally do. Bishop's first novel ends with the main character striking a noble pose as if he has figured out everything he needs. The revised version shows him wading into the confusing muck of real life, fighting for the people around him and (incidentally) for his own salvation. In *Eyes*, the possibilities of failure are much greater than in Bishop's first version of the story. But so are the possibilities of achievement.

Sensing, with desperate reluctance, the way he needs to grow, the hero of Bishop's first novel reaches the best resolution he could in the best novel Bishop could write at that time. The later version shows not just more novelistic skill but also a fuller understanding of how an unsatisfied, uncertain person could begin developing toward productive maturity. Grasping patterns of action and understanding is the work of all varieties of visionary. Like those who created the stories that are told within this novel, a writer should try to tell the truth. Bishop was discovering better ways to tell his readers what they needed to hear, even if they'd prefer not to. The novels demonstrate that humans need unity as much as they crave separation; that rejecting the demands of conscience to satisfy selfish whims is toxic; and that one should be willing to seize wisdom, compassion and purpose wherever they are to be found.

Although the first version of this story was good enough to be published and drew some very positive reviews, Bishop was so dissatisfied with it that he rethought the whole enterprise a few years later. A few decades after that, as part of the thorough revision of his body of work, he looked at the novel again and published yet a third version, returning to the original title *A Funeral for the Eyes of Fire*.

And then for something completely different ...

After his dramatic (and sometimes melodramatic) performance in the first version of *A Funeral for the Eyes of Fire*, Bishop experimented with a ruthlessly self-controlled, even repressed tone in his next novel. To understand what's going on in *And Strange at Ecbatan the Trees* (1976), readers must pay close attention to passing remarks by Ingram Marley, the tight-lipped narrator. The action evidently is set on an alien planet under a wan sun, circled by a ring of shattered moons. The characters appear to be normal humans who can refer to Earth's calendar and history, but who naturally are more concerned with matters in their own lives—"Atarites" and "Mansuecerians," "Pelagan reivers," "the Parfects," and the threat of the legendary, dreaded "sloak"—that are too familiar to need explanation for eavesdropping readers. But the novel does let Ingram share this background information early on:

> [T]here had been colonists on Mansueceria for six thousand of our years. We had been brought from Earth in starships conceived and constructed by a neo-human species whom our earliest records had always referred to as the Parfects—principally because Earth's last men had considered them free of all human a vices, cleansed of the quasi-mythical taint of Original Sin. It was the Parfects who had

saved mankind from ultimate extermination in the terra-cotta city of Windfall Last in the Carib Sea; who had redeemed us genetically, providing for two contrasting but complementary types of individual (the stoically disciplined Mansuecerians, or "maskers," and the more aggressive, more emotional Atarites); and who had then delivered this population of half a million to the rugged heartland of Ongladread, on a planet more than eight hundred light-years from Earth. Another chance. Yet another chance, in an isolation even more splendid than that the ambient sea had insured at Windfall Last. Then, the early records and later legends unanimously agreed, the Parfects themselves had left us, gone back to turn all of Earth into the gardens of Adam's first paradise. As for man, he had the rocks of Ongladred—and another chance.

In other words, the people in this novel have been *built* with limited ability to observe or act. If they seem to be unnaturally restrained, it's because natural responses were considered too dangerous to trust. As readers watch threatening events accumulate around the characters, the result is considerable, though carefully muted, tension.

This is a tricky approach to storytelling, not unlike Ernest Hemingway's "Big Two-Hearted River," in which obsessively meticulous description of Nick Adams' solitary fishing trip gradually reveals that Nick is forced to concentrate on what's immediately in front of because that's all he can handle at the moment, for memories of some traumatic events evidently are too difficult to confront directly. Yet. Readers of Hemingway's story, however, have a much easier time imagining what Nick could be repressing because they can refer to historical events such as World War I and to human concerns such as shameful cowardice. The world of Ingram Marley is harder to grasp, both because Ingram's terms of reference are different and because the Parfects designed him with limitations that prevent him from seeing things that the readers would—or from responding as readers might consider normal. Hemingway's story ends with a suggestion that Nick is healing, gaining calmness. After that, though it's quite beyond the story's scope, Nick may choose to return to normal society or not. In Bishop's novel, Ingram doesn't have that choice; his experiences must so totally change him that he must change his society. In short, he must learn to do the unimaginable and keep doing it.

Like the readers,' Ingram's understanding of his situation accumulates gradually. Early in the novel, he is satisfied with his place in life. He accepts what he has been told. Even if he is somewhat uneasy with how calmly a masker father accepts the death of his daughter at the hands of barbarian raiders (Pelagan reivers), Ingram he realizes that such calmness is normal because maskers are genetically programmed not to feel/display emotions. Ingram himself is capable of such observations because he is an Atarite, one of the minority genetically designed with more emotional range so that they can look after maskers, "the people of the hand."

Initially, as a low-level servant of the state, Ingram has grudgingly accepted the task of surveilling Gabriel Elk, Atarite former military hero and acknowledged genius whom government officials uneasily distrust because his current interests stretch the boundary of permissible behavior. Imaginative art is severely limited. One cannot, for example, step out of one's social identity by acting the part of a different person in a play. Nevertheless, Elk persists in reanimating corpses to perform dramas before audiences of maskers who display no emotional involvement in the dramas that they're seeing performed—but who nevertheless keep coming back to the theater. Someday, Elk insists, their masks will slip: They *will* respond openly. Ingram is puzzled but fascinated by a project that initially seems futile.

As a Pelagan invasion looms, the government that has uneasily disdained Elk's iconoclastic thinking is forced to ask him to rediscover a literally unthinkable weapon from humanity's past, a laser canon, to win the war. If it is beyond their imagination to conceive, it is beyond Elk's ability to actually *use* the thing. So it's a distraught Ingram who must cut Pelagan warships apart and watch fellow human beings drown.

This individual transformation throws in doubt the Parfects' whole enterprise—whether the attempt to tame basic human nature has any chance of success. Although Ingram doesn't notice it happening, readers have noted how the young man has been absorbing Elk's concerns and attitudes. It's also clear that the supposed distinction between Parfect-designed human species is illusory: Ingram notes that the corpse of the young woman that he and Elk purchase at the novel's beginning wears a disturbingly non-mansuecerian expression, for example, while Elk's shaved head reveals a Pelagan-like birthmark. And once Elk has made laser canons available to the Atarites, they don't meekly hand them back to him after the war is over. No, the Parfects actually *may* be monitoring what is going on, and the legendary sloak *may* be a device that those smug, supposedly-benign meddlers could use to destroy civilization and force humans to climb back from barbarianism again, but that ultimately, inevitably, won't stop humans from expressing themselves, even if that means their potential for violence has been unlocked. The novel clearly predicts that the theater audience will respond someday, and Ingram hopes eventually to "become the first living actor in all our history." He himself flatly declares that the audience will escape their programmed limits: "the day is coming when they will weep."

It might be better, or at least safer, if Ingram and the others accepted their assigned roles, but that doesn't appear to be possible. In

Robert A. Heinlein's *Have Space Suit, Will Travel*, the teenaged narrator watches as an interstellar tribunal disposes of one irredeemably hostile alien race by removing the sun from its home planet, then considers doing the same thing to humanity because of *its* potential for aggression, whereupon the young man explodes, "All right, take away our star—You will if you can and I guess you can. Go ahead! We'll make a star! Then, someday, we'll come back and hunt you down—all of you!" Bishop is too mature and Ingram is still too inhibited to make such a gloriously, heroically stupid boast. Bishop also leaves unstated the silent addendum by Heinlein's hero, "Oh, I didn't mean we could *do* it. Not yet. But we'd *try*. 'Die trying' is the proudest human thing." Nevertheless, when Ingram restates his explanation of how humanity came to its present condition, there seems to be more than a hint of resentment as he describes a body-preserving shell lying "like the casing of one of those fabled bombs that had so long virtually destroyed our spawning place, making our planet the home of a *preemptive neo-human species that had exiled us* [emphasis added], masker and Atarite, to the darkling islands of a northern sea on a world eight hundred light years from Earth." At the novel's conclusion, the Parfects' benevolence is less obvious than their presumption, the self-righteous way they took charge of human destiny and did things to us before casting us out of our rightful home.

*Can* humans be made less dangerous but still remain human? As usual, Bishop avoids offering a simple-minded, comforting answer to a complex, disturbing question. The novel leaves open the question of what's ahead for Ingram and the Parfects, whether it might be necessary to destroy humanity in order to save it from itself.

The situation looks even bleaker if the novel is read in the context of "The White Otters of Childhood" (*F&SF*, July 1973), a novella set on Earth just before the Parfects' "ultimate judgment upon mankind." As revenge-obsessed as an Elizabethan tragedy, that story shows a radiation-ruined remnant of humanity sinking into bloody stupor. The narrator eventually is so distressed by the loathsome things he has done as a man that he plans to have his body surgically altered into the form of a shark. In any event,

> I am convinced that we are the freaks of the universe; we were never meant to be. In our natures there is an improper balance of stardust and dross, too much of the one, too little of the other—but not enough of either to give us the perfection of the extreme.

He plans to end his life with a defiant, honest statement by beaching himself so that other creatures may be "aghast at so much unprincipled might," but this image of human futility does seem to limit the possibilities for Ingram's theater.

Looking at *Ecbatan* from decades later, Bishop left the story intact but polished the prose. Where the first version says that a horse "wickeringly barked," the revision says simply that the animal "whickered." Instead of using archaic language to say that his sense of direction "'never faileth,'" Gabriel Elk simply says that it "'rarely fails.'" And he alters the pacing/emphasis of the paragraph toward the end of chapter iii in which Ingram ends their expedition:

> I carried Bronwen Lief into this chamber, placed her on a table, opened the silken quilt away from her, and stared at her gowned body and her noncommittal lips. Still, the ability was there even yet, in death as well as in life she could betray. In the programming room, amid support consoles, minicomputers, oscilloscopes, and Elk's privately engineered neural-surrogate equipment, I associated Bronwen Lief with everything that was then threatening Ongladred's civilization: the barbarians of Angoromain Arachipelago, the mythical sloak, Elk's own wayward genius, and damn me for thinking it, maybe even the inflexibility of Atarite rule. Somehow Bronwein Lief was all of these things; somehow she embodied all the intangibles of the Halcyon Panic.

Here is the revised paragraph:

> I carried Bronwen Lief into this chamber, placed her on a table, opened her silken quilt, and gawped at her gowned body and noncommittal lips. Still, the ability to betray remained there yet; in death as well as in life, she could betray. In the programming room, amid support consoles, minicomputers, oscilloscopes, and Elk's privately engineered neural-surrogate equipment, I associated Bronwein Lief with everything that then menaced Ongdladred's civilization: the barbarians of the Angromain Archipelago, the mythical sloak, Elk's wayward genius. And, damn me for thinking it, even the inflexibility of Atarite rule. Somehow Bronwein Lief carried all these things within her and so embodied all the intangibles of the Halcyon Panic.

Consider how "gawped" is a more vivid word than "stared" and how making the last element in the list of threats into a separate sentence gives it greater, albeit consciously unwilling emphasis. Such small changes add up over the course of a story, especially a novel, to sharper focus and more direct storytelling. Bishop's revisions are full of such choices.

Continuing the arguably downbeat theme of *And Strange at Ecbatan the Trees*, *Stolen Faces* (1977) is possibly Bishop's grimmest novel, his bleakest examination of human nature. The book almost fits the classical definition of tragedy as the story of a great, or at least proud and confident, individual who is brought low because of a personal flaw. Almost-tragedy occurs on two levels in *Stolen Faces*, as the protagonist's collapse parallels the *moral* disintegration of human society.

Several of Bishop's early stories share the same interstellar civilization, Glaktik Komm. This book's earlier discussion of "Blooded on Arachne," for example, described a young cadet barely surviving a mortal test in order to advance in the service. Observing how clever but merciless the testing process is, readers might imagine that Glaktik Komm is deliberately encouraging ruthlessness, training young Nazis to rule space. Actually, the truth is even worse; GK is a vast bureaucratic system that is not so much cruel as uncaring. At some point, as departments and agencies spawned and respawned, the shared goal of running the organization efficiently blurred into an individual desire to avoid blame if anything went wrong. Now GK's complexity means that responsibility has been divided into such small components that no one person ever is blamed for whatever happens. The system's harsh, unstated rule for employees is simple: Accept those social limitations or recognize there's no place in society for you.

Learn or die.

Lucian Yeardance has somehow failed to learn that rule when he arrives on planet Tezcatl as the new kommissar of the Sancorage, a quarantine facility created over a century ago to care for the sufferers of muphormacy, a leprosy-like disease that left its victims hideously maimed. Although Yeardance has been demoted from GK's spacefleet due to minor personal conflicts with his superior officer, he is not bitter. He has an open mind about his new assignment. He intends to fulfill his duties conscientiously as soon as he can learn what they are, and "he still didn't intend to cry mercy of the system that had dropped him here." He now has command of a squad of young GK cadets, "civkis," in a structure that contains living quarters, infirmary, and store room. The Compound where the infected live is a short distance away, and the whole institution is safely remote from the planet's capitol city Town Tezcatl because "the disease had assumed slashingly epidemic proportions before survivors were rounded up and herded into the Tezcatlipocaa Reserve. The much heralded prophylactic symbody designed by the galens [physicians] of Glatik Komm was as fallable, apparently, as humankind itself, for the muphomers who lived in the Compound had still not been cured." This is the official information that Yeardance receives; readers should note that equivocal "apparently."

As, isolated but hopeful, Yeardance begins taking stock of his resources and of the new job's challenges, he is startled by a visit by a delegation of sufferers from the Compound who try to present him with a normal, unblemished baby who's just been born to them. Yeardance is repulsed but moved to pity by their physical and emotional deformities—unlike the Tezcatl civkis who simply loathe the murphormers as "animals." When Yeardance insists that the all the inmates actually be examined in the infirmary, the staffis are startled to find no trace of the muphormacy germ. (Like the novel, this essay will continue to refer to compound residents as muphormers because that's what other people call them and how they label themselves.) Though the Compound inmates' most extreme physical aberrations are inexplicable, much of their physical degeneration is the result of poor diet and harsh living conditions. At this point, like a good fledgling administrator, Yeardance supposes that the problem is inefficient administration, so he travels to Town Tezcatl to end the unnecessary quarantine or at the very least update the Compound's supply invoices. What he finds is that the people in authority understand the ugly situation but don't intend to correct it. Rather than dealing with Yeardance man to man, the colony's governor puts on "a 'plenipotentiary Komm-mask'" that hides the top part of his face: "The fitting of the mask meant that the judgment to issue from the man beneath it was a wholly impartial one conveyed by the man's sense of office rather than his own prejudices. In Yeardance's experience, however, the man behind the mask usually began to think himself infallible…" In fact, the governor reassures Yeardance that the "muphormers" should be happy where they are, safe from encroachment by settlers who would just steal their land. All the governor can or will do for Yeardance is direct him to the colony's bursar, who smoothly explains that food and drugs are so scarce that there just isn't any more that can be done for the people in the Compound. And so he is sent back to Sancorage, explicitly told to stay there and keep silent.

That is, of course, impossible for a genuinely empathetic human being, even though he is helplessly stunned by GK's determination to continue an inhuman policy. Yeardance tries to find some alternative course of action. Exploring Sancorage's records, he discovers that the kommissar before him had followed the official instructions exactly and so had served his time in ineffective isolation. The kommissar before that had gone to the other extreme; before she was caught and punished, she cared about the people in the compound so much that she stole from Glaktik Komm to buy extra food and drugs on the black market. Neither was effective in helping the sufferers. With no clear model to emulate, Yeardance becomes increasingly desperate and irrational. At this point, the novel's viewpoint often shifts from Yeardance to that of the young civkis, who formerly equated the muphormers' physical ugliness with moral degeneracy but who now have been impressed by Yeardance's passion and by his demonstration that the muphormers have normal emotions. Their sympathy awakened, the civkis unhappily watch Yearwood flailing around hopelessly—

—Until his despair reaches the depth of the Muphormers,' who have made a religion of worthlessness, the fact that mainstream society considers them "dung." They worship perfection by further debasing themselves, so that they faithfully enhance their loathsomeness by amputating digits or limbs, scarring their bodies or transposing bits of flesh to create the tumor-like growths that have simulated morphomacy since the disease itself ceased to ravage them. The medical staff couldn't explain this aspect of the sufferers' leper-like condition when they were checked in the infirmary, but Yeardance must suspect what is going on as he insists on being admitted to their annual religious festival. There, drunk and despairing, he watches as the inhabitants of the Compound perform more ritual mutilations, including the first on a little girl who has been kept unmarred until now, until the birth of the perfect baby boy whom Yeardance saw at the novel's opening. Then, sharing the muphormer's ecstatic hopelessness, Yeardance gouges out his eyes. The civkis break up the ceremony, but Yeardance escapes into the woods. He is last seen in the novel being stalked by a band of murderous muphormer children led by the little girl who has just received her first ritual mutilation.

The gruesome scene in which Yeardance blinds himself inevitably suggests the climax of *Oedipus Rex*. However, Oedipus is simply the victim of Fate, and his "flaw" consists of proudly boasting that he is in control of the situation. Yeardance understands that he is a minor official in a vast system, as superior officers blandly remind him. He himself accepts responsibility but has no power to act, while all the people who should have power deny personal responsibility. There simply and absolutely is no sane action he can take to correct a dreadful wrong, and he can't live with that realization.

Yeardance's personal failure is dreadful but not exactly tragic. On another level, however, Glaktik Komm's failure is closer to classic tragedy, the collapse of a proud but flawed entity. GK takes for granted that it is in firm control of planet Tezcatl. After all, it efficiently allocates all resources and manages all personnel for the colony's overall good. As part of its efficiency, it makes sure that no individual resistance accumulates. Thus, though the civkis at the Sancorage obey Yeardance's orders they still belong to GK so that each dutifully submits regular reports on Yeardance's behavior; it's unclear who actually pays attention to the reports, but such constant surveillance is typical inside a paranoid bureaucracy to remind members that no one is entitled to a private life, that no one is safe. Making the same point, when Yeardance is in Town Tezcatl, the colony's bursar treats him to a dinner theater performance representing a bloody Aztec ritual of submission and sacrifice before an audience of revelers. Readers must wonder how much GK actually knows about the muphormers' ghastly self-mutilation— or, rather, how much potential knowledge GK is repressing. And the muphormers themselves parody GK's attitude as they deny personal power and responsibility. So perhaps the novel does show the tragedy of a proud entity brought low by self-destructive pride, willful blindness. Except, of course, that GK isn't brought low. Readers see that GK's presumed moral authority has collapsed, but that doesn't matter inside the novel. No one with any kind of authority takes notice or cares.

Consider the story's conclusion. When the civkis break up the muphormers' orgy of self-mutilation and rescue the unharmed baby boy, and then when it's discovered that that Kommissar Lucian Yeardance has been killed by a muphormer, GK is forced to clean up the mess. Citizens are reassured that the governor, after all, is "not an unfeeling man." Hearing that official announcement, one of the civkis "listened with a corrosive cynicism she was appalled to discover in herself." So GK closes the Sancorage colony, and the civkis also are dispersed with the quiet understanding that their careers have been blighted because they are somehow associated with the scandal. The same civki who recognizes the glib phoniness of GK's official response does manage one defiant gesture by giving the rescued murphormer baby boy the name Lucian in honor of the man responsible for his salvation.

*Stolen Faces'* epilogue, however, carries the action farther into the future and suggests that Yeardance's efforts were absolutely futile in the long run. Most of the freed muphormers did not integrate successfully into society. Most of the Compound's children, in fact, voluntarily accepted sterilization because, without realizing or admitting it, they learned the lesson that GK teaches its members. "They had been raised in consonance with the Civi-Korps ethic of responsible self-denial ... and so they complied. Those who did not comply were given isolated duty-assignments, arbitrary punishments, or Komm-visas off-planet." In any case, they still are marked as muphormers: "They could not eradicate *every* trace of their origin, for the simple fact that regulations denied them access to prosthetic devices or plastic surgery. By contrast, the mark of Cain on the heads of their fellow 'Tezcatli was invisible.'" Following that angry condemnation of the general population is the novel's terse last paragraph:

> A century after the revelations of the "Sancorage Affair," almost everyone even remotely involved with it was dead. The planet had three new frontier cities already half the size of Town Tezcatl, and other problems had arisen to occupy people's hearts and minds.

"Winning hearts and minds" was a familiar phrase during the Vietnam War, describing propaganda campaigns against the Viet Cong; it assumed that passions and values were so superficial that they could easily be accessed and manipulated. Even without awareness of that topical reference, it's clear that Bishop is condemning human eagerness to be distracted, to accept comfortable lies rather than strain for truth that might lead to productive action. *Stolen Faces*' basic, genuine tragedy may be that no one really notices or learns from society's moral void. The novel's real climax is not a bloody catastrophe but an empty silence.

The recent republication (in revised form) of the 1979 novel *Transfigurations* lets readers appreciate how Michael Bishop concluded his writing apprenticeship with a masterful examination of the anthropology of fiction and the fiction of science.

In earlier novels, Bishop had tried out a variety of tones: Elizabethan melodrama (in *A Funeral for the Eyes of Fire*, 1975), emotional repression (*And Strange at Ecbatan the Trees*, 1976), Grand Guignol horror (*Stolen Faces*, 1977), and multi-protagonist dialogue (*A Little Knowledge*, 1977; to be considered later in this study). Overall, besides the stylistic versatility, reviewers noted how his early fiction frequently focused on characters who must find their way through a barrier that separates them from an alien social group—in short, its anthropological approach to science fiction.

Of course, any piece of fiction could be labeled "anthropological" if it uses extrapolation based on observation to depict individuals within a social group. Fiction, however, works deductively from general rules to individual cases, while anthropology attempts to proceed inductively from individual examples to the formation of general principles. Science in general tries to understand general principles, and science fiction is a branch of literature playing with the idea that humans can (or will be) able to understand and control their lives. The discipline of anthropology attempts to study the unique ways in which people behave in an alien culture, so that observers can increase their understanding of human nature in general. These observations may then suggest alternative behaviors within our own culture, as when Margaret Mead's study of healthy adolescence in the South Seas was used to argue for greater sexual freedom in America.

Bishop realized how difficult it could be to actually carry out anthropological research, but he was fascinated by the effort. In his earlier short fiction such as "Cathadonian Odyssey" and "The House of Compassionate Sharers," he had begun exploring the perilous but vital role of empathy in human life, the ways in which approaching someone else sympathetically can turn out to be deadly or revivifying. Thus, besides his natural human curiosity and his compulsion as a writer of fiction, Bishop was drawn to the discipline of anthropology in order to consider humans in different settings. In his earliest novels, he focused on characters who are forced into the role of anthropologists; in *Transfigurations*, for the first time, he dealt with people who are trained anthropologists. The novel grew out of "Death and Designation among the Asadi" (*If*, February 1973), a novella shortlisted for the Hugo and Nebula awards. David Hartwell's suggestion that Bishop consider expanding that original story led Bishop to consider first the technical difficulties of expanding a story that felt complete, albeit enigmatic, but also to ask himself in what direction that story actually was going.

"Death and Designation" is set on the newly discovered planet BoskVeld (landmass divided between woods and prairie), where explorers have discovered a tribe, the Asadi—one group on the whole planet—of approximately 500 hominid creatures who gather in a clearing every day for constant, asocial activity, then disperse into the surrounding forest at night. Scattered relics of a higher culture suggest that they have not always been brutal savages, but it is not clear why the Ur'Asadi had degenerated—or how the Asadi manage to survive at all in what looks like a state of barely repressed hostility. Glaktik Komm, the soulless bureaucracy that manages interstellar civilization, is uncertain how to treat the Asadi, which gives cultural xenologist Egan Chaney the chance to propose a plausible-sounding project to study them by going alone into the Calyptran Wild and insinuating himself into the tribe

The story is comprised of an assemblage of scholarly writings, jottings, and informal recordings that Chaney left behind when he abandoned his fellow humans and vanished into the wilderness.

Anthropology attempts to get past the notion that a culture must be inferior if it is different from our own. One possible problem with such an effort is that the empathetic anthropologist may discover tempting possibilities of behavior that subvert his/her position as an objective observer. Instead of observing others, then, the anthropologist winds up revealing himself. "Accepting a multitude of perspectives," as Chaney puts it, can go so far that the observer winds up becoming "subhuman" according to the dominant culture. The best literary depiction of this devolution is Joseph Conrad's "Heart of Darkness," in which the narrator searches along the Congo River for traces of Mr. Kurtz, a young man who went to Africa as more of a missionary than a commercial agent, intending to enter the native culture so he could transform it into a facsimile of Western European civilization. But Kurtz has lost himself utterly. His last scrawl, in the journal that began as a record of his idealistic enterprise, is the despairing cry, "'Exterminate the brutes.'"

Egan Chaney appears to be on the same trajectory from idealist to brute. It's clear from the beginning that he is dreadfully obsessed

## 2. Outside/In & Inside/Out

with the fate of the African pygmies, wiped out on Earth in the grinding process of Western civilization. Evidently, Chaney desperately wants to believe that humans may do a better job of understanding and protecting a vulnerable tribe on BoskVeld. He pretends to be a dedicated anthropologist, willing to submerge himself in Asadi daily life and absolutely minimizing contact with his human support system. Actually, as confirmed in *Transfigurations* by his daughter's description of his family life back on Earth, readers may suspect that Chaney's observation that the Asadi mob lives in dreadful isolation, in a state of "Indifferent Togetherness" could apply to Chaney himself. But he's not satisfied with that status; he wants to do more, to *be* more.

It's no surprise, then, that "Death and Designation" concludes with Chaney abandoning his research project and fleeing into the jungle. He has seen too much to maintain his guise of professional detachment. He has observed that the Asadi commit both murder and cannibalism, and his earlier academic ruminations on cannibalism in human society have been replaced by atavistic fury when he sees The Bachelor, the Asadi male to whom Chaney feel closest, standing over the butchered carcass of an Asadi female. Earlier, he had recognized what he was doing: "I now see them as alien projections of my own consciousness, and expecting better of myself, I expected better of them," so that "I belong among the Asadi," he says in a farewell note to the human he feels closest to, "not as an outcast and not as a chieftain—but as one of the milling throng." At the very end, then, Chaney deserts his fellow humans, rejecting the source of nourishment that could keep him alive, and disappears into the darkness. Readers of the novella could assume than Chaney finally is accepting his personal dissolution. "Death and Designation" leaves unexplained the description of baffling Asadi behavior at an elusive "pagoda" in the jungle, in the presence of malignant little creatures that Chaney labels "huri"—in short, a mass of puzzlement that the human witness finally would prefer to ignore altogether. Still, the story's action feels complete because Chaney has groped toward a more awful baseline than readers may be comfortable with, so that we may be relieved to imagine that his death is imminent. Out of sight, out of mind.

Or so readers of "Death and Designation" probably assumed.

In writing *Transfigurations*, however, Bishop chose not to expand the original novella but to enclose it in a larger story that would give Chaney's descent a larger context. The novel expands, contradicts, amplifies, and fulfills the novella's exploration of humanity's terrible and wonderful potential. It shows that dissolution isn't the only possible outcome of using empathy to open up a multitude of perspectives. The title, remember, is *Transfigurations*, suggesting that some people or things can be remade or at least seriously re-envisioned. And so they are, though sometimes unwillingly or unknowingly.

*Transfigurations* is narrated by Thomas "Ben" Benedict, Chaney's semi-friend who put together "Death and Designation among the Asadi" from the scraps of Chaney's desperate research. In the years since then, Ben has settled into a stale and sour bureaucratic routine, cynically observing how settlers come to BoskVeld with vague images of frontier adventure but actually wind up eagerly taming the place into a standard Glaktik Komm colony. He is jolted awake by a message from young Elegy Cather, who announces that she is Egan Chaney's daughter, that she has used royalties from the sale of the "Death and Designation" monograph to train as a primate ethnologist, and that she is on her way to BoskVeld to study the Asadi and to rescue her father.

At this point, Bishop craftily enlists readers as "anthropologists." Just as Egan Chaney tried to observe the Asadi by watching what they were doing and seeing what general principles described their behavior, readers of *Transfigurations* have an opportunity to watch how people behave as they try to reach past their preconceptions and find a livable way to accommodate with their surroundings. Watching Ben and Elegy study the Asadi, readers can study them to see what potential for transfiguration *these* primates might have.

The novel's human protagonists imagine that they are on relatively straightforward quests. Ben realizes that the monograph he assembled is tantalizingly incomplete, and he is galvanized by a chance to solve the Asadi riddle. Elegy professes the same goal, but she obviously cares about understanding the Asadi primarily as a means to find her father. She believes in the existence of the elusive, super-scientific, alien pagoda Egan Chaney inadvertently described, and she is sure, despite all logic, that he still is alive: He *must* be alive so that he can be vindicated and so that she can restore (or actually *create*) a loving family relationship with him.

Relationships are hard to build, not least because of humans' willful isolation. Elegy's confidence is based not only on belief that her father's reports are literally true but also on the fact that she has brought a new tool with which to pry open the Asadis' secrets. The tool's name is Kretzoi. He is a chimpoon, a hybrid of chimpanzee and baboon designed to resemble an Asadi; he bears a big mane and has had lenses surgically mounted over his eyes to mimic the Asadis' kaleidoscopic optics. He communicates with Elegy via sign language. Ben sometimes thinks of Kretzoi as an animal but at other times recognizes that he is capable of morally judging the humans around him—most of whom react with horror or disgust when they imagine that they are in the presence of an

Asadi. Although the real Asadi mob accepts Kretzoi readily enough, Ben is so impatient for results that he has Kretzoi capture an Asadi straggler for study back at the colonial city. That captive, nicknamed Bojangles, is murdered by one of the Glaktik Komm civkis who is supposed to be guarding him, "whose personal hatred of the Other had overcome both his early indoctrination in the Komm regs and his fear of a long, nightmare-ridden Punitive Sleep. Hatred and boredom." The murderer's punishment also reveals how impersonally the overall society treats its members. Tom sees him at the spaceship terminal, about to be shipped

> to a GK-world with rehabilitative/punitive Long Sleep facilities.... The next time he awoke to life he would do so on a strange world among strangers, an E-1 again, freshly indentured and as stingingly raw as an April onion.
> Reborn.
> Fifty years of salutary nightmares lay ahead of him. Dreams that beneficially terrorize the immobile sleeper: hypnopedagogic visions that insinuate a rejuvenated ethical awareness through a series of varied reenactments of the crime itself: painful neurological appeals to the heart and the head.... [sic] Only within the past three decades had the process become economically feasible.... I stood in something like awe as he passed—not for what he'd done, but for the dread justice that was about to befall him.

Glaktik Komm's "justice" is dictated by cost-effectiveness, and its goal is to produce another, more dependable component for its mechanically organized system. The end result may be a chastened, purified, reborn person, but the means used feel uncomfortably like those described in *A Clockwork Orange*. Evidently, the label "Indifferent Togetherness" can fit an entire society.

Fortunately, those intolerant, impersonal reactions aren't the limits of human possibility. Readers can observe how Ben and Elegy's relationship develops, beginning with their obsession with the Asadi, through a somewhat unlikely sexual fling (introduced by Ben's meditations on Asadi mating posture), into a prickly dependence and trust.

Along the way, both discover that their original goals can't be achieved. The novel gently suggests what is to come when, early in the story, when Elegy fails to find a restaurant in the port city by relying on an out-of-date guidebook she read before coming to BoskVeld. Ben remarks, "'you've found nothing but the shell of your expectations and something you didn't expect to find at all.'" In a similar way, the novel records Elegy's memories of how her physician mother tried to save the dying Pygmies who had been removed from their radioactive habitat in Africa but how she realized (against Egan Chaney's demand that they be preserved no matter what the cost) that what they really needed and deserved was not mere survival but the mercy of death.

Ben and Elegy must confront some uncomfortable discoveries. First of all, an autopsy on the corpse of Bojangles, the kidnapped Asadi, reveals that humans and Asadi probably had a common ancestor: the Ur'Asadi. Second, when they locate Bojangles' nest in the wild, they discover the partly devoured, trepanned, but still living body of his twin brother, for the Asadi not only devour their own dead but consume their blood kin over the course of years. Elegy tries to find the seed of genuine love in this practice; Ben appeals to the ideal of "mercy" and kills the maimed creature. And finally, after they impatiently have Kretzoi mimic the death rituals that Chaney had recorded, they are able to follow the Asadi through the jungle to the sometimes-invisible pagoda. And there they do discover Egon Chaney. Not, however, as Elegy has imagined him. The ugly little huri appear to be the psychic masters of the Asadi now, but they yearn to recreate genuine, more talented Ur'Asadi to enslave. Therefore, when they recognized Chaney's kinship to the Ur'Asadi, they sealed him in a cocoon that they imagined would transform him into one of his ancestors. The attempt failed. Chaney is stuck halfway between human and Ur'Asadi. He begs Elegy for mercy—release into death—and she eventually agrees.

What are readers, let alone Ben and Elegy, to make of this? For one thing, it's obvious that not all physical transfigurations work out. Besides the failure of Chaney's remake, Kretzoi is last seen about to have the fake-Asadi lenses removed from his eyes so that he can go back home. It's also clear that the anthropology in the novel is the equivalent of archeology as practiced haphazardly by Indiana Jones. These would-be anthropologists—Chaney, Ben, and Elegy—may have imagined that they could gather information about the Asadi, but they actually needed to discover truths about themselves. And eventually they realize as much. A short time before she gives her father the release he needs, Elegy berates Ben for relying too much on the rational half of his brain: "'You're dying of a disease—formulaic digital logic—that doesn't prevent you from behaving as an animal in moments of intuitive sanity.'" Just so, he calls her out for the obsession with a dead man that has distorted her planning. They learn to see and analyze in personal terms. And then they go on.

It's also obvious, by the end of the novel, that scientific exploration may fall short of understanding and controlling life. The elaborate theoretical reconstruction that Elegy and Ben create to explain the Asadis' dreadful condition—Ur'Asadi expeditions to Earth and BoskVeld, the proud Ur'Asadi's degeneration into bestial Asadi under the influence of the huri swarm, etc.—all remains elegant and ingenious but not especially convincing. The would-be anthropologists accept that fact.

Even though an unlikely presumed connection is "the only explanation" for something they've encountered, their suppositions are stuffed with qualifiers and conditional constructions. As Elegy finally admits, "'The facts are many and open to multiple interpretations. Not only that, Ben, in some cases they're not even facts, just suppositions arising from our bewilderment. They're seductive because we'd rather construct a theory than admit or live with our ignorance.'"

Somewhat earlier, Elegy dismissed Ben's elaborate scenario as "'Space opera,'" but that's not quite true; if this were a run-of-the-mill space opera it would conclude with Ben and Elegy united, as kindly Dr. Chaney's nods approval, while all the evil huri are appropriately destroyed and the downtrodden Asadi are redeemed. That would be a simple, satisfying conclusion. Instead, *Transfigurations* shows people unknowingly and unwillingly learning to admit and live with their ignorance, so that the "conclusion" is much looser and more confusing than readers may expect. The novel's last chapter, "Transfigured Lives," shows Ben arguing against Glaktik Komm's straightforward but mechanistic proposal to nuke the pagoda and wipe out the huri. That plan could prevent a future danger, since the huri might be capable of using humans' shared biological heritage with the Asadi to learn how to control our minds. Or such genocide might be unnecessary. There's no way to be sure. Ben uses his friendship with BoskVeld's governor to persuade GK to put that plan on hold for now, understanding that he may be making a mistake. But that's all right: "the fact that I could be wrong is what keeps the music so sprightly and the dance so hazardously sweet." Ben is satisfied to leave BoskVeld so that he can return to Earth and pursue "the remaining possibilities of my life." He reports that he is married now and that he, his wife, and Elegy are going on a fossil hunt to Lake Turkana, where they don't expect to make any new discoveries but where the sunsets are magnificent. He is content. In the novel's last paragraph, Ben contradicts the statement he made just above, anticipating that he and his wife "in the strange, uneasy hour before dawn ... will lie together anticipating sunrise. It's not so spectacular an event as sunset, perhaps, but it's just as dependable, and I've come to appreciate that quality in nature as well as in my fellows." In other words, Ben has learned to balance, uneasily but happily, his desire for certainty and his realization that he will never be able to understand and control everything in his life.

In short, anthropologically oriented readers have watched members of a tribe practice human behaviors that proved not to fit their situation or to increase their satisfaction. Readers have had a chance to watch as Ben and Elegy changed their approaches along with their attitudes. Unlike Bojangles' murderer, the two have had to discover the necessary changes for themselves. At the end, Ben reports that he has chosen "sanity vs. melodrama," and readers of *Transfigurations* are encouraged to do the same. Deftly playing with the practice of anthropology and exploring the limits of science, the novel is Michael Bishop's first fully controlled performance, the first book that could be considered a masterpiece.

The Ur-Nu sequence isn't quite a masterpiece. Still, Bishop's writing about the Urban Nucleus, major American cities that have isolated and sealed themselves under immense domes, spans the first part of his career, so the subject obviously let him return to several important themes. Gunnar and his brother refer briefly to Ur-Nu in the first version of *A Funeral for the Eyes of Fire* as the reason they dread returning to Earth. The main fictional sequence, however, consists of *Catacomb Years*, a fix-up narrative assembled out of seven short stories, and one novel, *A Little Knowledge*. The following list contains the stories set within or near Ur-Nu Atlanta, beginning with the construction of domes in and ending with the opening of Atlanta's dome:

> "If a Flower Could Eclipse" (*Worlds of Fantasy*, Winter 1970), set in 2034
> "Old Folks at Home" (*Universe 8*, 1978), set in 2040
> "The Windows in Dante's Hell" (*Orbit 12*, 1973), set in 2045
> "The Samurai and the Willows" (*F&SF*, February 1976), set in 2046
> "Allegiances" (*Galaxy* February 1975), set in 2066
> "At the Dixie-Apple with the Shoofly-Pie Kid" (*Cosmos SF & Fantasy*, November 1977), set in 2071
> *A Little Knowledge* (1977; according to Bishop, probably written between "Samurai" and "At the Dixie-Apple"), set in 2071
> "Death Rehearsals" (original to *Catacomb Years*, 1979), set in 2073–4

Note that the order of writing/publication sometimes doesn't always match the sequence of events in Bishop's future history—and that the novel *A Little Knowledge* falls toward, but not quite *at* the end of the larger story. Obviously Bishop kept returning to the Ur-Nu material for almost a decade, fitting in new pieces here and there, then stepping back and taking a dubious look at the assemblage, before eventually writing historical interludes to connect the shorter pieces and adding one new story to continue a chain of events after the end of the novel. Confusing as the facts of publication may seem to be, the sequence itself turns out to be messy and inconclusive but fascinating.

Bishop was part of a long tradition of sf writers who have been concerned about urban trends, especially as technological advances have made it possible to build ever more dense and more confining habitats for human beings. Gabriel de Tarde's *Underground Man*, published in 1905 with an Introduction by H.G. Wells, pictures humanity forced to create a new civilization beneath Earth's surface, and E.M. Forster's novella "The Machine Stops" (1909) shows feeble humans becoming so dependent on machinery that they cannot survive its breakdown. Forster's generally downbeat story does offer some hope with a glimpse of humans who have learned to live apart from the Machine. However, Bishop claims Robert Silverberg's fix-up novel *The World Inside* (1971), an exceptionally grim city-dystopia, as a primary inspiration for the Ur-Nu stories. Beginning with the story "A Happy Day in 2381" in 1970, Silverberg developed a vision of an Earth filled with Urban Monads, each towering for hundreds of stories and stuffed with hundreds of thousands of people. Looking backward, a researcher in one monad can realize how

> an ancient [i.e., a reader of Silverberg's story] would feel about Urbmon 116: it is a hellish place ... in which people live hideously cramped and brutal lives, in which every civilized philosophy is turned on its head, in which uncontrolled breeding is nightmarishly encouraged to serve some incredible concept of a deity eternally demanding more worshipers, in which dissent is ruthlessly stifled and dissenters are peremptorily destroyed.

But this monad dweller cannot truly feel as an "ancient" would, let alone take any corrective action based on that revulsion. One inhabitant who does venture outside, encountering a tribal society symbiotically allied with the monads, is disposed of as soon as he returns and tries to preach about new, alternative "possibilities" for living. No one wants to listen. The only escape for another disillusioned young man apparently on his way to moving up (figuratively and literally) is to leap off the top of the structure. There are no other possibilities. The monads will inevitably continue growing—along with their throngs of happy, happy dwellers. Silverberg's book is dourly impressive. The Urban Monads are carefully imagined, and the stories were written and published in a steady flow, so that the result is neat and smooth. Nevertheless, Bishop's uneven, off-and-on Ur-Nu sequence winds up being more memorable because it shows a writer considering and reconsidering what might have led to the inhabitants' confinement, how they managed to cope with it, and what kind of freedom they could hope for.

First, Bishop had to imagine *why* the people of Atlanta would want city-sealing domes to be built over themselves. In "Prelude: The Domes," a connective essay at the beginning of *Catacomb Years*, he offers several alternative or accumulating motives: (1) fear of pollution, (2) proud independence from other urban centers, and (3) "'Preemptive Isolation,' by which it was meant that America's major Cities were concertedly resisting foreign attempts to entangle them in a patently unworkable Government of the West." Later in the book, he suggests a quasi-religious motive: People need to ally themselves with something larger than individual humans, and a city certainly is large enough to inspire awe. In any event, the completed Domes "were unparalleled feats of engineering, prodigious works of art, and unutterably loony memorials to human folly."

Pure human looniness can almost, if not quite, explain why a lot of inconsistent, self-destructive actions happened. Referring to our embarrassing tendency to stumble into ill-considered actions may convince readers that Ur-Nu Atlanta is a believable place. The stories themselves don't offer enough physical details about the place's background, and they don't fit together very convincingly. Wondering just how large Atlanta's dome is and how it was constructed, how consumer goods are produced, where food comes from and where waste products go—considering such questions as this could bring readers to a crashing halt. Fortunately, Bishop's characters are believable enough to convince us that the setting *must* be real because these real people live there.

The early *Catacomb Years* stories study what confinement does to the human spirit, and the immediate answer must be "Nothing good!" The narrator of "The Windows of Dante's Hell," for example, hysterically expresses his anger at anyone daring to dream of space travel, of life outside the dome; only at the end does he come close to recognizing that it's his own dreams that he has learned to fear and hate. The city obviously survives by repressing natural instincts. As the last paragraph of "Prelude: The Domes" puts it,

> Living during the Catacomb Era, you could go crazy without ever realizing the depths of your own madness. The outwardly well-adjusted and the uncompromisingly deranged were often indistinguishable. You lived from day to day in the submerged hope that your old age would deliver you to the immaculate dignity of death under a clear blue sky. In the meantime, you tried to form fragile human alliances against the terms of your imprisonment.

That's accurate, but it's not quite all the truth. Several stories stress how the dome has failed to destroy the human spirit of its inhabitants. They yearn for more than oblivion. It is true that life inside the dome produces situations in which people are able and/or encouraged to do self-destructive things to themselves. But not always. As the discussion of "The Samurai and the Willows" earlier in this book showed, life wants to survive, to be reborn. And so it is. "Old Folks at Home," another story that Bishop wrote later but inserted early in the sequence is even more affirmative, with a title that balances the connotations of "old" and "home." Zoe Breedlove, the story's 67-year-old protagonist, gladly joins a gerontological group marriage temporarily sanctioned by the city as a merely temporary experiment; the project's purpose is to see what a random group of old people could accomplish if they were freed from the restraints of their (younger) families. As Dr. Leland Tanner, the project's originator tells Zoe, "'From now on ... we're going to be more interested in serving *you* right. And in permitting you to serve." The story shows Zoe physically and emotionally adjusting to the other members of the Phoenix family, demonstrating that she still can learn to serve others. In fact, of course, the members of Zoe's new family are old, so that they naturally die off; by the same token, the city kills the project as soon as it can. So a reader might ask how valuable was the service Zoe gave to Phoenix—what was the point of this whole effort? At the story's end, though, despite seemingly being defeated by age and social constraints, Zoe has one final piece of advice for her daughter who's just suffered a miscarriage: "'Tell her ... to try again." Human allegiances within the dome may not be as fragile as they look. Though humans may be frustrated within the Urban Nucleus, they somehow manage to remain resilient.

The Ur-Nu sequence shows two truths: People want to wall themselves off from others, but they also crave human contact; they are quite capable of creating a mammoth, soul-crushing system to subdue themselves, but at the same time they will stubbornly continue to discover ways to beat that system.

Characters in *A Little Knowledge* instinctively work to resolve this dichotomy. "Allegiances," in *Catacomb Years*, revealed that two former refugees from Atlanta are waiting to introduce non-human aliens into the city. The escapees traveled to a European society that has developed dynamically outward, into space exploration, rather than turning inward and stagnating like the Ur-Nu cities. The returned Atlanteans hope that meeting visitors from another solar system, the flesh/machine blended, inscrutable Cygnusians, will remind dome dwellers that a huge, interesting universe is waiting for them to explore. But it isn't that easy to open up rigid social barriers. The aliens' presence in Atlanta first results in uncertainty and tension, especially when one of them comes forward at the end of a religious service and commits himself to Christ. This appears to validate Atlanta's Ortho-Urbanist Church, yet it also suggests that beings from outside the city and with different physical forms have souls like ours so that shutting them away from us by the dome is *wrong*. A little knowledge can be truly dangerous in such a situation.

The official representatives of religion in *A Little Knowledge* vary from malevolent to innocently zany, from coldly dogmatic First Counselor Saganella Lesser to boisterous, buckskin-clad High Bishop Avery Holman. The novel's genuine religious dialogue, however, is to be found in the relationship of deacon-candidate Margot Eastwin and agnostic Julian Cawthorn. Neither "wins" the discussion. They respect each other's conscience, especially when they realize they are in love. The way Margot and Julian complement each other may seem like a pop-fiction cliché, but Bishop makes their coming together feel satisfyingly natural. Other parts of the story seem beyond natural, such as how Margot was nudged into a religious vocation by rescuing an abandoned baby, while fictions that Julian has written turn out to predict the aliens' names. Something uncanny seems to be happening. Furthermore, on the couple's wedding night, Lileplagak the Cygnusian visits them and causes them to share a vision—or perhaps just a dream—in which the soul of Julian's dead grandmother (Zoe, from "Old Folks at Home") tells him that humans are reincarnated as Cygnusians. They are stunned and perplexed:

> If Lileplagak had once been Parthena and Parthena had once been others, then Margot and Julian had also had previous aspects, identities, personalities. Avatars, one could say. Must they therefore believe that one day—how many incarnations hence?—they would tenant the same sort of cybergamic shells as did the Cygonsitkoi?.... Sleeping, dreaming, Margot/Julian realized they had just been privy to a revelation and a charge. In a way what they had just heard or dreamt, or absorbed through spiritual osmosis, was a contradiction of what each of their waking selves believed. Margot's faith was mocked, and Julian's absolute agnosticism, his Know-Nothing stance in the face of cosmic politics, was undermined by too exact a knowledge.... [stet] We've been fed answers we would rather have remained ignorant of. For what, what really, can we do? ... [stet]

Obviously, Margot and Julian's shared vision/dream raises more questions for them than it answers. They feel that they have been given "a charge," an obligation to do something, but they get no clear instructions or even suggestions of *what* that might be. The novel ends soon after, on Year Day, 2071, and Bishop's CHRONOLOGY at the very end of the book concludes with the cryptic word "Revelation."

"Death Rehearsals," the last story in *Catacomb Years*, carries the story a bit farther. It is set in 2073–74, and the book's Chronology indicates that it deals with "deaths, nativities, resurrections." First Counselor Lessor has been deposed, and the new ruling troika has expelled the Cygnusians from Atlanta, though two have been allowed to stay because they supposedly are at the point of death. Margot and Julian have settled into a calm but somewhat uneasy married life, still not sure whether or not to believe their super-logical message's content or its import in their lives. She is in the church; he is a journalist but also has been put in charge of the dying aliens. It would be exaggerating to call him a caregiver, since all he is able to do is visit their dark, bitterly cold, rubble-strewn hotel suite and verify that the motionless forms still somehow are alive. At this point, elderly gerontology researcher Dr. Leland Tanner reappears and begins happily working in the UrNu Geriatrics Hostel: "He lived simultaneously as if each day were his last and as if he were never going to die." Unfortunately, Tanner falls in love with the Hostel's new director Vivian Klemme, who looks "like an albino wren," and who turns out to be literally ageless: Her immortalist father started her on a regime that could theoretically keep her alive forever—as long as she avoids dangerous behaviors such as physical intimacy or emotional involvement with short-lived humans. After that rejection, Tanner asks to be taken into the suite where the Cygnusians lie in death-like repose, where he muses,

> The quest for immortality was a motive arising from profound, maybe even noble self-interest—but the quest for communion and adventure was a motive partaking of that inbred cooperativeness that had enabled humanity to evolve from a slouching primate to an angel of sublime contradictions. If you had to choose, if you were denied the option of synthesis, which motive was the more human and therefore ultimately the more noble?

Note that this meditation concludes with a question and that Tanner speaks of humanity evolving into "sublime contradictions" rather than achieving a synthesis of goals.

The story ends with Tanner's death, which quite possibly validates the message that Margot and Julian received. Earlier Margot has told Tanner that she could not accept that revelation because it seems to her that "'the forms of genuine reality—when revealed—strike us as so ludicrous that we deem it beneath our dignity to believe in them.'" She adds, "'I try to speak from the firm center of my faith.'" However, as Tanner physically declines, he observes, "'I dreamed I was being squeezed out of my present life and squeezed into another that didn't fit me.'" His death, shortly thereafter, coincides with the emergence of an infant Cygnusian, suggesting that his essence (soul) has been passed on (been reincarnated) into the alien body. Perhaps. Bishop avoids a clear conclusion. After Julian witnesses the birth, he hurries "from the scene of this fearful alien nativity like a man striding naked into the irresistible gales of Change." Shortly thereafter, the two young people witness the dreadful, hopeful opening of Atlanta's dome: "Holding hands, Julian and Margot stared up into the unfathomable artifice of the reborn night." And so *Catacomb Years* ends with many plot threads (many more than are discussed here) not so much dangling as waving defiantly in gales of Change. The Chronology in this book ends not with "Revelation" but the tantalizing but rather uneasy promise: "2075/ onward/ ERA OF MULTIPLE POSSIBILITIES."

Bishop's revision of these two books combines them in one volume, *The City and the Cygnets* (2019). No longer presented as a *future* but as an alternative history that might have occurred if exceptional paranoia had panicked America into stepping outside the flow of history and hiding. This continuity also makes it easier to see the aliens as a counter to the city's supposedly safe isolation—enigmatic, unsettling reminders that a literally wonderful (full of all kinds of wonders) is waiting for humans to explore.

Nineteen eighty-one saw the publication of *Under Heaven's Bridge*, a collaboration by Bishop and British writer Ian Watson that serves as an odd sidebar to the Ur-Nu sequence. The novel does not mention the Urban Nuclei at all, since the Japanese central character has no concern with America and since the main action shows humans investigating an alien planet. However, the aliens living on that planet are obviously the Cygnusians: bodies apparently mixtures of organic and mechanical, craving extreme cold, tantalizingly and irritatingly enigmatic, etc. Fitting the novel into the main sequence would require either imagining that this was the first contact between humans and Cygnusians, sometime before "Allegiances"—or that this novel's events occur some indeterminate time later, perhaps even after *A Little Knowledge*. Neither solution works very well. According to Bishop, he and Watson thought it would be interesting to kick ideas around in a trans-Atlantic collaboration, sending chunks of manuscript back and forth by mail. So perhaps the novel can be seen as an alternative version of events, continuing the mood of the overall sequence by seriously playing with multiple possibilities. The short book doesn't have room to develop characters or to dramatize ideas so much as talk about them—though those ideas are quite dramatic in themselves.

After a prologue set in Japan that shows seven-year-old Keiko Takahashi's encounter with a foreign tourist who wants to take her picture, making her imagine "what a great thing it might be to speak with aliens," the novel jumps ahead several years. Keiko is now a linguist aboard the spaceship *Heavenbridge*, frustrated like the other scientists on board by their inability to understand the natives of the planet they call Onogoro. As the back cover blurb on the American first edition succinctly says, "The Kybers are an unnerving sight for human eyes, more like Giacometti sculpture than living beings." The exasperated humans aren't even sure whether they are basically organic, machine, or cyborg—the label

## 2. Outside/In & Inside/Out

"Kyber" suggests that they suspect the last. On the surface, Keiko has made more progress than the others, since one Kyber has taken to dropping by the expedition's base for language lessons; actually, though, the alien has absorbed huge amounts of data but has revealed almost nothing about itself and its kin. Rather, the Kyber seems to have leapt far ahead of her conceptually: "It absorbed and processed vocabularies as if its mind—its watch movements of concept and reason—were specifically geared to a universal grammar still more or less opaque to human understanding." She goes on to speculate that the Kybers' "universal grammar" might be "*literally* universal ... a grammar programmed into the very data of which the cosmos was composed." But where could that ability/understanding have originated? Echoing William Blake's "Tyger, Tyger," she uneasily wonders, "Had the Kybers coagulated naturally out of primal protoplasm? What lance had stirred them? Whose hand had held it?"

The other expedition members respond to the Kybers according to their own natures. Farrell Sixkiller, pilot of one of the "floaters" that carries scientists from one site to another, sees the Kybers as evil, mere machines that killed their organic creators and now only mimic life while they tempt humans to submit to rigid stasis. On the other hand, Xenologist Andrik Norn, Keiko's lover, believes that the Kybers "'have struck through the mask of our illusory reality to what's truly real.'" The novel's action shows, unfortunately, that the only way to partake of the Kybers' understanding is to leave one's humanity behind: Humans and Kybers view experience in irreconcilably different ways. When the scientists discover that one of the suns in this binary system is about to go nova and that only an almost absolutely impossible chance could shield the planet from a burst of massive, fatal radiation, they learn that the Kybers already are aware of the impending solar crisis but are certain that they will survive. They say they know because their united consciousness has communed with the God-Behind-the-Galaxies, though it's unclear whether that took the form of pleading with the supreme power to manipulate future events or simply of being informed that their planet *will* be at exactly in the right place at the right time to be safe.

It's hard to be certain exactly what the Kybers are trying to say, since their speech is so full of puns and Zen-like *koans*, as well as references to religious rituals, as when one tears off a bit of its leathery flesh and invites Keiko to ingest it in a parallel to Christian communion.

Keiko ultimately is appalled by the notion of connecting with such a "god," let alone worshipping it. She sees the Rite of Conjoining, to which Andrik submits himself, as "an activator of continent wide-data exchange," so she fears that "if God was a control system, God was infinitely more alien than the Kybers. You could never attain perfect union with that which lay above and beyond you, *outside* you, manipulative and dictatorial rather than serenely existent and quiescently complementary. Andrik, a Westerner, might approve the concept of such a god; but how could she ... ever surrender to so impersonal a cosmology?" Keiko lets Andrik choose to become part of the Rite because, although she loves him, she does not *possess* him; just so, later in the book, she is both amused and outraged by Sixkiller's overture, "DR TAKAHASHI PLEASE BE MINE." Like Margot in *A Little Knowledge*, Keiko realizes that even if the vision of reality that the aliens offer is genuine it is not one that human beings dare try to accept.

Nevertheless.... The *Heavenbridge* returns to Earth before the nova, leaving uncertain whether the Kybers' assurance of safety was correct. Aboard the ship are six Kyber refugees (less than the full family unit seen in *A Little Knowledge*). They are in their dormant state, so after one is dissected the other five are put in rotating exhibit as curiosities/works of art in public halls and museums throughout Earth's cities. So, after another time jump, an elderly Keiko journeys to Sanjusangendo, to the Hall of Mercy she visited in the novel's prologue. There she views the motionless Kyber and sees—or imagines—that "one of its peripheral eye-bulbs" comes to life and momentarily glows for her. Time has come full circle, from the past when she realized how wonderful it would be to talk with an alien to the present after such communication apparently proved futile. And now? "She would come again. The promise was there." As with *A Little Knowledge*, the story stretches past its last words.

Neither Bishop nor Watson considers *Under Heaven's Bridge* a major work, and it's not. But, despite its brevity, talkiness, and sketchy characterization, it's not negligible either.

## Part II

# Discovering Stranger Worlds Next Door

At one time, a space ship on the cover of a book or magazine was a reasonably safe indication of the presence of science fiction—or at least "sci-fi." Readers imagined that sf dealt with the achievement or consequences of space travel, or sometimes with the circumstances that prevented such an achievement. As a young sf writer, Bishop frequently found himself writing stories set on alien planets, though the human characters were his real concern. See, for example, how *Transfigurations* shows the main character on an anthropological mission on a distant planet that turns back into himself and the people who come after him. Written a few years later, *No Enemy but Time* is set up as an anthropological inquiry on Earth but is actually an exploration of the main character's inner space.

# 3

# Surreal Estates
## *Short Fiction, 1981–1994*

Bishop's short fiction had shifted away from spacefaring before his novels did. Continuing the interest in human obsessions seen in "Within the Walls of Tyre" and "Storming the Bijou," his stories over the next few years explored mortal striving and consolations on Earth.

"The Quickening" is an oddly perfect, perfectly enigmatic novella that appeared first in the 11th volume of *Universe* (1981), a series of original-story anthologies edited by Terry Carr. It since has appeared in several reprint anthologies, including Arthur Saha's *The Year's Best Fantasy Stories* and Terry Carr's *Fantasy Annual V*.

We eventually will consider how the story is related to its title; for now, let's simply note that "quickening" indicates fresh animation, new energy, especially a milestone in a healthy pregnancy. That seems, at first glance, to have nothing to do with how "The Quickening" shows the aftermath of an abrupt, terrifying geographical shuffling of all human beings, so that everyone suddenly and inexplicably is moved to a new location on Earth. Lawson, the viewpoint character (his first name is never given), fell asleep in Lynchburg, Virginia, but wakes up in Seville, Spain. At least he is clever enough to recognize where he is; many in the scrambled mob around him die in blind panic because of their sudden displacement before they even can try to group together according to shared language. By shouting "'English here!'" Lawson connects with Dai Secombe, a Welsh philosophy teacher who sympathizes with the American's desire to reunite with his wife and little daughters but who can't offer any real encouragement. Instead, he advises Lawson to look calmly at their new reality and adjust to it. Secombe is able to verbalize what Lawson already has realized: The vulnerable people who have been arbitrarily shuffled about, such as Lawson's children and Secombe's elderly father, are on their own, cut off from dependable protection and thus probably are doomed. There's no use imagining that they can be rescued.

Moreover, human civilization as a whole is doomed too. If communication between members of the Seville crowd is obviously almost futile, each gathering place within the old human civilization must have been catastrophically disrupted too. That leaves individual humans on their own, without support and without rules. Therefore, Secombe and Lawson should stop yearning for what's lost and discover what's usable now.

Readers probably want a more comfortable conclusion than that. Although the story gives a convincing description of chaos in one city, there's no way to tell with certainty that the same thing happened worldwide—or *how* it happened at all—or how the change might be reversed. Once the basic situation is clearly established, in the formulaic sf story readers may be expecting, the main character should start figuring out the answers to those puzzles. He and his laconic sidekick should examine the evidence, hypothesize, and construct a gadget that would return all the survivors safely to their homes. And the hero should find his own family waiting for him. "The Quickening," on the other hand, demonstrates that Secombe's comfortless analysis is correct.

As a matter of fact, Lawson himself soon demonstrates a surprisingly realistic but rather callous reaction to the change. In his initial conversation with Secombe, he startles the Welshman by asking:

"Do you have a family?"
"Only my father. He's eighty-four."
"You're lucky—not to have anyone else to worry about, I mean."
"Perhaps," Dai Secombe said, a trace of sharpness in his voice. "Yesterday I would not have thought so."

Lawson does weep—and not only for his own loss—and he briefly feels guilty about surviving the change; however, that doesn't strongly motivate him to aid other survivors. Soon after awakening, as he recognizes that there's nothing he can do to protect his family, he sees "a movement in the river" next to him, "a bundle of some sort floated in the greasy water below the wall: a baby clad only in a shirt. The tie-strings on the shirt trailed out behind the child like the severed legs of a water-walker. Lawson wondered if Spain even had water-walkers." And so the incident ends with a dismissive comment about local insects; Lawson takes no action to determine whether the "movement" was caused by the struggles of a drowning child. Later, while walking with Secombe, still protesting that he wants to go home to his wife and little daughters, "they passed a white-skinned child lying in an alley doorway opening onto a courtyard festooned with dingy laundry and overrun by orphaned dogs. A coat covered her head, but she seemed to be breathing. Lawson felt no temptation to examine her more closely, however. He kept his eyes resolutely on the map."

Lawson knows more than he will let himself understand, though his realization of how thoroughly the old order has been disrupted shows itself rather haphazardly. He throws away his watch *before* being bothered by the new uncertainty about a base for time since "no one knew how long the redistribution of the world's population had gone on," so that counting "time" is impossible. In the same dazed way, he follows the English-speaking crowd to an airfield but gives up his place on the plane that will attempt to carry people on their way back home but that actually crashes on takeoff, killing all the deluded passengers. Then Lawson walks back to the city alone.

"The Quickening" doesn't condemn Lawson for being self-centered. Each individual's self, after all, is the only thing these literally displaced persons have left—whatever that "self" might be. But the way some people like Lawson are able to adapt to life after the change does suggest that their alliances to other people and to their former ways of living were more superficial than they would have declared. Now that these fragile connections have been violently broken, individuals are free to find new, simpler, perhaps healthier ways to live. Perhaps. If they could just get past their horror at the sight and smell of all those dead people....

So Lawson's behavior may be perfectly natural under the circumstances. The circumstances are so extraordinary that Lawson would have to be a phenomenally gifted human not to be stunned by the prospect of creating a new order. And so he simply accepts the ramshackle order that falls together in Seville. He settles into a living arrangement with the other survivors. A kind of social system somehow occurs in the city, and people find themselves speaking a shared dialect. Meanwhile, other aspects of the old life are disappearing. When Secombe reappears, Lawson barely recognizes him and can scarcely find the words or concepts needed to conduct a conversation. Though in his former life he had been teaching his daughters to play chess, now he can't remember the rules well enough to have a match with Secombe. On the whole, he is more comfortable when Secombe goes away, just as the rest of his pre-change memories are fading. He is "[p]roud of his adaptability."

One rather puzzling remark by Secombe is that he is working in "'demolition. As we'll all be soon. It's the only constructive job of work going.'" In fact, Lawson has already begun taking apart his dwelling place; next, he and the Mongolian woman who is now his mate join the crowd taking down the city's cathedral. That includes destroying the tomb of Christopher Columbus:

> Together, Lawson thought, they would dismantle the mausoleum of the discoverer of the New World and bring his corrupt remains out into the street. After all these centuries, they would free the man. Then the bronze statue of Faith atop the

bell tower would come down, followed by the lovely bell tower itself, the flying buttresses, the balconies, the walls, every beautiful, tainted stone.

It would hurt like hell to destroy the cathedral, and it would take a long time—but, considering everything, it was the only meaningful option they had. Lawson raised his pickax.

How can "demolition" be "constructive"? In what sense is Lawson's project "meaningful"? How are the stones both "tainted" and "beautiful"? Is the emergence of this spontaneous mass movement the reason humanity was reshuffled and "leveled"? Are humans discovering a new way to live—and was that opportunity worth all the death and suffering? There's no way to be sure. The story doesn't say.

Robert Silverberg, one of the editors of another anthology that reprinted "The Quickening," suggested that Bishop use it as the basis for a novel. Though that might have been an interesting project and might even have been a commercial success, Bishop comments that he "felt, and still feel, that the story accomplishes just about what I want it to." He's right. For "The Quickening" to be expanded into a novel, the basic situation would have had to be developed, and the point of the story is that some unstoppable, unimaginable development *may* be beginning. But what that could be remains unknown and probably unknowable for us. The story's title suggests that a new energy from somewhere has somehow entered our world; however, we modern-day humans simply cannot foresee what rough beast is slouching toward Seville to be born.

That frightening hope is missing in "A Gift from the Graylanders," one of Bishop's most deliberately painful stories, first published in *Isaac Asimov's Science Fiction Magazine*, September 1985. Decades later, it is difficult to appreciate the insanity that possessed Americans during the Cold War. Publicly, we applauded our development of ever-more sophisticated nuclear weapons and proclaimed that our fallout shelters and duck-and-cover drills would let us survive an attack. Robert A. Heinlein, in *Farnham's Freehold* (1964), even suggested that nuclear war would be useful for getting rid of weaklings. Privately we all knew better; in fact, we never tried to build enough fallout shelters to protect many of us, and we certainly didn't take civil defense drills seriously. We lived in tacit denial. We sat out in the open and distracted ourselves as best we could while waiting for the bombs to fall. We might have realized that this behavior was insane, but we didn't let ourselves be bothered enough to admit that.

Cory, the viewpoint character of Bishop's story, is only seven years old, in a terribly restrictive situation and altogether at the mercy of more powerful people. He and his mother are living in Denver with her sister and an at-best-indifferent family, in a house so small that Cory has to sleep on a cot in the dank basement. He worries that Graylander monsters—"Clay People, Earth Zombies, Bone Puppets"—are trying to scratch their way through the basement walls and snatch him away. In fact, Cory has a lot to be anxious about, and his Mommy can't do anything to help him. She can't—or won't let herself—understand how deeply he's disturbed and shifts the focus of their conversation to her problems. To his plea for his missing daddy, she replies that the man fled his family responsibilities and tried to kidnap Cory only to hurt *her*. Sadly, he has no comforting memories that could counter that accusation. In fact, Cory remembers that when his dad tried to snatch him away by lunging at him out of a dark room, he screamed at the "monster." Actually, he's surrounded by a variety of monsters, the Graylanders being only slightly more terrifying than the people upstairs.

But events beyond the house's upstairs interrupt Cory's fearful routine. While he is being ridiculed for trying to decipher messages the Graylanders have left in scratches on the basement wall, one of the hateful upstairs children sarcastically asks, "'Is war gonna break out? Ask your stupid wall if the Rooshuns plan to bomb us?'" And while Marty, the upstairs father, is locking Cory in the basement for using the family's surplus paint to cover the Graylanders' messages and make the basement more cheerful, his wife interrupts, "'Marty, don't! Something's happening on the news. You like the news. Come see what's going on.'" Sealed in darkness, Cory hears his Mommy come home and state her intention to free him. Then the house shakes violently, and after that no one upstairs answers his cries for help. Sometime later, accompanied by a blinding flash of light, an even more violent impact destroys the upper part of the house and opens Cory's prison.

And so he is set free. Readers recognize what Cory can't consciously quite admit, that nuclear war has obliterated all the things that confined him or might conceivably have liberated him. Of course, none of his earlier appeals for help succeeded very well. His family didn't cherish him effectively. The Graylanders didn't listen to his appeals to leave him alone. Even God, Who seemed to endorse Cory's painting a big yellow sun on the basement wall—"Let there be light"—shows up only in the nuclear explosion, a burst of light that irradiates the basement, endowing "with blinding brightness the symbols of life and sunshine that Cory had splashed all about." Now, walking almost naked through the radioactive rubble and breathing in glittering fallout, he meets a maimed, dying survivor, whom he can recognize only as a Graylander. The other may be a woman, could even be his Mommy, but Cory can't accept that. He refuses to interpret the Graylander's plea for help, rejects its "gift"—an eyeball that has fallen out of its skull, and runs away into the radioactive ruins.

Earlier in the story, Cory tried to use his seven-year-old's reasoning to figure out what was on the other side of the wall and what the Graylanders were trying to say. Even when he's imprisoned in the dark basement, he goes on trying to understand his surroundings in the belief that "it was better to know than not to know, even if what you learned made your gut turn over and the hair in the small of your back prickle." But he's forced to do this "on his own ... because he'd been locked in a place he couldn't escape without the help of the adults upstairs—grownups a kid would ordinarily expect to make some responsible decisions for him and maybe for themselves too." But that's the problem: The adults in this story haven't been making responsible decisions for themselves—not in Marty's house, not in Denver, and not anywhere in their adult world. Cory reasonably enough supposes that Graylanders may have eyes, "but years of living in the dark, ignoring the kingdoms of light above their heads, had robbed them of the ability to see."

That's what happened to the Graylanders. But what, the story asks, is *our* excuse? What are we turning a blind eye to today?

"Taccati's Tomorrow" first appeared in *F&SF*, June 1986, and was reprinted in a slim collection of Bishop's mainstream stories as part of the Author's Choice Monthly series, *Emphatically Not SF, Almost*. "Taccati's" was the "almost" story because, rather than being sf per se, it is concerned with sf *people*, the relationships between sf readers and writers. The fact that Bishop first submitted the story unsuccessfully to mainstream literary magazines may reflect how complicated this analysis turned out to be, how difficult it is for cosmic-minded people to get along with average folks.

We sf fans recognize that we're different from most people. To quote George Bernard Shaw's *Back to Methuselah*, "You see things; and you say 'why?' But I dream things that never were; and I say 'why not?'" The great theme of sf is change, and long-term sf readers are more willing than the general crowd to accept the idea that human society and the humans in it are likely to change. Sometimes the result of this open mindedness is acceptable, as "Taccati's" viewpoint character Beverly Jefferds cherishes the "fragile optimism" of her boyfriend Gil Vannoy; however, most people would rather not exercise their imaginations so freely. It makes them uncomfortable. Because sf fans tend not to be quite at ease with their "more realistic" neighbors, they appreciate the chance to validate their interests by gathering in regular sf conventions, such as the unfortunate Deep South Con depicted in Bishop's story.

Bev has accompanied Gil to the con unwillingly, with as little teeth-gritted grace as she can. She acknowledges that fans ignore her by labeling her a "mundane," which she correctly interprets as meaning not just "typical" but "ordinary"—i.e., merely boring. She, in return observes how ridiculous some of the fans look in their sfish costumes, how many of them seem to be more interested in partying than in sharing their enthusiasm for sf, and how every convention's programming is full of the same boring stuff. The reason she and Gil are at this con, however, is that the guest of honor is Nathan Taccati, a writer of "philosophical science fiction" with whom Gil corresponded in the late 1970s. He wants "to meet one of the writers who had meant something to him as a shy high-school kid and, later, an idealistic young adult." Bev mentions that Gil is now almost 38 to suggest how immature he still is. At his urging, Bev has just read a paperback of Taccati's, "one of at least twenty novels that he'd hacked out during the years of the Vietnam conflict." Predictably, she hated the book for its poor attention to detail and sloppy writing. Despising Taccati, she can tolerate the con only because she needs to keep her lover from making a fool of himself by demanding an affirmation of undying fellowship from the hack writer.

Readers' first impressions of Taccati, though colored by Bev's negative attitude, do suggest that he is a verbose, insincere poseur, propped on a pile of his past accomplishments that *she*—and quite possibly he too—knows are crap. However, by desperate groveling, Gil does penetrate Taccati's reserve, forcing his idol to see "him as a *person* rather than a bipedal annoyance," so that they set up a breakfast meeting at a nearby McDonald's. Bev observes that Taccati is keeping this conversation insincere and superficial: "Nothing at all about Gil's favorite topics: the inevitability of a single worldwide government, the infinite promise of space travel, the genetic perfectibility of the human species…. Bev suspected that he was purposely avoiding matters of substance, holding Gil at arm's length with fake intimacies that really divulged nothing but his social awkwardness and his lack of human warmth." Then they are interrupted by a disheveled, angry young African-American man who rudely demands that Gil lend him a pen. When Gil rebukes the fellow for bad manners, Taccati seems ready to give away his own pen until Bev warns him, "'Don't you dare.'" The confrontation ends as the other man wanders away, cursing, and Taccati tells Gil, "'I admire your courage…. But it isn't much to loan a man a pen.'" Later, along with a paperback copy of his only Hugo-winning novel, he sends a note to Gil that expands his reaction:

> "It seems to me that the whole incident was avoidable….
> Misunderstandings of this kind trouble me because they're precisely what keeps the different racial, religious, and political factions of our species at loggerheads.

*And Gil, it's people who think and perceive as we do who have the major responsibility to build bridges of understanding that others lack the background, the fellow feeling, or the will to engineer. I hope you'll think a little more about the way you handled the man's simple request."*

Predictably, Gil is furious that his one good memory of reconnecting with Taccati is tainted. He tears the novel literally to shreds, and he and Bev immediately check out of the hotel and start driving home. She is pleased: "Sometimes you lost, sometimes you won, and sometimes you drew even. On this occasion, maybe she and Gil had come out a little ahead."

It's uncertain how fully readers should accept that upbeat mood. That Taccati is personally unlikeable makes his unsolicited gush of pontification especially unpleasant, besides the fact that he is delivering it at a safe distance, by writing rather than advising Gil directly, and safely well after the incident itself. (That "a stomach problem" excuses his subsequent disappearance from the con program may be another way of saying that there's something wrong with his guts.) What Taccati is saying may be good advice, but the way it's offered makes it impossible to accept. On the other hand, it *is* good advice if the alternative is macho posturing. The story begins with Gil in the grip of road rage so that he is ready to ram a pickup truck from the back of which unruly kids—"Mexican or Vietnamese, Bev decided"—have thrown a cherry bomb at their car. Bev tries to calm him down to prevent an accident. In McDonald's, on the other hand, she is "disgusted" by Taccati's willingness to appease the rude outsider, exclaiming, "'Money isn't the issue.'" The fact that violence doesn't break out doesn't mean that the potential for violence wasn't real. So the story leaves us with the question of how people who want to believe in the perfectibility of the human species can live up to that hope: How can we match our faith with our deeds? In other words, can we imagine a world in which Taccati's vision is not foolish? In the meantime, what does Bev believe she and Gil have won? And what could Gil have lost?

Bishop admits that the story has unresolved issues. That may be unavoidable. After all, a popular interlineation, one of the space-filler gag phrases that floated about in mimeographed sf fanzines, was "I have a cosmic mind—what do I do now?"

The odd little story "Alien Graffiti (A Personal History of Vagrant Intrusions)" first appeared in the June 1986 issue of *Asimov's*. At first glance, it reads more like an essay than a story. In that, it resembles Borges' "The Library of Babel," an apparently emotionally detached description of a place where all truths, half-truths, garbled truths, and purely chaotic drivel are stored for the elucidation and frustration of mankind. Bishop in turn describes a situation in which observers try to interact with objects that might be meaningful—in the same way that someone might guess that the shapes spray-painted on the sides of railroad cars speeding by *must* mean something. Actually, Bishop lists this story among several of his that reflect J.G. Ballard's coolly reptilian attitude toward all futile human endeavor—or perhaps, if we're groping for additional literary antecedents, of the baffled frustration felt by people in Arkady and Boris Strugatsky's *Roadside Picnic*. In any event, the story continues Bishop's fascination with unresolvable puzzles.

The person who tries to describe the basic situation to us readers is Jemmi Nakuru. When he was nine, he and his mother were on a beach at Cadiz when "baffling iridescent hieroglyphics started appearing in our world." No one was frightened by the beautiful shapes hanging in the sky until they disappeared a short time later. Decades later, however, people have developed an obsessive wonder at the fascinating variety of the objects, whatever they could be, that have appeared in the sky or on objects scattered around the world. Jemmi himself has spent his life in baffling fascination, now as head of the UN's Department of Vagrant-Intrusion [a more official, objective-sounding label than "alien graffiti"] Analysis. He writes this expository essay to share his understanding and his frustration—much more of the latter than the former. If this were a comfortable sf "story," it would describe the steps by which how humans have come to understand the VIs. The reason the piece feels like an essay is that nothing has or can be done to resolve the situation. We can record the appearance of each manifestation, where it appeared, and how long it materialized. We have not learned, though, what each is composed of, where and when the next one will appear (a serious concern since people have died in collisions with the things), where they come from, or what they *mean*!

Jemmi lists the various suggestions concerning the VI's import. They might be meaningless byproducts of a previously-unknown chemical process. They could, as in the Strugatskys' novel, have nothing at all to do with humans, just debris shed by alien tourists. Like most people, Jemmi needs an explanation with more human significance than that, as shown by his first labeling the things "hieroglyphs." They may be baffling now, but he can't accept that they'll remain unintelligible. He is more respectful of people who find religious significance in the VIs, for example those who believe that the VIs are translations of holy scriptures—which would, of course, validate the existing faiths if they could be deciphered. And then there's Escribienismo, the new religion that believes the VIs are offering new sacred texts. Now, at his mother's invitation, Jemmi is attending an Escribieno conference at the same Cadiz hotel. His emotion erupts in the next to last paragraph, as he remembers

> past theophanies, beautiful midnight exfoliations, great terrible letters burning our our deserts, inarticulate parables of hope illuminating the walls of crypts or subway stations, brief *billets-doux* from God-knows-who and God-knows-where glittering over tepui or tenement; and in spite of what of what I know and in obedience to what I remember, I am here to celebrate my ignorance and purge my heartache.

The congregation is waiting, probably in vain, for the appearance of a new sample of VI/alien graffiti to tantalizingly offer "mystery, beauty, awe, and humbling sense of awe"—but never satisfaction. Echoing her reaction from the story's opening, our viewpoint character's mother remarks, "'How wonderful.... Didn't I tell you you'd have fun here, Jemmi?'" So the characters, like all the rest of us have come full circle, back where we started.

Bishop's novella "Apartheid, Superstrings, and Mordecai Thubana" was first published as a separate little book by Pulphouse Publishing (Axoltl Press #10, July 1989). In that volume's introduction, Lewis Shiner congratulates himself for prodding Bishop into massively revising an early version of the story but also gives Bishop credit for settling down and writing "the best damned Michael Bishop story I've ever read." At least on the surface, "Apartheid" certainly is one of Bishop's darkest stories, describing how members of the South African security police sadistically torture and eventually kill a young black man. It does, however, try to assert that humans naturally *will* struggle, albeit painfully, to formulate and answer questions about the purpose of their existence.

At the story's beginning, smug white Afrikaner Gerrit Myburgh is jolted out of his comfort zone when his car collides with an elephant, late at night and far from a town. In order to get back to civilization, Myburgh is forced to hail one of the ramshackle buses normally reserved for native African laborers; he is rude to the driver and the other passengers because he is the only white man present, uneasily surrounded by resentful strangers whom he fears are about to attack him. Instead, young Mordecai Thubana tries to put Myburgh at ease and to engage him in a conversation about the theory of superstrings and the search for a GUT (Grand Unifying Theory) or TOE (Theory of Everything) that would explain how everything in the universe works together. Myburgh scoffs at the notion, partly because it is outside his mundane concerns but also because he is bothered to think that a black man could be able to consider such profound issues. Still, without his being aware of it, Myburgh does make a personal connection with Thubana that leads him to follow the young man when he is picked up by the state security police, to witness his suffering and murder, and finally to hijack the bus and take the native passengers on a wild ride through town before he too is taken into government custody.

Exactly how Mygurgh and Thubana ever become connected remains somewhat mysterious. The story chooses to give only a sketchy background for the former—"a thirty-eight-year-old banker," driving an "imported cranberry Cadillac"—and not much more for the latter: Thubana currently is working as a roofer, but he attended university at least briefly and has read and reread a little pop-science paperback titled *SUPERSTRINGS: A Theory of Everything*; "'Under a different set of circumstances,'" he tells Myburgh, "'maybe I *would* be a physicist.'" Thubana's loquaciousness with the obnoxious white businessman is difficult to imagine; he should know better than to waste his time; moreover, he should be careful about exposing too much of himself to a racist stranger. By the same token, Myburgh (the story uses only the characters' last names throughout in order to keep readers distanced from them), develops an unlikely, enduring bond with the young black man. Readers recognize that the real reason Myburgh behaves so hatefully when he climbs aboard the bus is not so much because he is secure in his racial superiority as because he feels outnumbered and vulnerable. This unspoken recognition may also explain the cruelty of the security police later in the story, since they represent a racial minority that uses violence to control the majority population. But Myburgh, who reasonably would be expected to side with the police, soon shows empathy for Thubana.

But this is far from the story's most obvious stretching of probability. There is, first of all, the question of the elephant that suddenly "blossomed" in Myburgh's headlights. Right after the accident, as he surveys his ruined car and shredded clothing, Myburgh realizes that "there weren't any elephants in this part of South Africa." And he can find no evidence that the beast was ever there—no carcass, no blood, etc. Much later, when Myburgh describes the event to the security police, they offer a mundane explanation: He hit an escaped circus animal; at least one officer approvingly calls that scenario "Not unlikely." Most people are eager, even anxious, to find—or invent—natural explanations for unnatural events. Just so, when the bus is stopped by the security police, Myburgh desperately tries to suppose that there must be natural, believable reasons why the white officers, his presumed allies, can't hear him as they sift through the black passengers in search of a terrorist. He doesn't want to realize that his body has become intangible, "ghost matter," which means that he can't significantly interact with the people in authority. And this happens, of course, after the bus on which he was riding apparently suffered a fatal collision with another bus—which fortunately turns out also to be composed of more ghost matter. Not to mention the bus' stopping by Myburgh's wrecked car in which he sees his corpse, dead of a heart attack....

Bishop's overwhelmingly effective massing of realistic detail in "Apartheid" keeps the action from feeling preposterous, but the shifts in perspective may be as confusing to readers as they are to Myburgh. Perhaps at this point readers should turn back a few pages to when that somewhat-untrustworthy viewpoint character resisted hearing Thubana's attempt to introduce the speculations of theoretical physics, including vocabulary such as "ghost matter." The problem is that Myburgh doesn't want to listen to new ideas, let alone apply them in his own experience. Actually, beginning with how the title shoves disparate elements together, Bishop's story demonstrates *Superstring*'s speculation about our efforts to discover how everything in the universe is connected—realizing, of course, that these speculations still are incomplete and wildly contradictory. According to the theoretical physicists, there may be overlapping, alternative versions of reality; after all, it is much more reasonable to believe in a different set of circumstances, under which Myburgh died of a heart attack while driving, than the one in which he lived after his car collided with an elephant. According to the same theoretical uncertainty, there may be ghost matter coexisting with what we call the real matter that makes up busses and human bodies. And genuine connections may show up between obviously, "really" separate objects or people.

If the connection between Myburgh and Thubana is difficult to explain in realistic terms but is definitely *real*, that fact seems to validate speculation in superstring theory and to encourage Thubana's search for a Theory of Everything that insists everything is connected. Such a belief does not fit common sense, especially in South Africa, where Apartheid is based on keeping people separate on the basis of their race, then encouraging them to distrust each other. This situation should make it unreasonable for Myburgh to attach himself to Thubana; still the connection is real. In the same way, Thubana must realize that attaching himself to Mpandhlani, the bus passenger/terrorist who is the security police's prey is at least unwise; nevertheless, he defies the police and accompanies the other to police headquarters where he is tortured and murdered. And Myburgh, as an invisible ghost of himself, goes with the two blacks to witness their undeserved suffering. His black cohorts beg him not to abandon them, not to deny what he is observing, even though "what happened from that moment on, Myburgh received as if dreaming—a long hallucination that complemented his selective invisibility." The security police, meanwhile, can believe only in a very elementary kind of connection, insisting that the TOE symbols on Thubana's tee-shirt must be some kind of subversive African nationalist code. If they could see Myburgh physically in his ghost-matter condition, they would be able to interpret his presence only as a collaborator with the black saboteurs. But the officers' common/comfortable sense is mistaken, criminally *wrong*. Even though he did not witness the crime, Myburgh knows that Thubana was murdered because his naked body is hanging from the belt the police confiscated before beginning to physically abuse him. The police, who committed the crime, insist that the young man committed suicide: After all, natives in their custody do kill themselves frequently. In short, the behavior of South African authorities shows that it is possible to be solidly realistic and thoroughly stupid. What is needed—for justice, practical understanding, and pure decency—is willingness to recognize existing connections, however unlikely or impossible they appear, and reconcile them in a Theory of Everything.

That TOE is what Myburgh is groping for at the story's end. Intermittently restored to physical tangibility, he is visited in his apartment by Thubana's spirit (who is solid enough to feed the goldfish and to wear a robe that Myburgh lends him). When he learns that the driver of the bus GRIM BOY'S TOE was the one who pointed Mpanhlani out to the police in the first place, Myburgh commandeers the bus, which by then has had part of its name painted out so that it now is labeled simply TOE. He takes the native passengers on a ride through brightly lit downtown Pretoria until the police stop the bus and throw him to the pavement. Readers must assume that Myburgh's life will be much harsher and probably shorter after this demonstration of common humanity. However, at the very end, for the first time in the story, he exclaims "'Mordecai,'" his cohort's Christian name, "and he had the distinct sense that someone had heard him." So the connection evidently holds, from one reality to another, from death to life. This validates Myburgh's experiment. He may not have arrived at a Grand Unified Theory of Everything, but at least he has been moving in the right direction.

Bishop's story did not become of merely historical interest when Apartheid was (with a miraculous minimum of violence) put to rest. Its point is not simply political, that Apartheid was a bad system of government. Worse than being evil, it was an especially *stupid* example of the many ways people distract themselves from the real human task of understanding ourselves and our place in the universe. The story insists that people who do try to recognize their true purpose may be destroyed but not quite, not finally defeated.

The outcome is much grimmer in "Life Regarded as a Jigsaw Puzzle of Highly Lustrous Cats" (*Omni*, September 1991). In form, this story most resembles "Dog's Lives," a heap of fragments that requires some assembly by readers. But where the earlier story appeared to end optimistically, pointed up and onward, "Cats" subsides into darkness.

The story's fragmentary structure resembles one of the big jigsaw puzzles that the narrator's father-in-law works every Christmas season; like its chunks of narrative, the puzzle box's lid "lacks any background ... a serious obstacle to quick assembly." The fact that all the pieces of the story are written in the present tense also makes a coherent whole difficult to assemble—obscuring, for example, the important fact that the puzzle worker is the narrator's *former* father-in-law, that a family relationship has been broken.

What emerges from a careful reading of "Cats" is first of all that readers are getting only glimpses of the nameless narrator's life because he is being forced to recall times he has interacted with cats, as if those are the only significant things he's ever done. And so it is—to Penfield, "a.k.a. the Zoo Cop," the person directing this brutal interrogation. Penfield is an animal-rights zealot who is obsessed with getting evidence against the narrator's employer, Rockdale Biological Medical Supply, for committing cruelty to animals as it supplies school biology classes with dissection specimens. Everything else about the narrator is irrelevant to the Zoo Cop. Scraps of personal history adhering to the cat data reveal that the narrator's parents separated during his childhood, that he struggled to connect with people while growing up, that his own marriage failed, and that he spent some time in the Adolescent Wing of the Quiet Harbor Psychiatric Center. Whatever led to that incarceration isn't included in the story, though he does report a childhood episode in which he barely (but sincerely) resists the impulse to throw a newborn kitten against the wall. At QHPC, he is medicated with the antipsychotic drug haloperidol. Sometime later, after his marriage has failed and he is off his meds, he lives rough on the streets of Atlanta until a friend from school recognizes him and offers him a job at Rockdale Biological Medical Supply. Following that, he is snatched up by Penfield and is being subjected to Electrical Stimulation of the Brain (ESB) to dig out whatever he's done with/to cats.

The job at OHPC is the only part of the narrator's life that matters to Penfield, the process by which he converted live cats to specimen cats. In excruciating but affectless present tense, he describes receiving cages of cats at the RBMS loading dock and setting them in a gas chamber, listening until their "yowling and tumbling" stops, then submerging them in water to wash away fleas and finish killing any cats who survived the gas, and finally laying the bodies out on the platform to dry. When he was in a high school biology course, he was horrified when he had to dissect a cat; now he appears to perform his job mechanically. He may be in that condition because his dosage of meds has been reduced by his employer. And he may actually be more disturbed than he appears. When Penfield complains at this point that his recorded testimony is becoming "almost intelligible," the technician controlling the ESB that is forcing the narrator to recall painful memories replies, "He's replaying the experience inwardly.... But he's starting to go autistic."

Essentially, the narrator is just a victim. He is at the nonexistent mercy of his bad genes, his brain chemistry, his untrustworthy buddy at RBMS—and, at this moment, of Penfield, whose self-righteous cruelty resembles that of the South African security police. The story's ESB scenes also resemble Alex's "therapy" in *A Clockwork Orange*, especially as seen in Stanley Kubrick's movie version. The image of the narrator being tortured within a mechanism also fits his vision of himself as a homeless person being manipulated by the artificial people around him, "androids programmed to keep you dirty and hungry by programming your actions with remote-control devices that look like wrist watches and key rings." Eventually, when Penfield despairs of getting useful testimony from the narrator, he simply discards the man: "Christ, Penfield says, unhook the bastard and carry him upstairs. Dump him somewhere remote, somewhere rural." In the larger framework of the story, the narrator is like one of his (former) father-in-law's jigsaw puzzle pieces that don't fit unless they're trimmed with a razor blade; however, when the narrator tries to help with that, the blade slips and he cuts his finger. So that's how the bleak story ends, with a nameless individual being cast aside/off, abandoned and bleeding.

The narrator realizes that he's done dreadful things, "no argument there. None." The story, however, hints that there might be reasons, even excuses for the unthinking cruelty of his actions. But what about the people who have mechanically ignored or misunderstood his needs? Doesn't that constitute unthinking cruelty too? And what about Penfield?

# 4

# Family Reunions
## *Novels, 1982–1994*

These are the novels for which Bishop is best known, his fully mature and accomplished work.

*No Enemy but Time* was a milestone in Bishop's career. It is the only one of his novels to win the Nebula Award; it is the only Bishop novel selected by David Pringle for discussion in *Science Fiction: The 100 Best Novels*; and it is the only Bishop novel bearing a "first-purchase (best buy)" in *Anatomy of Wonder*. Moreover, in the print *The Encyclopedia of Science Fiction*, John Clute magisterially certifies *No Enemy* as Bishop's "most public success" since it has "a protagonist of sufficient racial (and mental) complexity to carry a storyline immured in the particular and haunted by the exotic," with the result that he not only can father a child in the remote past but can bring the baby back "to the battering world" of our present.

In many ways, *No Enemy* is a wonderful book, skillfully constructed according to the image of shuffled photo slides in its Prologue and full of wonder as protagonist Joshua Kampa explores the prehistoric world he has dreamed of/been dropped into. Still, somehow, the novel doesn't quite ring true. To consider how this can be, let's consider how the storyline follows a human process to which readers *must* respond. That may give a better idea of what Bishop's protagonist is looking for and also of what he ultimately fails to hold onto.

Clute is right in saying that we respond to Bishop's protagonist first of all as a "particular" individual. At the same time, Joshua is undertaking the timeless human quest discussed by Joseph Campbell in his synthesis of myths *The Hero with a Thousand Faces*. This is not to say that Bishop was deliberately following Campbell's agenda. He had not read *The Hero* itself at that time, though he vaguely remembered looking through Campbell's *The Masks of God* back when he was beginning to think of himself as a writer. But conscious intent doesn't matter. If

Campbell is right, any storyteller will find that stories naturally follow similar paths, simply because certain patterns of thought and action are fundamental to being human.

Everyone, according to Campbell, is hardwired the same. We have the same needs, and we attempt to satisfy them in much the same ways. First of all, as infants we need protection and encouragement. But after childhood each of us must break free from parental control. By doing so, the adolescent individual becomes triumphantly independent, yet isolated and somehow anxious about that condition. Genuine maturity, therefore, means learning to temper one's individuality by recognizing one's membership in a group. We need to balance our separate identities with the recognition that we also are part of a larger unity (family, tribe, race, conscious living beings, etc.). Achieving this balance is our ultimate concern, our sacred goal. Campbell's "heroes" are the people who have reached this recognition, and the heroic stories we tell and the rituals we practice are intended to demonstrate his process of discovery and to initiate individuals into it. Today, however, cultural continuity has been interrupted, traditional myths and rituals are taken less seriously, and many people remain stranded as perpetual, anxious adolescents, their social "values" borrowed from the lonely crowd around them. Despite this, the impulses of such people still produce the same images that show up in the myths Campbell studied. Contemporary would-be heroes thus reflect our present confusion but still, inescapably, seek self-understanding and self-mastery in much the same ways other humans have in many other lands and times.

This seems to be true in *No Enemy*, though myths that appear in contemporary fiction have become so garbled that rituals have become ineffective parodies of themselves. For example, Campbell describes how a native Australian circumcision ritual accomplishes boys' transition to manhood. Details of the sacred ceremony are kept secret from the uninitiated, so that young men are awed and frightened by the impending transformation and try to flee back to the women who sheltered them as children. When they discover that this protection is no longer available but that they can survive a mysterious threat, surrounded by others, they become men, independent but also interdependent with their fellow tribe members. In Bishop's novel, Joshua Kampa also undergoes ritual circumcision. However, because the young man has not grown up in the African tribe that performs the ceremony, it has little personal significance for him. Moreover, although it matters a great deal to the old native who is Joshua's current mentor, ritual circumcision's diminished significance for other tribe members is shown by how they turn it into a show for a busload of tourists. Overall, this

## 4. Family Reunions

supposed of rite of passage gives distinctly confused signals about what maturity and common humanity can mean today, even when it unconsciously reflects the true dynamic of the ritual. Among the tourists, for example, Joshua even recognizes a woman from one of the places where he grew up. But he can't turn to her for kinship or shelter. She was a hateful, small-town bigot then, and when he approaches her during the ceremony she exclaims, "I've never seen him before," and calls him "an impudent little nigger." It is difficult for anything deeply meaningful to be recognized at such a time, surrounded by such people.

And yet, despite all distraction, Joshua catches a glimpse of superhuman truth just before he passes out, murmuring words that Joseph Campbell would approve: "Everyone wants a piece of the sacred.... Even if it isn't sacred. Dreaming makes it so, and the dreaming goes on and on until it's a habit." Overall, Joshua's story illustrates this hunger to obtain—or create—the sacred, as details and themes from Campbell's study constantly turn up in *No Enemy but Time*. Above all, the structure of Bishop's novel follows Campbell's synthesis of heroic myth. In *The Hero with a Thousand Faces*, the hero's mission occurs in three stages: (1) leaving home and setting forth, (2) facing challenges and learning from what happens, and (3) returning home with prizes to share. This is the journey that Joshua undertakes.

It couldn't be otherwise. Besides unknowingly echoing Campbell's observations about the heroic quest because he is a storyteller, Bishop is himself. At the beginning of "Military Brat: A Memoir," an autobiographical essay, Bishop describes his first childhood memory of waking up and finding himself alone in the house, apparently abandoned: "the memory of this orphan lostness endured through an otherwise happy childhood whose sole major disappointment lay in my parents' divorce. I begin with it not because it traumatized me forever, but because I can recall nothing earlier and because the search for belonging and place surely marks every human life." Another memory, from shortly before his parents' divorce, is of a nightmare quarrel during which the little boy was tugged back and forth between the two, so that "this midnight set-to seared into my heart the knowledge that the single flesh of one's mother and father could rip like a decaying rag." In any event, Bishop's mature fiction frequently contains the theme of the shattered home, especially the missing father.

The raw experience underlying a writer's recurring themes is less important than how he is able to use them as a storyteller. What Bishop accomplishes at the beginning of *No Enemy* is to demonstrate how someone who feels profoundly the absence of a nurturing family can begin doing something, consciously or not, to obtain what he lacks.

According to Campbell, a hero begins his quest by being summoned away from routine activities; in *No Enemy*, the protagonist grows up excluded from the surrounding society. Joshua is first seen as the mulatto child of a mute Spanish prostitute whose neighbors shun her as a witch who created the child as a tool of sorcery. When she realizes she can't raise the boy herself, she leaves him with residents of a United States Air Force base in Spain. Everyone there assumes that he must have been fathered by an African American serviceman who has since departed for another base. However, the child is adopted by Jeanette and Hugo Monegal, an American woman and her Panamanian husband, and he moves with them from one military assignment to another. Besides this rootlessness, at various times in the novel, bystanders call the boy Spanish, American, Indian, or Mexican. He finds himself called by different names—John-John, Johnny, or Juanito—until he chooses the *nom de guerre* Juan Ocampo and still later the adult name Joshua Kampa. All in all, the society around Bishop's protagonist gives him little help in figuring out where he belongs or what social label fits him. "You can't go home again," he later reflects, "particularly if you've never had one."

Nor does he have materials with which to build a personal identity. During the fever and delirium following his circumcision, when he imagines his father's ghost visiting him, Joshua can picture only "a young black infantry man with no head." Although physically whole, his adopted father Hugo Monegal is not a very useful model as an adult male either. He is likable and well-meaning, but he doesn't understand himself very well or deal with the world around him very competently. The way Hugo dies illustrates his incompleteness. Joshua's adoptive mother has gone to stay with the editor who is helping her produce her first book, a move toward independence that Hugo would have liked to prevent on several counts, although he "never had that kind of power." To make up for that supposed slight to his male authority, Hugo insists that the two men of the family will prove *they* can have fun by touring Florida's roadside tourist attractions. At a wretched little "animal ranch," Hugo torments a pair of rhesus monkeys until the male snatches and splinters his beloved meerschaum pipe; the phallic association is unavoidable since Bishop describes Hugo's pipe as "a comfort and a crutch from the days he had *manfully* [emphasis added] struggled to give up cigarettes." Hugo is too abashed—unmanned—to take revenge immediately, but he sneaks back that night, after his adopted son is asleep. He shoots into the monkey cage, killing the female ("ironically"?), but is fatally injured in a car wreck as he flees. His embarrassingly pathetic death encourages Joshua "to close the door on his life with the Monegals and to run away from home."

### 4. Family Reunions

In fact, that hasn't been Joshua's real home for some time. While he was still with his birth mother and long before he had language to communicate his observations, the boy began dreaming of prehistoric life in Africa, in what is now the country of Zarakal. By the time he is a young man, his dreams have given him a vivid and detailed picture of long-vanished wildlife and people that is at least as coherent as his own patchwork life and that feels more significant. Looking back at his behavior later, Jeanette Monegal dispassionately remarks that her adopted son "cherished the idea of an identity separate from the bourgeois one with which we had saddled [him], and ... one day [he] might try to *inherit* [emphasis added] this alternative life." For a while after leaving the Monegals' home, Joshua feels himself to be drifting purposelessly. His first lover, however, assures him that his life has a purpose: "'Think about those dreams you have, Joshua. The apemen in them— the apemen trying to become human—they're the key. You want what they want, but you don't know how to get there any better than they do.'" Later, Joshua accepts that he does have "a mission foreordained for him at birth," and demonstrated, though not explained, by his dreams.

But it is not simple for Joshua to start becoming more human. Though his "mission" involves personal, individual development, Joshua also is troubled because he is *only* an individual. Immediately after accepting his quest, "[a]lmost against his will," Joshua finds himself thinking of reconnecting with the family he has rejected, then reminds himself that the Monegals are just his *adopted* family; whatever he feels for them as people, they aren't his kin, and he can live without them. His mood is less dispassionate when he learns that Alastair Patrick Blair, eccentric hominid paleontologist and member of the Zarakal government, will be lecturing at a nearby college. In the grip of excitement that he recognizes is irrational but that he cannot resist—convinced that "his entire previous life had been pointing him toward this meeting with Blair"—Joshua rushes to the auditorium. He interrupts the lecture by sometimes confirming but also contradicting Blair; the scientist has only reconstructions of prehistoric life, while Joshua can rely on his firsthand dream observations. To some extent, Blair is a father figure whom Joshua respects but must supersede. But Blair accepts rude corrections from Joshua because he recognizes that both of them are obsessed with the same goal, revealed in Blair's lecture when he describes the habiline Zarakali Man as "'[o]ur foremost *father* [emphasis added] in the apeman line.'" The shared quest for ancestry, however, is less vital to Blair than it is to Joshua. Blair wants to trace humanity's bloodline intellectually, but Joshua's need to physically reacquire his inheritance is the core of the young man's being, the heart of his dreams.

Joshua's dreams make him the only person who *can* return to the distant African past, in a time-travel experiment sponsored by the Zarakal government at the behest of its vain president.

The novel emphasizes how thoroughly personal and subjective Joshua's quest is. It is not the relatively straightforward jaunt through time that most characters (and readers too) might suppose. That's camouflage. While Joshua is discussing the theoretical basis of time travel with the project's lead scientist Woody Kaprow, the latter admits that returning to Earth's actual past is impossible. Instead, Joshua will be entering a world objectified out of the past as he has dreamed it. Blair is horrified at this news, since he has been counting on his own theories being verified by Josh's direct observations, a validation that is impossible if Joshua will see only "'a bloody diorama of the Pleistocene.'" In his prospectus for the novel, Bishop suggested that it could exploit uncertainty about the same issue: "has the protagonist really gone back in time, or is his total immersion in the past a protracted and convincing fever dream." But Kaprow adroitly sidesteps this uncertainty by insisting that Joshua may be going back to a

> Diorama of Pleistocene or a "simulacrum," to use another of your words, but it's going to be a *living* diorama, a *perfect* simulacrum.... Time travel as H.G. Wells envisioned it is an utter impossibility. The future is forever inaccessible because it hasn't happened yet. It has no pursuable resonances. The past is accessible only because of adepts like Joshua here, a person whose collective unconscious—whose psyche, if you prefer—establishes an attunement to a particular place at a particular time.

As Kaprow further speculates after Joshua's return, "terminology's of no consequence. The dreamfarer is himself the key to the journey, because time, like our universe, is an atttribute of consciousness. In fact, it's possible that it has no significant meaning apart from consciousness."

Blair is pacified with suspicious ease. So are readers. Most commentary on *No Enemy* describes it as a story about travel through time, not into the unconscious of the protagonist. This is a dazzling fast shuffle by Kaprow—and by Bishop also. To accommodate Joshua's unstated needs, the novel shows its protagonist riding machinery to a place different from his contemporary surroundings. The "scientific" justification for the story's action essentially stops there, with the assertion that something's working somehow. As Kaprow says, "terminology's of no consequence." And so the distinction between "genuine" and "accurate" becomes blurred or lost, along with a reader's ability to tell what's inside or outside Joshua's consciousness. Blair simply accepts that the "past" Joshua will travel to is simultaneously subjective *and* objective but still useful for validating Blair's theories—a remarkable concession since

## 4. Family Reunions

Joshua has told Blair that his dreams have included watching astronauts land in the prehistoric veldt and seeing the Snuffleupagus from *Sesame Street* being butchered by hominids. It's impossible to be sure where the raw material for Joshua's dreams originated, and it's startling that his dreams correspond closely to Blair's reconstructions of the past. But it's clear that this "past" has been created by Joshua's unconscious psyche to supply a space in which he can satisfy his needs.

At this point in the novel's action, we should consider Joseph Campbell's explanation of what happens to the hero during the quest's central phase: the tests he faces and the prize he finally wins. The mythic hero in Campbell's *The Hero with a Thousand Faces* also learns that terminology is meaningless. "Interior" and "exterior" reality are equivalent but equally useless notions. Daunting as they seem at first to be, the difficulties a hero must overcome merely test his will to overcome. Belief *is* the deed. The power to penetrate barriers is natural for one destined to be a hero, "for his passing and returning demonstrate that through all the phenomenality the Uncreate-Imperishable remains, and there is nothing to fear." From that perspective, David Pringle's observation that the world Joshua visits "is in some sense imaginary" is correct but irrelevant. In other words, thinking of "subjective" vs. "objective"—or "real" vs. "imaginary," for that matter—is useless. By breaking through the shell of our phenomenal reality, the hero discovers that the difficulties humans encounter are just ideas. "Time" is just a concept, as is "matter." "The hero finds that even when the universe around him dissolves, his imperishable self remains constant—then discovers that 'self' is a concept too." Once he reaches this point, according to Campbell, "[t]he hero has died as modern man; but as eternal man—perfected, unspecific, universal man—he has been reborn." To reach this state, the mythic questor releases himself from himself through various poetic frenzies and sensual ecstasies, in particular "the frenzy of love, as illustrations of that divine 'enthusiasm' that overturns the reason and releases the forces of the destructive-creative dark."

This description fits remarkably well what happens as Joshua explores the world created out of his dreams. It's not that Joshua is leaving a real world to explore his fantasies, as opposed to facing real dangers in an objectively existing situation. Rather, the novel's consensus reality is as much an artificial, frivolous construct as the frivolous f/x "past" that disturbs Blair. But even though the dangers Joshua faces are at least subjectively "real" to him, the jocular tone of his observations suggests that he never loses confidence that he will prevail. Once he has gotten past some preliminary dangers, he joins a tribe of hominids and wins one of them, whom he names Helen, to be his mate. Following this, he releases himself into frenzies as he ecstatically introduces the others to the taste of roast meat, recites one of his poems so that he "projected [his] very soul into the words and the Minids listened ... with rapt self-extinction," and he himself becomes the creator inspiriting myths—all leading up to the realization that "I was dreaming myself into being out of the forgotten material of pre-consciousness, and Helen was my guide through the dark." Later still, when he dreams of being killed by a leopard, the consciousness that once was Joshua and more recently a nameless hominid simply expands again: "Neither terrified nor pain-racked, I died into the night." Immediately, now in the identity of the leopard, he races through the night with Helen on his back, until he stops so that "[w]e fed our passions beyond the limits of her former lover's appetite. Thus did we cuckold the dead. Afterward, we curled together in a ball and jointly dreamed this dream."

Accomplishing his first goal, Joshua has found the family niche he was looking for, and he responds by giving up his adult identity. As the habilines settle into sleep,

> The Minids and I were Children of Eve Together, Sons and Daughters of the Dawn.... we lay down like siblings on the hilltop.
> I was happy; supremely, unconditionally happy.

Besides family kinship, this escape from the limits of his modern, conscious self is also inspired by what Campbell calls "the frenzy of love"—the moment of orgasm—demonstrating "that divine 'enthusiasm' that overturns the reason and releases the forces of the destructive-creative dark." Joshua is enough of a conscious observer to report that Helen's labia are farther forward on her body than that of the other female Minids, permitting the lovers to "consummate our mutual lusts face to face." Despite this rather cold and graphic description Joshua attributes considerable significance to their relationship, for he goes on to say that "Helen was a human being in my sight, and our love was not bestial but sublime."

While Joshua simultaneously is fitting in with his newfound siblings and regaining childlike acceptance of life's fluidity, he also is taking adult responsibility, especially when he realizes that he has made Helen pregnant. Another part of Campbell's explication of heroic myth is useful in explaining Joshua's relationship with Helen, because their union appears to be what Campbell calls "[t]he ultimate adventure ... [that] is commonly represented as a mystical marriage ... of the triumphant hero-soul with the Queen Goddess of the World." Campbell stresses the significance of this relationship by calling it "the crisis at the nadir, the zenith, or at the uttermost edge of the earth, at the central point of the cosmos, in the tabernacle of the temple, or within the darkness of the deepest chambers of the heart." This seems a fair description of how thoroughly Joshua's marriage with Helen helps satisfy some of his deepest needs. The fact that individual consciousness can change masks or merge, as Joshua imagines himself becoming the leopard who then dreams together with Helen, again demonstrates Campbell's point that our conceptions of identity are as arbitrary as those of time, matter, reality, etc. Campbell describes the hero's bride, thus, as "the paragon of all paragons of beauty, the reply to all desire, the bliss-bestowing goal of every hero's earthly and unearthly quest. She is mother, sister, mistress, bride." In fact, she represents all of the mother's aspects. She is threatening and forbidden—yet tempting—the woman who belongs to the father. She also is "the comforting, the nourishing, the 'good' mother ... who was known to us, and even tasted, in the remotest past." Helen, the woman Joshua finds in the remote past that has just been created out of his dreams, can satisfy both his immediate lusts and his larger appetites. She is essentially non-verbal; the only sentence she learns to parrot is "I love you."

Helen's most independent pursuit, which appears to surprise Joshua each time it appears, is her maternal yearnings. She evidently is sterile with the Minids of her tribe, so she first steals a baby baboon, then an australopithecine infant. Helen sets this child down between herself and Joshua and, while patting him on the back and "gibbering a series of syllables that had little relation to any I had taught her," communicates that "[a]s surely as if we had conceived this child ourselves, Helen and I were the australopithecine's mother and father. It was our responsibility to see that she grew into a healthy adult." Joshua reasonably objects, declaring that even if the baby survives it won't have an easy life: "She'll be lucky if the Minids tolerate her presence, much less accept her as one of their own.... She'll be despised by *hablis* and *africanus* alike, Helen, just as if she were a half-breed." He should know. Joshua himself was a despised half-breed who lacked support from the people around him as he grew up.

If Joshua is not rejecting what he learned in his own childhood, he must be suggesting that his childhood could have been happier and his development easier if he had received more benevolent attention. Helen's first "children" are incapable of responding to such attention because their bodies and minds are prehuman, limited. But Joshua's *own* child would be more able to carry the best of his potential into the future, even if the "present" is all he consciously cares about at the moment. Therefore, his objections to Helen's desire to be a mother or to see himself as a father show again the divergence between conscious attitudes and unconscious needs. Since Joshua has dreamed Helen into existence, she cannot want what he doesn't, even if his desires are hidden within the darkness through which Helen guides him. Her feelings of incompleteness reveal his own. One thing Joshua has craved is to meet his father face to face. Returning to Campbell again, we find that although the hero imagines his father to be a rival, the older man actually turns out to be "the initiating priest through which the young being passes on into the large world." As he enters the larger world by freeing himself from his initial limitations, the hero becomes more comprehensive; in fact, he discovers that the role of father is yet another potential facet of his own personality:

> The mystical marriage with the queen goddess of the world represents the hero's total mastery of life; for the woman is life, the hero its knower and master. And the testings of the hero, which were preliminary to his ultimate experience and deed, were symbolical of those crises of realization by means of which his consciousness came to be amplified and made capable of enduring the full possession of the mother-destroyer, his inevitable bride. With that he knows that he and the father are one: he is in the father's place.

So Joshua gets the child he needs.

Along with his possession of home and family, Helen's pregnancy completes Joshua's set of prizes. Now he has a sure foundation as he goes about what his teenaged lover back in Florida suggested was his goal, "trying to become more human." He is at peace. An "unexpected rainfall" eases the existence of Joshua and his adopted kin: "Our little village became Shangri-La.... I was dreaming this idyll. Submerged in my experience without benefit of continuous, rational consciousness, I may have been more alive, alert, and accepting than at any other time in either of my pasts." It also is during this period that his dreams no longer show a distant land to which he'd have to travel for fulfillment; now he dreams about his immediate surroundings, including his dream of becoming the leopard and achieving even more total intercourse with Helen.

Now that Joshua has become a more complete human being, at least theoretically he should be able to do what no parent did for him: protect and nurture, provide continuity in a chaotic world, and—in Campbell's sense—guide and liberate. In short, he should be able to do whatever he imagines a "father" ideally doing. So the issue becomes what Joshua can do with the role he has created. For he does not consciously realize his power as creator. Still burdened with incomplete and contradictory role models from his own past, operating in a setting limited only by his dreams, and without understanding to match his cunning—what will Joshua be able to do for (or to) his child? And where will those actions leave him?

## 4. Family Reunions

The first signs are not encouraging. Now that "the past" has supplied what Joshua needed, he can abandon it. And so a volcanic eruption drives the tribe from their home and scatters them across the burning veldt. Before this, however, Helen dies just after giving birth to their daughter. Her pelvic structure is too narrow to let the baby's head out, so she is doomed by not being quite human enough to accommodate Joshua's seed. Naturally enough, he initially is inclined to reject the baby responsible for his lover's death, calling her an "unappetizing little grub." Remembering that the Minids actually do eat insects, including larvae, readers may suspect that Joshua again is revealing conflicting appetites of which he is unaware. In particular, since he compares the baby's pale skin color unfavorably to that of the albino hippo he had just refused to eat because he felt it was too closely connected to him and his dreams ("the hippo and I had an affinity of which I was ignorant"), Joshua is drawing an analogy between absorbing physically and nurturing: "The mired hippopotamus that the Minids had eaten had been a lovelier hue, a more comprehensible variety of mutant. I had refused to eat of it for fear of violating the integrity of one of my dreams—but this creature, my daughter, how was I ever going to be able to love her?" Nevertheless, with the mountain trembling above them, Joshua manages to remove the child from Helen's corpse: "Come here, baby. Come to Poppa."

In his prospectus for the novel, Bishop imagined the protagonist apparently dying "alone with no surviving family" in our reality but also imagined at least that his subconscious could escape "to the ancient African grasslands where Helen Habiline has borne their hybrid child." The novel itself goes much farther. With Joshua in possession of family memories and of the child who validates him as family head, it is time to return home. The novel must take on the considerable task of physically transporting him from the past to the present—or, as I would argue, from a subjective, dream-created simulation of the past to a more objective, shared-world reality. This is accomplished, incongruously, by a Zarakali space module landing in the prehistoric veldt next to Joshua and carrying him and his baby back to the time machine. Joshua himself recognizes how unbelievable the event is, and he records several alternative semi-rationalizations for it. But he also recognizes when to stop worrying about it—he senses, in other words, that he shouldn't think too deeply about what happened:

> What ... occurred will strike many as an improbably *deus ex machina* solution to our dilemma. I cannot effectively counter this complaint. To argue that I dreamed this solution is to cast into doubt everything else that happened during my sojourn in Pleistocene East Africa. (However, it is entirely possible that I foresaw this solution in a childhood spirit-tainted or impure dream.) On the other hand, to insist

on the absolute reality of this occurrence is to violate the self-consistent world to which the director of the White Sphinx Project posted me. Let me, therefore, justify the following strange events in the only way possible, by declaring that they conform to the reality of my subjective experience.... If they have any other justification, I do not intend to record it here.

No matter. As we've seen, the novel is Joshua's story in more ways than one, and he can steer it any way he wishes. In any event, however, now that he's back in the less subjective here-and-how, Joshua will have to do something about filling the roles of hero and father. He will have to integrate his understanding of the larger, freer world of his adventures with the more limited setting to which he has returned. And, perhaps most important of all, he must try to bring the knowledge he explored in the formless darkness into the light of consciousness.

Or perhaps not. Perhaps he will be able to evade these demands.

Instead of relaxing into well-earned contentment at the end of his adventures, a hero faces new and especially demanding trials now. Homecoming may be the most challenging test of all. Even Joseph Campbell has trouble explaining this stage of the hero's quest. Since, after all, the quest has brought the hero to where he most deeply wants and needs to be, why should he even return to everyday reality? Campbell would answer that the hero returns "from that abyss to the plane of contemporary life ... to serve as a human transformer of demiurgic potential." As Bodhisattva or Christ, he reveals to ordinary humans their potential to transcend their limits. And yet, because he is returning to the constricting shell of individual consciousness, the hero may try to make everyone else submit to his singular vision. He must give up that egotistical control: "the hero of yesterday becomes the tyrant of tomorrow, unless he crucifies *himself* today."

In the last pages of *No Enemy but Time*, Joshua works out his role as well as he can. But he does so within the limits of his experience in non-dream reality and of his conscious understanding.

After a couple of chapters set in the 1987 from which the experiment was launched, the novel jumps to 2002. Joshua has written a book about what he unequivocally calls "my adventures in prehistoric East Africa" but has titled it somewhat more ambiguously *Eden in My Dreams*. He has reared his daughter Monicah and served as Zarakal's Minister of Tourism and Intercultural Affairs. As a politician, he has had to practice the art of the possible, reassuring himself that what he is doing will encourage progress eventually. On the fifteenth anniversary of his return from the Pleistocene, chosen by Monicah as her official birthday, they return to the site of his departure to celebrate the opening of "the spanking-new Sambusi Sands Convention and Recreational

### 4. Family Reunions

Centre." This resort's glitziness seems out of place in the austere landscape described earlier in *No Enemy*, let alone the Pleistocene veldt. When Joshua is singled out for applause at the opening gala as "the man whose mind conceived" the place, he flinches inwardly: "The Centre, I wanted to tell them, was not entirely my fault."

But he does not object publicly. On the contrary, he sits through a program that includes a reenactment of his rescue, as performed by Lisa Chagula and the Gombe Stream Chimps: "Five chimpanzees swaggered in from stage-right, one of them having been shaved to simulate a quasi-human nakedness. I saw through the chimp's imposture immediately, and so did everyone else who knew the details of my legendary trip into the distant past, i.e., everyone in attendance. The ape was supposed to be me." And so on. This travesty is not, remember, intended to humiliate Joshua; the show is the best these people can do in celebrating a transcendent event. But Joshua does not interrupt to suggest that they could have done better if they had stretched their imaginations. He does not even try to be "a human transformer of demiurgic potential." Instead, he accepts his role as a public figure and so feels that he must simply smile and applaud the show.

Monicah reacts differently, escaping with the comment that the depiction of her and her father is violating at least the chimpanzees' dignity. At this point, if not sooner, readers become aware how little the last section of *No Enemy* has shown of Monicah. After his initial desperation to get custody of his daughter after they return, Joshua describes almost nothing of how he actually has behaved as her father. One such almost-omission is especially troubling. Joshua observed, even when Monicah was a newborn, that "her translucent eyelids flickered," suggesting the behaviors that signaled the beginnings of Joshua's own dreaming. In the book's last sequence, he reports that Monicah "dreamed as I had once dreamed. Not of her mother's cat-eat-chalicothere grasslands, however, but of a vivid utopian tomorrow whose inaccessibility sometimes frustrated her beyond bearing. I, the past; she, the future." The notion of such dreaming violates Kaprow's theory that "the future is forever inaccessible because it hasn't happened yet," but of course that was just a theory, mere "terminology." In any event, Joshua doesn't seem especially curious, since he reports no further details; the nature of the Utopia in Monicah's dreams is left vague, even though her father ought to have sympathized with her intense frustration, considering his own childhood. For that matter, the relationship between parent and child is left vague generally. Joshua doesn't describe how he shared his own childhood experiences and what he learned of himself on his journey, to help Monicah grow up. In fact, he does not contradict a later accusation that he has never even spoken to her about her mother.

Overall, Joshua doesn't describe how he helped Monicah get a solid sense of herself in a family so that someday she would be able to stand apart from it. Any parent of a teenager has trouble noticing when the child develops independent ideas that deserve attention. Instead, Joshua sloughs off Monicah's angry comments at the gala, tacitly accepting the official judgment that she is just showing "adolescent irresponsibility." He obviously assumes that she is not yet ready to be viewed as a responsible adult.

Complicating and highlighting Joshua's dilemma of whether to release Monicah or continue to possess her is the presence of Dirk Akuj, a young man who claims also to dream of a utopian future and who has been extremely anxious to meet Monicah. Akuj's interest in Monicah frightens Joshua for reasons that show how thoroughly he is confusing the roles of nurturing father and triumphant hero. In fact, he sees the stranger as a rival for his daughter's affections: "his interest in my daughter, just fifteen today, struck me as ominous, something other than the tardy fibrillations of a young man's fancy. After all, the Ugandan was not that much younger than I." Though Joshua may reassure himself that he still is in his prime and that in any case Monicah is not old enough to choose to leave him, he still is disturbed by the notion that he might someday be replaced.

Joshua's unrecognized need to possess Monicah, along with his experience of living in dreams, figure in a disturbing, enigmatic scene between the two. *How* disturbing readers will find that scene depends on how they read it. Michael Bishop personally disagrees with the interpretation offered here; he says directly that it goes "against the grain of my conscious intentions." He does affirm that a writer is not always conscious of the full import of what he is creating. So readers should approach the following discussion with all possible, reluctant skepticism.

What I believe happens is that Joshua has sex with his daughter. What Joshua believes—well, that's much harder to guess. At a critical point in the action, he enters a drug-induced dream state in which, he says, "time ceased to have any conventional meaning.... I was alone but in a place with neither substance nor dimension." Earlier, Joshua dismissed Akuj's questions about his own journey by saying that he tries not to think of it "[b]ecause it's grown more and more remote with each passing year, and I'm afraid half of it never really happened." At this point, thus, the novel appears to be warning readers not to assume that everything shown in the narration is what it seems to be.

## 4. Family Reunions

Here is what the novel's conclusion gives readers to work with. His official duties over, Joshua returns to the suite he and his daughter share. It is 2:30 a.m. He finds Dirk Akkuj in the room and immediately becomes suspicious of sexual activity between the two young people. Dirk is standing, but Monicah is lying, semi-conscious, on the bed; the man is fully dressed, but the girl's native costume leaves "her tiny breasts ... exposed." While talking with "the intruder," his "nemesis," Joshua lies down beside Monicah. He takes her hand, which is "warm and poignantly soft," while rejecting Akuj's request that the girl be allowed to leave with him to take part in a revival of the White Sphinx Project intended to let dreamers travel into the future so that they can "make the future their present." Joshua reminds Akuj that Monicah is a minor and insists that he will not consent. But Akuj replies that he has dreamed that Joshua will agree that very night in order to regain Monicah's respect, lost because she realizes that her father has "tried to take advantage of [their] relationship for certain unworthy, short-term ends." Moreover, Akuj says that he has drugged Monicah so that she can enter a trance state and communicate with her mother's spirit; in fact, since Helen's spirit entered her body, Monicah has "become her mother." Even before this, Joshua has observed how much his daughter "looked like Helen," adding that "[t]he strange glint in her eye bewitched as well as terrified me." When Joshua demands that he bring Monicah back to her body, Akuj counters by offering him the opportunity to enter a trance himself and "touch the spirit of your habiline wife." Unnerved by the other's taunting, Joshua agrees, whereupon he sees Helen in the doorway, dressed as a hotel maid. Almost blinded by tears, he draws her into the darkness by the bed and undresses her:

> I stood, embraced her for an infinite moment, just to feel her body against mine, and rocked her in my arms *like a father holding his child* [emphasis added]. Her starched clothing began to annoy me, too, and I loosened the knot supporting her apron, expertly unbuttoned her dress and swept these items down her flanks to the floor, there to join my V-necked T-shirt and my beautiful Fruit of the Looms. She regarded me with tender puzzlement, but did not scold me for returning us to the innocent nakedness of beasts and Minids. Instead she closed my eyelids with her fingertips and settled one gnarled fist on my heart.

When he opens his eyes again, he is in bed with Helen Habiline. And the next time he becomes conscious, it is midday, Monicah and Dirk Akuj are gone, and he is looking up at a hotel maid who is standing by the bed and politely inquiring whether she can leave the room. As far as Joshua is concerned, the maid is the woman who shared his bed. That was Bishop's conscious intent, on the assumption that Joshua "insists on mistaking her for Helen."

But the maid says that she has been in the room for only about two hours, and it is almost noon.

And the maid is fully dressed, although the woman in bed with Joshua was as naked as he was.

And, above all, the maid doesn't resemble Helen or Monicah physically or spiritually.

If incest did occur, as I believe, that never will trouble Joshua's conscience because it never will emerge into his consciousness. Still, the subject is worth brief speculation. Incest is barely mentioned in *The Hero with a Thousand Faces*, for the shame and guilt of committing this taboo act would distract any hero from his quest. Incest is even more taboo when the parent consciously initiates it. When Campbell describes the hero's female prize as summing up the roles of "mother, mistress, bride," he omits "daughter" from the list. Sir James Frazer, one of Campbell's sources, is somewhat less squeamish, but he explains that a father might have sex with his daughter as a tactic to maintain control. An insecure king, for example, might hold on to power by marrying the daughter who was immediate heir to the throne through her mother the queen. Seen from that angle, sex with Monicah might be a way for Joshua to reassure himself of his continuing command. Permitting her to depart with Akuj, thus, might be expelling a rival that the ruler is too proud to fear. Then again, using a somewhat healthier interpretation, Joshua may not just be rationalizing when he sees Helen in Monicah; he may genuinely be convinced that he is touching his wife and thus restoring what Bishop calls "the single flesh ... of father and mother."

Or, if the notion of incest is totally mistaken, it may be that Monicah's disappearance after the gala shows that Joshua finally recognizes that she needs to begin her own search for meaning. If so, Joshua may finally be fulfilling the hero's ultimate responsibility of starting others off on their own quests.

I doubt it. Joshua's treatment of Monicah has been described only sketchily, but the available specifics—such as his refusal to talk about her mother—don't show recognition that she needs the kind of family security that he did as a child, or that such certainty could become the basis for mature independence. The book gives him—or he gives himself—no opportunity to reflect on the personal significance of her departure with Akuj. Overall, he does not appear to have grasped a vision of life that he could try to share with his own child, let alone with people more remote from him. And unless he can deal with what happened to him, how can he help anyone create a better future? The novel ends almost immediately afterward. There is no opportunity to reconcile the contradictory evidence—which includes an upbeat, affectionate note that Monicah leaves for her father. The conclusion's abruptness simply demonstrates that Joshua is ready for the story to be over so that he can stop thinking about what has happened. Instead, at the very end, he is swinging from the support rods under the resort's water tower, just as he did back in Florida before he caught sight of his "mission": "For the duration of my stunt, at least, I was a very happy man." The mention of a time limit and the further-qualifying "at least" may or may not be significant to Joshua.

Has Joshua's quest brought him to increased self-awareness, or has he simply been swept through a process without realizing what it means? Has he become significantly more human or not? I suspect the latter. Looking at the first version of *Transfigurations*, John Clute is unconvinced by its insistence that the protagonist has been transformed; even though the character has gone "as far as the novel can go … it's not far enough. He understands no more than we do. He can ape but he cannot speak the language of metamorphosis, and stands, at the novel's close, as a sign of the prison house." Sadly, that judgment seems to fit *No Enemy but Time* even better. Like Joshua himself, this novel's reach has exceeded its grasp. The more one considers its happy ending, the sadder it feels. What Joshua has accomplished, finally, is reburying the truth he has sought and briefly held.

Even so, *No Enemy* still is an important effort. It should be taken seriously because it struggles with concerns that are especially relevant not only to Bishop but to all readers. Bishop's later novels are more successful in showing genuine heroism and the rebuilding of human relationships in uncertain times. Nevertheless, this was a book he probably needed to write as part of his quest to become a large-souled, honest writer. Unlike Joshua, Bishop was able to make sense of where he had been in order to get a feel for where he was going.

Bishop's next novel was a surprise to his readers. Rather than return to the sf territory of prehistoric anthropology that he had begun exploring in *No Enemy but Time*, *Who Made Stevie Crye?* (1984) is a parody of contemporary horror fiction. In particular, *Stevie* takes off on Stephen King's habitual transformations of routine, small-town life into gaudy nightmare. The novel was less than successful commercially. After appearing in hardcover from prestigious small press publisher Arkham House, it had no American paperback edition; in the UK, it first appeared only in paperback. The novel's critical reception also was mixed, though David Pringle listed it in *Modern Fantasy: The Hundred Best Novels, an English Language Selection, 1947–1987*.

Actually, different as it initially appears, *Stevie* is a perfectly natural successor to *No Enemy but Time*, continuing Bishop's consideration of the seductive power of the creative imagination.

In this story, the imagination belongs to (or vice versa) "Stevenson Crye—her friends call her Stevie," who is the still-distressed and -angry widow of Ted Crye as well as the mother of 13-year-old Ted Jr. and eight-year-old Marella. She is barely holding her family together by free-lance journalism for local Georgia publications. When her electric typewriter, a high-tech PDE "Exceleriter" goes haywire, Stevie is forced to take it for repair to Seaton Benecke, an almost threateningly affectless young man who says that he's a fan of her writing but that he really prefers "'the personal-experience columns ... sometimes they get close to what I'm talking about, when you exaggerate things to make them deeper, when you confess your feelings.... Deepness is what I really like. Not being afraid to write about fears and dark desires. Nitty-gritty stuff.'" Stevie extricates herself as soon as she can and returns to her safe little home.

And then the fun begins: the nitty-gritty stuff.

As the Exceleriter begins to type taunting messages for Stevie, transcribe her dreams, and then to offer bits of narrative that repeat or *predict* "real life" events, it become virtually impossible to summarize the novel's action. Rather than linear chronology, manuscript divisions sometimes organize the action. Late in the story, for example, Stevie remembers that Seaton has invaded her house—but needs confirmation from the friendly neighborhood psychic whose typewriter has also started participating in the action:

> "Please, Betty, is Seaton upstairs or not? I've been going crazy for a week. You've got to help me, not make me crazier."
> 
> "Well, child, he is and he ain't. Chapter Forty-four says he is. If we drop out that chapter, though, and start this one over, with me arrivin' at your kitchen door, well, then, he ain't." Sister C. leaned, folding her arms beneath her bosom. "What do you want to do? We can renumber this chapter so there's no hiccup in the story. We can renumber all the chapters right to the end, closing things up as tightly sweet as you like."
> 
> "Betty, you can't tear up a piece of someone's life and throw it away like a sheet of typing paper."
> 
> "Happens all the time."

As this exchange demonstrates, *Stevie* is balanced precariously between horror and humor. From Stevie's perspective, as her belief in her self-control disintegrates and even her sense of her own identity evaporates, this is a moment of absolute horror. But it also resembles slapstick farce—or Marx Brothers surrealism such as Chico's smug observation that when you get right down to it "there ain't no sanity clause." If Stevie is learning that she can't trust her memory, how can readers guess what's real or not? For that matter, of course, remember that this is a novel. It's *fiction*. None of it is "real," but *Who Made Stevie Crye?* goes out of its way to remind readers that one sequence of events, set of words, typed symbols on paper, is not more worth taking seriously than another. The fact that Stevie looks through one of Ted's old sf paperbacks, a battered copy of *The Grasshopper Lies Heavy*—actually a part of Philip K. Dick's alternative world novel *The Man in the High Castle*—could hint that Stevie is living in an alternative world too. Or it could be just evidence of Michael Bishop's playfulness. There's no way to be sure.

The title itself can be read two ways: as "Who upset Stevie?" or as "Who created Stevie?" Late in the action, Stevie's daughter Marella brings up the latter question directly by reciting William Blake's poem "The Lamb": "Little Lamb, who made thee? / Dost thou know who made thee?" Rather than being reassured by the conclusion that God is responsible for the lamb's innocence, Stevie wonders whether she and Marella have had this conversation earlier or whether the Exceleriter imagined it. And a page or so later she finds herself sitting on the edge of Teddy's bed, remembering "the awe-begotten words" of Blake's "The Tiger": "Tiger! Tiger! Burning bright / In the forests of the night, / What immortal hand or eye / *Dare* frame thy fearful symmetry?" This question remains unanswered. Songs of innocence and experience indeed....

Consider the novel's incest scene between Stevie and her 13-year-old son Teddy. Early in the book, Stevie looks into the boy's freezing cold bedroom and sees him sleeping with the covers off and no pajama top on. He reminds her of her dead husband, Ted:

> Beneath his right arm, which he had just flung over his head, Stevie could see a delicate brunet curl, a clock-spring of hair—symbolic, maybe, of his burgeoning maturity. His face still looked callow, the endearing mug of a wiseacre juvenile (its dearness a function of family connection, Stevie knew, and probably not readily evident to strangers), but his body was acquiring strength and something like an admirable classical purity. As she drew his blanket over his shoulders, Stevie kissed him lightly on the brow.

All this scene shows is normal loving-mother concern and pride. However, several nights later, after several Exceleriter-nudged nightmares featuring appearances by the revenant of a maddeningly-uncommunicative Ted, Teddy appears at the door of Stevie's bedroom. He is very cold and wearing only underpants, so she invites him into the warm bed with her, where he complains that he wishes he could talk to his father. "'You wish Dad were here. So do I, Teddy. For both our sakes,' Stevie replies. Teddy's problem, it turns out is that he has no one to talk to about his sexual development, the adequacy of his genital equipment. And so,

> Stevie leaned over her son's face and kissed him on the brow. Her kisses descended casually to his eyelids, his nose, his cheeks, and finally the soft chilly bud of his mouth. She nibbled on his bottom lip and, using one arm to keep the electric blanket over them, slid her right hand down the porcelain smoothness of his chest and stomach. Her fingers curled back inside the elastic of his bikini briefs (the very brand that Baltimore Orioles pitcher Jim Palmer, a hunk if Stevie had ever seen one, modeled in full-color one-page advertisements in a variety of national magazines), and her tongue flicked out to lay a trail of saliva from Teddy's chin to the base of his throat. Eventually her fingers achieved purchase, closing on a masculine knot that burned her palm by exerting an acute reflexive pressure of its own.

Consciously, by having sex with her son Stevie is reassuring him that he is masculine enough so that he can stop worrying about that and just continue growing up. In addition, though, as she calls her son by his father's name, she is after something else for herself: "'I'm not your mother. You're my lover. You're my beautiful, passionate, ever-faithful demon lover. We've waited nearly two years for this reunion. Finally it's here, Ted. Finally it's here.' ... A little death, the English metaphysical poets had called the moment of orgasm. Well, that was what she and Ted, with Teddy as the bodily agent of their reunion, had achieved."

At first glance, this scene seems uncomfortably, unequivocally true. But not quite. As Stevie drifts off to sleep, she congratulates herself on having overcome "middle-class values," but when she is awakened by the sound of the Exceleriter typing away she realizes that their lovemaking was "a fit of inexplicable self-indulgence and depravity." She is relieved to find herself alone in bed and convinces herself that her memory of what happened in the darkness was just a nightmare—until Teddy thanks her for what she did during the night. She won't admit to him or even to herself that the sex really did happen. What readers believed they witnessed is almost literally unthinkable for Stevie, and Bishop works very hard to both build *and* also deflate readers' belief—both our identification with Stevie and our acceptance that she would do what the novel shows her doing. Or imagining that she is doing.... We can't be any surer than Stevie of how seriously scenes like this should be taken. Notice, In the paragraph above, how the erotic tension is broken by the interruption of a parenthetical comment that pulls readers away from touching the physical body of this one, particular partner to imagining multiple, mass-produced images of a sports celebrity. Whatever is on Stevie's mind at this moment, it is unlikely to be the brand of underwear her fingers are invading.

On the one hand, Bishop does everything he can to make the action convincing and increase reader involvement; on the other, he undercuts the apparent realism and sabotages that involvement. This is related to how *Stevie* mixes humor and horror. Both humor and horror depend on surprise, the discovery that an expected event or a presumed situation are *not* what naturally was supposed. The chief difference is that in humor no one who matters is seriously injured; prejudices and paraphernalia may be ruined, but the action concludes with a feeling of gain, not loss. In horror, on the other hand, the people readers are supposed to care about may lose everything, including the system of belief that lets them go on living from day to day.

Stevie, like *Stevie*, winds up having it both ways. She has been trying to assemble a collection of her wry, upbeat newspaper columns for an Atlanta publisher, and she receives—or imagines that she does—a phone call offering her a contract but suggesting that she should try her hand at fiction. What she produces, in a sustained burst of inspiration, is a modernized, personalized version of "Beauty and the Beast," that Bishop published as a separate story (*Heroic Visions*, 1983). For Stevie, this reveals her own changing attitudes toward the forces disrupting her original position. One of Seaton Benecke's more disturbing aspects has been the ubiquitous presence of his pet monkey Certs, a Capuchin whose face resembles a skull; Stevie sees—or imagines—that Certs is scampering everywhere around her, and she both fears and loathes it. In her story "The Monkey's Bride," however, the strong-willed heroine Cathinka is forced to marry "Don Ignacio," a repulsive monkey-man. Isolated in her husband's remote estate, Cathinka avoids physical intimacy until he offers to grant her three wishes. Her first wish is that he fall asleep for ten years; her second is that her beloved Waldemar be delivered to the estate; she holds the third in reserve. With Don Ignacio comatose but ailing, Cathinka discovers that Waldemar is so shallow and selfish that she must send him away. She begins spending time naked and notices that fur is growing on her body. And so she holds her husband's hand and makes the final wish.... This conclusion is obviously closer to *Shrek* than *Beauty and the Beast* (at least the Disney version). It echoes Seaton's preference for deepness, "when you exaggerate things to make them deeper, when you confess your feelings." It is a real question whether the threatening, disturbing interruptions in Stevie's normal life have been imposed on her from outside—or whether they have seeped out of her own deep fears and desires. By writing this story, she is tacitly admitting as much.

Seaton still is too much of a yucky creep to easily be incorporated into a happy ending for the novel. He needs an explanation and a makeover, so he first reveals his motivation for tormenting Stevie, the fact that as a vulnerable teenager he stumbled on his mother and Ted Crye having sex. This inspires Stevie to exorcise the negative presences from her life by drenching both the Exceleriter and Ted's tombstone with a can of red paint. Shortly thereafter, Seaton sends Stevie a repentant letter:

> After you chased me off last night.... I began to see what a drain on my energy bugging you day in and day out was getting to be. It's hard work being a container for cosmic evil, harder than repairing typewriters.... That's why, later this week, I'm leaving for Arizona to enroll in the Mormon Lake Nondenominational Halfway House for Satan's Scions (they sent me a brochure back in '79), where I hope to shake my addiction and start a writing career.

If this didn't sound ridiculous enough, the parenthetical interruption again makes the message difficult to take seriously—except that Seaton is as good as his word—in the procession of words that make up the novel. His final gift to Stevie is six typewriters that she installs in her attic along with six Capuchin monkeys, supervised by Certs, whom she sets to typing at random. When she checks on them later, one is already working on a contemporary horror novel, and Stevie is happy to think that she herself may be able to avoid touching a typewriter ever again.

Forced and unbelievable as this conclusion is, the novel insists that it is more than satisfactory. It *must* be. The monkeys will be happy as long as Stevie feeds them. Stevie herself will not have to exert herself as a writer; she has had more than enough of going deep, admitting her fears and desires. And so, "she went downstairs into the many, many happy days remaining to her in this life, all of which were of her own composition...."

At least that's what the last paragraph says.

Bishop's next novel was *Ancient of Days* in 1985. Only two years earlier, *No Enemy but Time* had won the Nebula Award for its depiction of an alienated man who finds identity by travelling back in time to live with a tribe of ancient habilines. Bishop's new novel seemed to play a variation on this theme by depicting a present-day habiline's efforts to discover his identity, and its first section ("Her Habiline Husband," 1983) was nominated for a Nebula Award for best novella. However, though reviews were positive, *Ancient of Days* won no awards. The novel's long-term reputation also has been lackluster. According to the third edition of *Anatomy of Wonder*, *Ancient of Days* is merely a "more lighthearted" continuation of *No Enemy*'s themes, and *The Encyclopedia of Science Fiction* dismisses it as "less successful [than the other novel] and overextended." In part, this somewhat disappointing critical response to *Ancient of Days* may be due to Bishop's decision not to present the story of Adam, the habiline, directly but to have it narrated by a character who is not present during crucial events and—even more damagingly—is not only unreliable but also an unpleasant jerk. But these choices finally

## 4. Family Reunions

prove to be effective, so that *Ancient of Days* turns out to be one of Bishop's most satisfactorily developed novels.

Readers who are curious about how Adam develops will be frustrated by how narrator Paul Lloyd is not present when Adam and RuthClaire (Paul's ex-wife) are courting, when Adam confronts the man who has killed his and RuthClaire's son, and when Tonton Macoutes (Haitian secret police) raid the last band of habilines. As one character comments, Paul has only "peripheral importance to the whole affair"; a less sympathetic person even taunts him: "'You're hardly even a walk-on in this—hardly even a walk-on.'" More seriously, Paul is an uncomfortable person for readers to be with. As RuthClaire comments early in the action, "'In comparison to you, Paul, Adam's all courtliness and chivalry and consideration.... Why are you being such a jackass?'" Despite this, Paul's presence as the novel's narrator makes him unavoidable. As Bishop directs readers' attention away from the story they thought they were interested in, it becomes clear that, like it or not, *Ancient of Days* is about whether *Paul* rather than Adam deserves to be called "human."

Although Robert A. Heinlein identified "the man who learned better" as an essential sf plot, deeply flawed sf characters tend to be either doomed or easily redeemable. If the former, as in Bishop's own *Stolen Faces* or "The White Otters of Childhood," readers can watch them disintegrate. If the latter, we wait impatiently for their transformation; they may grate on our nerves a bit, but they're obviously just unaware of their true nature, carefully set up to confront a crisis that will let their glorious true selves burst out. By contrast, in *Ancient of Days*, Paul is self-aware, securely established, and well-fortified. Trapped in his presence for page after page, a reader can't imagine him falling apart, but also can't imagine—any more than Paul himself can—how *he* could evolve.

Paul's problems appear in the novel's first sentence, which introduces RuthClaire as "my ex-wife." Throughout the novel but obsessively in the first section, Paul is concerned with his relationship—past, present, and imagined—with RuthClaire. He is angry that she has left him, and he yearns for her to acknowledge her error and return. Actually compounding this problem is the way Paul uses his superior intelligence to hold it away from him; he uses wit and wordplay to keep from feeling too much, as in alliterative references to Adam as RuthClaire's "'ballsy bantam in blackface'" or "'prehistoric paramour.'" At the same time, compounding his snooty attitude, Paul knows that he is being foolishly disagreeable. As narrator, he records the negative comments that RuthClaire and others make about him, adds some of his own, and reports enough details to let readers draw even more negative conclusions. His unstated complaint throughout the novel's opening section is that he wouldn't be so offensive if only RuthClaire would take him back, but he actually shows and even knows better.

As an example of Paul at his best and worst, consider a telephone conversation between him and RuthClaire after Adam has settled into RuthClaire's house and they have visited Paul's restaurant, The West Bank, during which meal the imperfectly socialized Adam disgraced himself by vomiting all over the table. During their phone conversation, for the first time, Paul directly asks RuthClaire whether Adam is sleeping with her, but she evades him with a verbal maneuver of her own: "'In this kind of weather, Paul, he won't stay in a bed. He's sleeping on the linoleum in the kitchen where it's cool.'" Paul reacts with a sneer, "'You've finally got your own intramural United Nations relief agency, don't you? With a single live-in recipient.'" This is too raw for RuthClaire, who threatens to break off the conversation, so Paul

> apologized—quickly and effusively—for my sarcasm. It was, I admitted, rude and inexcusable. It would devastate me if she cut me off. My tone was mock-pathetic rather than sappily beseeching, and she let me get away with it. How many times had we bantered in this way in the past? So long as I did not overstep a certain hazily drawn line, she welcomed the familiar repartee. It was, I knew, my one clear leg up on the uninitiated, inarticulate Adam.
> "How's he doing?" I asked, mostly because it would please her.

A few moments later, though, as RuthClaire brags about Adam's progress, Paul interrupts, "'Bring him to the West Bank again,' I said impulsively." Paul doesn't say whether his impulse is intended to humiliate Adam further or to give him a chance to show his development. However, he at least sounds sincere when he explains why he won't come out to their former home: "'I just don't belong out there anymore, RuthClaire. It isn't mine, and it hurts to walk around the place. It's yours, yours and Adam's.'" Then he concludes the conversation by exclaiming, "'I've missed you, Ruthie Cee. God Almighty, how I've missed you.'" During these few minutes, Paul has been insincere, greedy, and insulting. He also has been calmly reasonable and has expressed an apparently honest interest in the welfare of the same people he has just insulted and verbally tried to manipulate.

Instead of being able to follow Adam's more-or-less steady progress, readers are distracted by Paul's erratic darting from sleazy to noble and back again. Still, if we would rather watch Adam embodying our higher aspirations, we are uneasily aware that our actual performance usually is closer to Paul's. Another Paul, in the Biblical "Letter to the Romans," describes how he is torn by conflicting drives: "I do not understand my own actions. For I do not do what I want, but I do the very thing I hate.... For I know that nothing good dwells within me, that is in my flesh. I can will what is right, but I cannot do it" (NRSV; 7: 15, 18). Bishop's Paul shows much the same realization at the end of the novel's first section when he exclaims, parodying Kipling, "'You're a better man than I am, Adam M,'" then adds a rueful comment to the reader, "For a time, anyway, I actually meant it. It is not always possible, I'm afraid, to be as good as you should be." In fact, he fits Ian Watson's description of Bishop's early short fiction as centered on "alienation—from one's fellows, one's feelings, one's world, one's body—and of the struggle to redeem those lives, a struggle often tragic, sometimes foolhardy or grotesque, occasionally a bittersweet success."

To get a better perspective on Paul's tangle of confused and contradictory impulses, yearnings, and defenses, let's consider some of the surrounding characters who echo his needs—whether or not those needs are healthy.

One of Paul's less healthy needs is to maintain his privileged position by attacking intruders. The teenage Klansmen E.L. Teavers and Craig Puddicombe crudely express this attitude when they try to make Paul their ally by appealing to the notion that his "'rights are being violated.'" Paul is just mature enough to reject this appeal; even when they repeatedly refer to RuthClaire as his wife, his recurring fantasy, Paul corrects them with "'ex-wife.'" But even though he mocks them, they make him uneasy. They are simultaneously absurd and dangerous. E.L. and Craig lead the Klan attempt to murder Adam, and the even more violently resentful Craig later kidnaps and murders T. P., Adam and RuthClaire's infant son. Nevertheless, Paul can't feel simple hatred for them, because he understands how such people are "fighting to make sense of events and attitudes that they haven't all that well by themselves," a description that could apply to Paul himself. Much of Paul's behavior early in the novel shows the same type of juvenile spite, and even in the novel's last section, remarried and successful, he still can lapse into a mood that resembles that of the juvenile Klansmen:

> Self-doubt. Paranoia. An absence of charity. I was the possessor of all these negative attributes.... I was a teenager again, a teenager not terribly shy of his fiftieth birthday, and the fact that I was living a kind of oblique Lose Race fiction right out of Bulwer-Lytton and H. Rider Haggard merely heightened my adolescent self-doubt.

Even if he can control his urgent need to physically attack an imagined threat, Paul also feels a selfish need to exploit his surroundings. Representing that aspect of his consciousness is anthropologist Brian Nollinger, whom Paul approaches early in the novel to pry Adam away from Ruth Claire. Paul imagines that this will clear his path back to her. Nollinger's prize would be possession of a habiline specimen to study and write about; as A.P. Blair (making a cameo appearance from *No Enemy but Time*) has demonstrated, skillful exploitation of the media can lead to academic status. As with the racist teenagers, Paul is able to reject this attitude when he sees it in action. Nollinger is such a selfish and insensitive exploiter that Paul finds himself siding with RuthClaire when Nollinger sneers at her with the same kind of alliterative insult, "'her habiline houseboy,'" that he himself had used earlier. Still, when Nollinger doggedly continues pursuing Adam for fame and glory, Paul is uneasily aware of his link to the man, for "it was no comfort remembering that but for my own jealous meddling Nollinger might not have come into any of our lives. In a sense, I had created him." Appropriately, it finally is up to Paul to keep Nollinger from revealing the existence of other surviving habilines. He does so by threatening to kill him if he talks. And it works, because the two really do think alike, so that Nollinger believes that the threat is real.

Hearing his own words and seeing his own attitudes in action, Paul is repulsed and impelled to try something else. Self-disgust, however, can't guide him out of his tangle of mixed motives. What he needs—to get beyond expressing resentment and exploiting situations for his own profit—is represented by Adam. Considering that Adam also represents the end of Paul's comforting fantasy of reclaiming RuthClaire and that seeing him as a person means that he can't easily be exploited, it is surprising that Paul accepts him as rapidly as he does. This does suggest that there may be more to Paul than the unhealthy traits noted above. His resentment and greed are complicated and sometime defeated by clear vision and generous impulses. But even when Paul realizes that the way he is living is unsatisfactory and self-defeating, he can't seem to change it. He needs a chance to witness someone else transforming himself for the better. Adam fills that role, as he struggles to grow in understanding and transcend his earlier limitations. That is why, at the end of the novel's first section, Paul can acknowledge that Adam is "'a better man'" than he is and why he later can reflect, after receiving one of Adam's naively open letters, "What wouldn't a reporter give to lay hands on this extraordinary document? I thought briefly of letting different outfits bid for it, but once I had rejected this course of action as vile beyond even *my* notorious reverence for the profit motive, I never looked back. Adam was no longer my rival, he was my friend."

This is not to say that it is easy for Paul to recognize his kinship with Adam or simple for him to act on that recognition. For that matter, Adam's progress is not without lapses. Although he tries to develop a higher moral sense, when he tries to express it by burying Craig Puddicombe next to T. P., the joint funeral turns into a wild mixture of tragedy and farce, climaxed by Adam's leaping onto an intruding TV newscaster. When Paul realizes that the assault is intended merely to terrify the man, he intervenes, but Adam responds: "'I am not a goddamn saint,' Adam growled defiantly. 'I am only human.' ... This admission rang in my ears with the unmistakable tenor of bitterness and regret. I am only human. An odd feeing came over me. It pained him that he was one of us."

Like Paul's explosion of paranoid resentment in the novel's last section, Adam's outburst shows that humans can't convincingly deny the unpleasant foundations of their glittering consciousness. We can't say, "Oh, I was never like *that*." We can't even get away with "Maybe I *used* to be like that, but I'm not anymore." What Paul and Adam discover and demonstrate for readers is more like "Yes, that's a part of me, though I know/hope to show that there's more to me now." Paul says much the same thing when he tries to explain to his new wife Caroline how in his delirious ravings he could have revealed that he still imagines himself and RuthClaire as mates:

> "A man's not responsible for *all* the crap in his subconscious, Caroline. I loved RuthClaire for a long time. We lived with each other for ten years. I was still in love with her when we divorced. I'll never utterly eradicate those feelings. I really don't think you'd want me to either. So long as you realize that here and now, it's all you, Caroline, every bit of it."

In *Ancient of Days*, evolution is not so much a physical process as an accretion of layers of consciousness, different levels of understanding that are higher because they overlay other layers. Maturity doesn't mean rejecting earlier parts of consciousness but somehow assimilating them; the most fully "human" human beings are those who have successfully integrated the levels of their nature. And encouraging that evolutionary process is the motive force behind all generous or destructive impulses, the Ancient of Days Itself (Daniel 7: 9ff). It is appropriate, then, that when Paul eventually stumbles and/or is driven into the presence of God Almighty he sees first the hyena-headed creature that tore open its breast to feed prehistoric habilines, then watches as the Deity removes that mask to reveal Craig Puddicombe's mutilated face.

Thinking of himself as a skeptical pagan and clinging to his immediate and limited sense of self, Paul tries to refuse what he hears from God, even though what God says matches readers' observations of Paul's fumbling attempts to become something more than he is now:

> Your species' hunger for the sacred, going back even to Pleistocene times, doesn't arise in the absence of satisfying spiritual meat, but in response to its availability in the miraculous slaughterhouse of creation. I AM that meat. I AM the architect of the sacred abbatoir. Those who refuse to ignore their hunger will eventually find me.

After all, God reminds Paul that as a restaurant owner he must have observed mortals' hunger; can't he see that as a metaphor for their recognition of incompleteness as human beings? Is it impossible to see that a hyena-headed creature literally offering its heart to protohumans is echoed in Christ's instituting Holy Communion at the Last Supper—or in the distress of a Georgia businessman who wants desperately to stay the same small person he is even while he also struggles to grow?

Paul would rather evade these questions. He would prefer to consider this God merely a hallucination, the product of fatigue and drugs. However, God's remarks contain too many surprises for a reader to accept this interpretation; if those thoughts are coming from Paul's subconscious, he must have been pondering his most basic needs far more than his skeptical consciousness would like. Moreover, what Paul sees early in his vision echoes one of Adam's paintings that is mentioned earlier in the book but not identified as a "sacred disclosure event." So it does appear that Bishop intends readers to take this particular close encounter with a Deity as objectively real for Paul, Adam, and the rest of humanity.

If this exuberant, bloodstained God is hard for Paul to accept, living up to His message is even harder. If God is telling the truth, all human suffering matters because our struggles "resonate forever in the all-encompassing Mind of God." If follows that we readers should care about each other too, and the novel shows how difficult that can be for someone like Paul—or the rest of us.

But the novel also shows that it is possible. Paul may dismiss Adam as a "nigger kid" at first glance, but at the same time he recognizes his Afro-American cook Livia George as a full-fledged person, to whom he later can turn over The West Bank. Evidently, the need to enlarge ourselves by empathy can occasionally overcome our mistaken belief that we'll be safe if we remain isolated.

Such equivocal victories may be as much as humans can expect. In the world of *Ancient of Days*, only temporary solutions are possible, as the process of yearning and growing continues. Thus, at the novel's end, the threatening Tonton Macoutes are bribed or intimidated "[f]or the time being at least." Nothing is or can be settled finally. It's a bit like RuthClaire's progress as an artist. At the novel's beginning, she is at work on a series of ceramic plates depicting the Heavenly Host; later, with Adam as inspiration, she does a popular series on the family of man; still later, she turns out a much less accessible group of works called "Souls" that offend Paul by their dull murkiness—until he sees them briefly in exactly the right light to reveal their beauty; at the very end of the book, though, she uses those pictures to fuel a bonfire on the beach for the enjoyment of people she cares about. As Paul describes the scene, "They burned very well. In fact, in the fire they had the kind of stunning luminous beauty that they had had for me only on one previous occasion." The fact that RuthClaire is drunk when she destroys her latest work does not mean she is wrong in her judgment. As she says,

> What I mean is, the pastels were to show the insubstantiality, the immaterialness, of souls—but souls are living bodies, and so my stupid concept is all wrong. My stupid paintings never lived except when the light hit 'em just right, and they looked better burning than they ever did in the morgue of my studio gallery. I had to get rid of 'em, I have to start over, thash—*that's*—all there is to it.

In fact, *Ancient of Days*' form itself demonstrates how conclusions clear the way for new beginnings, since the first section was published independently as "Her Habiline Husband," then incorporated into this book with two more alliteratively titled parts.

As usual, readers may finish this novel with the feeling that the conclusion has been left extremely loose. Bishop would argue, as he did in a 1993 phone interview with students, that he didn't *want* to claim to know everything about what his characters could or should do. In this novel, however, he is uncommonly successful in showing how such looseness is a necessary outcome of the action, as Paul ends up by trying "like crazy to believe" that T. P.'s scattered ashes—and the very existence of any humans—continues to matter "in the consciousness of God." With this ramshackle confidence, based on painful experience, Paul can appreciate that an ending is not the place where anything stops but simply a sign that now it's time to start over.

Bishop continued to play with the same subject, our quest for an authentic purpose, but from a different angel (not *entirely* my typographical error) in his next novel. *Philip K. Dick Is Dead, Alas* (1978) demonstrates how a story can be disconcertingly wacky—as when one main character receives vital information and advice from a spirit-possessed boa constrictor—and deeply felt—as when the same man agonizingly remembers a patriotic celebration in Denver where he saw his parents being stoned to death as traitors.

The novel first of all is a loving pastiche of Philip K. Dick's sf, not just in superficial mannerisms but in its fundamental viewpoint: When he looked at the world around him, Dick asked, "How can this be all there is?" and answered, "No, there must be something more—more satisfying, more *real*—hidden under the tawdry and superficial existence that most people accept." His writing tried obsessively to share that dissatisfaction with readers so that they too would scratch at the scab-like crust of ordinary life.

The opening of Bishop's novel effectively pulls readers away from ordinary life. First, it is an "alien pink Moon" that peers into Philip K. Dick's Santa Anna flat; then, the date is given as 1982 but with the parenthetical note that this is "not the 1982 of most history books." The writer has just suffered a stroke. But his essence—soul, spirit, whatever—looks down at the dying body, gets dressed, comments morosely on his futile career, and sits down at the typewriter anyway. This sometimes-tangible ghost is furiously typing "on erasable parchment, invisible bond" while Dick's corpse is buried and while he, the mysteriously-surviving consciousness, is whisked to a distant star system "to meet the Entity sustaining this entire irreal Cosmos." The other being is capitalized as "Entity" or "God," while Dick himself is labeled merely "the ghost at the machine" (in this case, an electric typewriter), but not *deus ex machina*, the god *in* the machine. Readers don't get to eavesdrop on the "chat" between the ghost and the Deity, but immediately thereafter Dick's ghost is brainlaundered and sent back to Earth, no longer bearing the burden of his frustrations but with an impulse to travel—

—to Georgia, where unwillingly transplanted Colorado Cowhand Cal Pickford is cleaning out urine-saturated litter in a pet ship, deeply aware of how tawdry and superficial life in America has become. Family obligations forced Cal's psychotherapist wife Dr. Lia Bonner back home to Pine Mountain (Bishop's home in *our* reality), but even if she were willing to leave, the Travel Restrictions Act would keep them from moving away. The story is set during Richard Nixon's fourth consecutive term as President. Since he masterminded America's brutal bombing strategy that won the Vietnam War, Nixon has become increasingly withdrawn and dictatorial, and the U.S. government is cancelling the Constitution bit by bit. Moreover, Cal and Lia find themselves trapped by Grace Rinehart—rabid patriot, former Hollywood star, and current wife of Nixon's Secretary of Agriculture—who likes compelling Lia to accompany her as a paid confidant and who also enjoys forcing Cal to follow distasteful orders.

Apparently, it seems all too natural for people like Grace to demand that others share their perception of reality, in effect creating a personal false cosmos where they can relax. On a much larger scale, Nixon's America uses the threat of force to create the irreality of a contented, prosperous and above all *united* state. And Cal and Lia know better than to protest very strenuously, for the U.S. government knows how to enforce its false reality. People who complained loudly (such as Jane Fonda, Bob Dylan, and Cal's parents) have simply—disappeared. Like 30,000 opponents of the Argentine junta during the "Dirty War" (1978–83), they have vanished. No one knows where the missing Americans are, and no one in authority admits having anything to do with

## 4. Family Reunions 117

whatever might have happened. The probable fate of the people who were disappeared is left to bystanders' uneasy imagination, until Cal's buried memory surfaces of watching his parents' being murdered by a mob. In Argentina relatives of the disappeared formed a protest movement that marched in the streets and painted body outlines on the pavement of Buenos Aires to remind onlookers that the missing people once existed, but Nixon's America is effective in keeping citizens from working together. All Cal and Lia can do is keep their heads down and trudge ahead, resentful but too frightened to act. The last thing they want to do is attract the government's attention.

Cal manages to keep a faint hope and a smoldering anger alive by dipping into his collection of clandestinely copied manuscripts by Philip K. Dick, who in this novel's cosmos was once a respected writer of mainstream fiction but who became a pariah when he started writing loony, anti-establishment sf. Cal admires Dick's independent viewpoint, especially in one gonzo novel that imagines the impeachment of an insanely dictatorial U.S. President. Discovering Dick's obituary in one of the urine-soaked newspapers he's scraping out of a pet cage disturbs Cal's stoicism, and starting to read another of Dick's novels triggers the memory of his parents' murder and encourages him to refuse Grace's attempt at seduction, a betrayal that would have fastened him even more firmly in *her* reality.

The force that prods Cal, Lia, and a motley crowd of other malcontents into positive action is the manifestation of Philip K. Dick's transcendent persona. Readers may suspect that Dick—whether wearing the appearance of the deceased writer, speaking through the mouth of a boa constrictor, or possessing (like one of the voodoo loas in *Ancient of Days*) the body of an African-American dwarf stable hand—is an angel or at least a messenger from the divine. Dick himself resists such comfortable categorization. He never gives a name to the Entity he represents; in this novel, "My God!" expresses anguish rather than worship. Appearing in the guise of the black stable hand to anti–Nixon members of the staff of Von Branunville, America's Moonbase, he rejects their calling him Elijah, Christ, or Thomas Merton: "'All Merton and I have in common is our unshakable faith that the Transcendent exists and that It will talk to you if ever It decides you're worth the effort. And that's about it. That and a quest to understand whatever the fuck the Transcendent is handing us when It finally deigns to speak.'"

What Dick offers his audience in this scene, speaking to Cal through the pet shop's boa constrictor, is a chance to "engineer [a] redemptive shift" into a (possibly) better reality. When Cal exasperatedly asks how that can be accomplished, Dick-in-the-snake replies,

"By taking risks," the snake said, bumping the glass. "Don't let yourself get too cozy."

"Cozy?"

"Opportunities will soon appear. Your first response to most of these will probably be distaste. A reluctance to follow through. It's easier to stay in a rut—to get out of bed at the same hour, eat the same old cereal, and totter off to work just like you've been doing for the past ten years."

"I've only been working here since Christmas."

"Coziness sets in—that's all I mean. And it's the archenemy of evolution, of healthy change. Look for chances to defy it. From whatever unlikely quarter they may come."

"All right. I will."

"Prove it."

Cal gets his chance when he is selected to accompany Nixon on a trip to the Moon. It is revealed that the President intends to launch nuclear war against his enemies on Earth, which probably will wipe out humanity. The men Dick has brought together attempt to perform an exorcism to drive out the demon that they believe is controlling Nixon; however, they discover that this is impossible because, instead of fighting against demonic possession Nixon welcomed Satan when he realized that the intruding Entity perfectly embodied his own paranoid impulses. At the very end of the story, Cal clings to the foot of an inflated, defiant Nixon pressed against the roof of a sub-Lunar cavern. He stabs upward at the demonically-possessed President. And all the novel's characters and settings disappear while this particular irreal Cosmos evaporates as the redemptive shift occurs.

*Philip K. Dick Is Dead, Alas* contains a Coda set in the redeemed Cosmos, in which readers may recognize characters from the main story as they might have developed in a different environment. For the most part, they are better off than they were in the main story. At first, it appears that the action has circled back to the novel's beginning, for the Moon has changed color. But this Moon no longer belongs to Earth; it has been occupied/transformed by aliens, the Choir, who have placated humanity by sharing bits of advanced technology that have made human life much easier. We don't need to struggle to explore space. In fact, we don't need to exert ourselves very much mentally or spiritually. That's over. The Choir also is offering select humans a ride back to their star system (a different one than referred to in the novel's opening) "to meet God." Not everyone is comfortable with this happy-happy resolution. Dolf, the Coda's version of Cal, resents the Choir's "meddling"; he thinks it would have been better for humans to do their own exploring.

He's not the only one not quite satisfied with the novel's cozy conclusion. The last paragraph describes "an insurgent" sitting in a Trappist monastery in Georgia: "God or the demiurge put a hand on his

## 4. Family Reunions

shoulder, giving him to know that this oddball reality was still not the one he wanted to live in.... And so Philip Kyle Dick put pen to paper to alter, painstakingly, the basic lineaments of the universe." In fact—whatever *that* means—Phil Dick's middle name was Kindred in our universe, signaling again that this story has been set in a Cosmos that merely echoes our own. In any case, readers may see Dick's persistence as futile, hopeless. Or brave. Or hopelessly brave. Bishop is careful to leave the outcome ambiguous. To remind readers that not all opposition to authority is fruitful, the novel shows Grace intimidating hyper-Americanism-indoctrinated Vietnamese Le Boi Loan into stealing Cal's stash of forbidden Dick novels. Although Le identifies with Daredevil, a masked comic book superhero, his attempt to punish Grace for her cruelty (by leaving the story's ubiquitous boa constrictor in the private screening room where she will be watching the image of her younger self perform) results merely in her death, then his own. So some solitary protests may not make much difference. Still, Dick's efforts within this novel *do* make a significant difference: The inflated Nixon is punctured, the demon expelled, and an extremely anti-human Cosmos erased. If this new Cosmos is unsatisfying, well, if Dick keeps trying perhaps he can help produce a better one next time....

The novel insists that writing and reading imaginative literature can make a difference. The more disconcerting the better, in fact. Just before the confrontation with Nixon/Satan, one of the anti–Nixon conspirators realizes that "none of this adds up to diddlysquat"; moments later, another thinks to himself that their plan "could only work in a storybook." For, of course, Bishop's novel *is* a storybook. Like all unconventional thinkers, echoing Glen Runsiter in Dick's own novel *UBIK*, Bishop might say that "we … are in a line of business that surpasses all rational understanding." The depiction of Richard Nixon in *Philip K. Dick Is Dead, Alas* certainly is exaggerated, but unfortunately it does reflect the truth that many people do live in false, selfish "realities" that they have constructed to avoid meaningful human contact. When he is asked why he has possessed the man's body, Satan replies that it's a way for one "'to kill many,'" and when asked why he wants to do that the President/Devil replies, "'Because I loathe the many who hate me.'" It's not simply "hate" that disturbs the malign Entity but the fact that a separate, independent "many" even exists. Much earlier in the novel, in a therapy session with Lia, the amnesiac Dick advocates not Nixon's assassination but neutralization, "'the elimination of a mind-set that won't grant the legitimacy of other mind-sets.'" One of the purposes of fiction is to bring readers into contact—or collision—with other mind-sets. *Philip K. Dick Is Dead, Alas* is Bishop's superficially playful but painfully earnest effort to make readers reexamine how they're living, ask whether they haven't become too cozy, and look for helpful ways to take risks. And, please God, to keep looking.

*Unicorn Mountain* (1988) continues juggling diverse characters and the differing realities they believe in. As two characters drive toward what should be a safe haven in Colorado, one of them, even remarks that he "'can't help feeling that we've both just entered an alternative reality. You know, a Phil Dickean world a couple of nudges past the twentieth century we've all come to know and love.'" Unlike *PKDID,A*, however, Bishop's new novel shows different planes coexisting, so that it's possible for unicorns to move back and forth between their native reality and ours. But *Unicorn*'s main focus is on how individuals' self-centered "realities" keep them from interacting usefully. Like Grace Rinehart (who appears briefly here as JFK's mistress in an uncanny late-night TV broadcast from a different plane), people tend to assumethat everyone else should/*must* see experience the same way they do. And so they create personal planes, mental and emotional fortresses for themselves that can be both defensive retreats and bases for offensive action against other people.

Most people in *Unicorn* do manage to share a view of experience that lets them coexist while exploiting their surroundings. Sexuality is one aspect of common-sense reality about which most of the novel's characters seem, at least initially, to agree. Most Americans accept that there naturally are two different but complementary genders. Therefore, it is natural for the stronger males to be practical and active and for the weaker females to be decorative and passive. Men act; women watch. Different viewpoints about sexual identity can barely be recognized let alone tolerated; they are unnatural, undependable, and disturbing: queer. Society runs on that basis. For example, a quarrel between two Chicano boys escalates into a real fight as one of them hurls the ultimate insult, "'You lying cocksucker.'" According to the shared viewpoint, adjective and noun belong together in this epithet, since anyone who doesn't fit one sexual role or the other obviously is untrustworthy or, as oafish Gary Quarles labels his gay, AIDS-stricken cousin Bo Gavin, "an in-between kind of monster."

The novel shows the unreliability of this categorization. Even before Gary approaches his ex-wife Libby in a small Colorado town and blurts out the news about Bo, the characters have been introduced as the reverse of he-man male and cute female stereotypes. *He* is tarted up like a fashion plate cowboy. She, on the other hand, is dressed like a working rancher, "wearing jeans, a flannel shirt, a navy pea jacket that had once belonged to her father, a floppy-brimmed leather hat, two pairs of socks, long johns, and some well-scuffed boots." As a matter of fact, the reason Gary accosts Libby is to get reassurance about his own masculinity. Since Bo is his cousin, is there any chance that he himself might be subconsciously a homo? Could swishy genes run in the family? Libby jeers at his ignorance and insecurity, but she also picks up on the fact that Bo's family has turned its back on him so that he is dying alone in Atlanta, since at the time *Unicorn* was written AIDS was an inevitably fatal disease. Whereupon, leaving Gary to stew and fret, she heads down to pick up the no-relation AIDS sufferer and bring him home to her Tipsy Q ranch. The woman acts; the man watches.

Besides explicitly showing the foolishness of common-sensibly separating the sexes, the novel implicitly demonstrates that people can share by shifting the narrative viewpoint among many characters, showing that a lot of people can connect empathetically—more than readers might suppose. Bishop wants to demonstrate that private planes can merge. To do that, he needs a *lot* of strongly individualistic characters, owning a lot of personal, isolated planes.

In addition to questioning personal sexual/social roles, *UM* also attacks the common sense distinction between "real" and "fantastic." At the novel's beginning, Libby is tempted to buy a paperback horror novel as an escape from all her worries: "Reading it tonight might blunt the horror of this run-in with Gary—and briefly obliterate the drudgery of winter ranch work—by immersing her in a spooky story with no immediate connection to the farrago of her private life." It's all very well for lovers of the fantastic to argue that the only people who object to "escape" are jailers, but fiction that merely obliterates a reader's personal concerns for a short time is unlikely to be memorable let alone (however unlikely or literally inconceivable) useful in examining the *need* for escape and the *methods* to be employed. Consequently, readers may feel guilty about giving in to once-powerful symbols that have become shopworn while acquiring connotations of utter irresponsibility. Even writers open to intrusions of the fantastic may feel this way. Jane Yollen, for example, initially recoils when elves pop up in a story she is writing; she does not want a novel about real people to be taken over by "little humanoid creatures of an attenuated beauty [who] caper about making white fire and singing in tongues." Unicorns have become so banal that Diana Wynne Jones just makes them part of the stuff customers usually encounter during group tours of Fantasyland: "Their horns … are to be found quite often, and you may use them both for healing and as a magic wand." Consequently, when Bishop read the draft of a chapter of *UM* at a writers' conference, Lewis Shiner responded that "the very mention of unicorns made me gag."

In fact, the unicorns in Bishop's novel are not there to provide care-free diversion. Thinking about them doesn't let Libby escape from her ranching worries; those beautiful but diseased creatures are part of her practical problems. Still, the novel's abundance of purposes may account for reviewers' uneasiness. No everyone was willing to accept what looks at first like an aimlessly sprawling plot, presented in a cacophony of tones. And even though Gwyneth Jones can accept (grudgingly) the unicorns, she concludes that *UM* "is finally only a book in which the magic tries just a little too hard." In fact, surveying Bishop's career, George Kelly complains that "[a]t times, the novel is almost too rich in detail." Moreover, Bishop's characters sometimes speak in a florid style that makes Lew Shiner explode: "Use simple English: real words for real people."

But these reactions miss the point of *Unicorn*'s profusion of tones, images, and ideas. It's necessary for the novel to bulge at the seams, for Bishop is attempting to explore two extremely difficult but somehow related human concepts: reconciliation and redemption.

Let's consider reconciliation first. A lot happens, at irregular rates and in different places, throughout the novel, because characters are colliding sometimes to comic, sometimes to painful effect. Besides Libby Quarles and Gary, other main characters include the following: Bo Gavin, the warily grateful, young gay man whom Libby barely knows but brings back to the Tipsy Q when she hears that he has been disowned by his parents; Sam Coldpony, Libby's middle-aged Ute ranch hand, who shares her concern about the unicorns that are sick and dying in the mountains but who also is nagged by guilt for having abandoned his wife and infant daughter years before; Paisley Coldpony, Sam's teenaged daughter, grieving over the recent suicide of her mother and responding to dreams that summon her to new challenges.

Other significant characters include Bo's desperately straight brother Ned, the vengeful and headless ghost of Sam's wife D'lo, the dyspeptic veterinarian Doc Brinkley, and various cowboys, Indians, and newscasters. Not to mention the unicorns themselves. Etc.

Yet, the very fact that the novel sometimes feels chaotic helps demonstrates Bishop's vision of the complexity, both real and imaginary, of human experience. To read *Unicorn*, one must trust the story—be willing to shift moods abruptly, to relate characters and concerns with confidence that the novel is whatever it needs to be at any moment. Characters themselves are less adept at shifting and accepting. Trust doesn't come easily to them, for they are not especially confident that they'll be able to face whatever comes along. Consequently, they fall back on simplistic patterns by which to prejudge new experiences. Readers soon notice not only how the novel's characters must endure confusing experiences but how often they busily make their lives more confusing by trying to force complexities into simplistic patterns.

*Unicorn* shows the consequences of seeing life in sets of opposing absolutes. The simplistic notion of sexual roles was discussed above, and the novel implies that if the squabbling boys grow up to be Real Men like Gary Quarles they'll use women for sex while refusing any deeper commitment. After all, if men and women have little in common, there's not much point in trying to communicate. Throughout, the novel shows the suffering fragments of several broken families to demonstrate how thoroughly human beings have become separated from one another. As often is the case in Bishop's fiction, parents—especially fathers—have withdrawn from their children or even denied them. This always is an admission of failure, no matter if people like Bo's parents call their rejection of him a necessary moral choice because they abominate his homosexuality. The lasting pain caused by such a separation actually proves how much people need to be reunited; at the same time, their fear of questioning personal absolutes makes it almost impossible for them to think of reunion.

One way the novel shows this conflict is in Bo's flamboyant, angry rhetoric. In a recent e-mail, Bishop speaks of looking forward to revising *Unicorn* and in particular to toning down Bo's verbosity. Although this would make novel smoother to read (and might satisfy Lewis Shiner's demand to "use simple English"), Bo's ornate speech is useful in revealing his pain through the cynical wit he wields like a whip. Comedy, like tragedy, is based on recognition of the gap between the ideal and the actual, between what we expect and what actually happens. We must be aware of both extremes simultaneously before we can react. When we can laugh because neither we ourselves nor someone we care positively about is injured, that's comedy. When we're hurt too much too laugh, that's tragedy. But when we're trying to deny how much we're suffering, bitter "humor" lets us hit back at those we hold responsible for our injury. Thus Bo, who has been hurt too deeply to laugh, delivers many of his remarks early in *Unicorn* with a languid sneer. Bo calls his attitude "honest cynicism" and believes that it demonstrates his refusal to be taken in by false appearances. It actually seems to be a defensive/aggressive response to the way he has been excluded by his family and the rest of "normal" society. His response to forcible isolation is to attack anything handy, especially anyone who has the nerve to approach him now in his pain. If some people have excluded *him*, he'll exclude everyone else right back.

Actually, Bo is unable initially to get past stereotypes of his own. The way he sees everything in terms of smart gay vs. dumb homophobe resembles how Gary contrasts normal vs. queer. At the beginning of *UM*, Bo too sees experience in terms of opposed absolutes. He is the one who compares contemporary America to a Phil Dick world or to an episode of *The Twilight Zone*. Because most people around him can't appreciate this disjuncture, Bo shows his superior understanding by using unusual language to separate himself from them. In addition to "sarcastic puns," Bo likes to make listeners struggle to understand him, so that Libby observes that "there was something egotistical and self-congratulatory about Bo's phrasing." Speaking of his brother Ned, for example, Bo comments that their parents are "militantly straight, and Ned always has been the apple of their rose-colored optical equipment." Conflating "apple of their eye" and "rose-colored glasses" and then using an elaborate euphemism for "glasses," Bo is saying that his parents can't see correctly and can't put a proper name on the things around them. But he says this in a way that challenges less verbally adept listeners to grasp the thought.

In addition, since he sees himself as apart from modern times since he's suffering from the equivalent of a medieval plague, Bo ostentatiously uses archaic language to show that he has a larger vocabulary than the people around him, that he can see through their shoddy pretense, and that overall he doesn't especially like or trust them. When, for example, he and Libby are caught in a blizzard on the way back to the ranch, a concerned gas station attendant advises them not to drive any farther that night, so Bo sneers, "'Why wouldn't we? ... You got a brother in the hostelry business or something?'" Even Libby is not spared. Beginning with his declaration that the existence of AIDS, "'a Thing of the Past,'" is proof that his world is not "'the twentieth century we've all come to know and love,'" Bo begins to address her as "m'lady," which could indicate respect but which also suggests how helplessly dependent Bo finds himself on Libby's bounty. Furthermore, when he finds Libby's drawings of unicorns but before he realizes that she had sketched them from life, Bo sneers at the whole subject as "unicorn-y nonsense" and mocks her as "Unicorn Libby Quarles," last of the hippies. Though unicorns might seem appropriate parts of a medieval worldview. Bo is especially savage toward anything that invades his disdainful isolation, and believing in unicorns would be too much like hoping for his own survival.

It seems unfair of Bo to sneer at Libby. After all, she impulsively went halfway across the country to bring a sick man she barely knew back to her home just because she didn't like the way that people more closely related to him were behaving and she didn't want him to feel like an outcast when he died. It seems ridiculous for Bo to consider her, as he does, a closet homophobe. Yet, ugly as that is, Bo's distrust is not wholly inaccurate. Libby sometimes thinks in narrow categories too. When one of her cows produces a stillborn, two-headed creature that also is a hermaphrodite, she calls the thing an "'abomination'" and orders Sam to get it buried and out of sight as fast as possible: "'Abominations can't live,' she said. 'The world rejects them. Hermaphrodites can't live. Nature weeds them out.'" Not surprisingly, Bo takes this personally. "'Fuck you, m'lady!' He flicked her on the cheek with his finger. 'You're a bigoted cowgirl puritan!'" To end this outburst, Sam wrestles him away.

Separation—of roles, concerns, and individuals—appears to be a constant part of the human condition. The feelings of anger, guilt, pain, and despair that accompany this alienation all reinforce each other. Sam Coldpony, for example, needs to reapproach his daughter Paisley. However, he realizes that he is to blame for their estrangement because he ran out on her and her mother, so he is frightened that it may be too late to reconcile with her. Despite his yearnings, he is hesitant to look further. Paisley, meanwhile, can't see past her isolation either. She yearns to reconnect with her father, as shown by the fact that she insists on using the name he gave her rather than "Alma," her mother's choice. However, since her mother's suicide, Paisley has had a series of dreams that indicate she must participate in the next Ute Sun Dance. This ceremony if intended to give the participants supernatural understanding and to grant rest to recently deceased tribe members. Actually, in Paisley's dreams two spectators at the dance are non–Utes: one is a near-middle-aged woman who looks like a fading hippy; the other is an extremely gaunt young man. Since, at that moment, she has no knowledge of Libby or Bo, however, Paisley has no idea how they could be important in her growth. At this point in the novel, she sees her responsibility wholly in terms of satisfying the needs of her dead mother's unquiet spirit and of her purpose-seeking tribe.

Bishop's novel repeatedly and convincingly shows how people have become separated from one another. Human relationships are tentative and fumbling, easily broken. And once a relationship has been broken, people fear that the pain of attempting to mend it would be even worse than the status quo. But *Unicorn* also says that this familiar picture may not be inevitable. Our isolation is real, but that may not be all that's real.

Readers can see that, while the novel's characters bicker, they do not represent separate sets of values as they imagine. In fact, as people spend time together and truly begin to pay heed to each other, they discover that each person has many sides; thus they realize that each is a mixture of unclassifiable traits that cannot be judged easily. Bo must admit that Libby's impulse to bring him home was as genuine as her revulsion at sight of the abomination. Just so, Libby must accept that Bo is not only a victim of betrayal but a betrayer himself, when he reveals that while he still seemed healthy he deserted his AIDS-stricken, dying lover Keith. And each also begins to accept the extremes of his or her own complicated nature, as when Libby admits that Bo's accusations of hidden homophobia "weren't just pretty damn crappy, but pretty damn insightful." Thus Libby learns to stretch her imagination through the extremes of human behavior, and thus Bo grudgingly begins to realize he was too hasty in assuming that unicorns were just a fantasy to let Libby escape from reality.

Recognizing and accepting the complexity of other people and of themselves, the characters can begin reevaluating what's possible for them to do. Thus Sam recognizes that "he wanted to be both a bona fide Ute and the person he had become during his long self-exile. He wanted to bring the two types of experience together and begin the process of reclaiming his daughter."

If recognizing and accepting the different facets of oneself may lead toward reconciliation with others, the change also can lead to redemption, rejuvenating parts of experience that must be denied in order to fit life into rigid categories. We need, in other words, to rediscover the power of something as shopworn as a unicorn. Libby, who has seen real unicorns, is appalled to discover "an entire paddock of [the] mythological beasties made of either pewter or glass" in the glitzy boutique where she is nervously shopping for a cheer-up present for Bo before making her offer of sanctuary. She finds the little statuettes both "beautiful" and "phony," impulsively shoplifts several, and leaves them in the grubby men's room of a gas station, with the message "THESE AREN'T UNICORNS—THEY'RE COMMERCIAL STEREOTYPES. REDEEM THEM WITH OUR ATTENDANT FOR A FREE GALLON OF GAS OR A STRONG DOSE OF REALITY." As mere commercial stereotypes, "unicorns" deserve only contempt; they have lost all significance, let alone magic. However, one of those little pewter figurines somehow survives, to be passed hand to hand (along with a foil-wrapped rubber from a vending machine in the gas-station toilet) among the characters—so that each person is free to attribute different significance to it and sometimes may even discover stirrings of magic.

Typically, in *Unicorn* the living unicorns are difficult to categorize. As Libby originally observed, they are "half-fragile, half-indomitable." They are wonderful beings that have strayed into our world from another reality, but they also are mortal animals. They are glamorous, but their glittering eyes are oozing matter while snot bubbles out of their nostrils. Essentially, the unicorns are a catalyst for the growth of characters who look at them with wonder but who also figure out practical steps to keep them alive. Even if a unicorn's horn is traditionally a magical object with healing powers, that doesn't help the unicorn itself. Unicorns must be protected, fed, and tended; they need the attention of foul-mouthed but empathetic Doc Brinkley, not some wizard. Yes, unicorns shimmer in daylight, and the bodies of those who die of their plague dissolve (except for the horn) to prove that they aren't part of this reality; nevertheless, the only way to save them is to treat them like mundane, vulnerable livestock.

And yet, also typically in *UM*, the extreme opposite also is true. Extremes balance each other in startling juxtaposition rather than cancelling each other out. Seeing unicorns for the first time and watching a pair copulate, Bo classifies them as "among the most beautiful animals he had ever seen" and redeems his earlier insult by admitting that "Unicorn Libby Quarles ... was truly Unicorn Libby Quarles." At the same time, Bo is spiritually moved, calling what he has just seen "a miracle" and feeling that "[i]t was as if God had arranged the constellations over Colorado to spell out, in English, the unequivocal declaration, I AM." This reaction is echoed later in the novel, when a self-centered female newscaster who has just seen a stampeding herd of unicorns exclaims that it was "[l]ike being visited by God." But this response does not remain ethereal and "pure." In Bo's case, while he is viewing the unicorns he also is eating "strawberry snow" that will give him diarrhea. Furthermore, Bo's epiphany is likened to the memory of his first sight of an unashamedly naked man that revealed/confirmed his homosexuality: "My feeling ... was one of ... [sic] comfortable awe, I guess. Something was right with the universe, and I sensed it at once. I knew that specific sense of rightness would draw me toward it as long as I lived."

The balance of opposites that *UM* strives toward is shown in Bo's feeling of "comfortable awe," an apparent oxymoron. The novel insists that such verbal contradictions may accurately describe our experience if we can escape narrow categories of thinking long enough to notice. For example, Sam discovers himself "in a mood somewhere between joy and funk." His daughter Paisley feels much the same way after she somehow has traced the sacred path across the god sheet (a Ute sacred relic that supposedly bears Jesus' walking footprints, much as the Shroud of Turin supposedly shows the imprint of His corpse), an ordeal that proved she should take part in the Sun Dance; she judges that her success was "simultaneously a remarkable achievement and a con." When Libby sees Sam riding bareback on an elk, it strikes her as "at once magnificent and comic." This discovery that presumed opposites can share space is comic in the healthiest sense. Rather than cancelling each other by their apparent contradiction, the juxtaposed extremes produce genuine, clean laughter, as Bo concludes that "[i]t was hilarious, the counterpoints life could throw at you."

Earlier, Libby worried that unless Bo could believe her and Sam about the existence of the unicorns or learn to trust "the evidence of his own senses—should he ever acquire any—well, he'll die thinking the universe is just as tawdry and predictable a joke as he's undoubtedly convinced it is right now." What Bo learns, thanks to his rediscovery of the wildly diverse human universe through—and past—his senses, is that life can truly be hilarious but the joke is only partly tawdry and hardly ever predictable. Early in the novel, the fact that Bo has kept a gallery of family photos hints that even though they have "excommunicated" him for his sin he still has hope of "forgiving their holier-than-thou asses." Observing Bo during that period of anger and alienation, though, it is difficult to anticipate that he actually will someday be able to confront his mother with love as well as anger: "Listen, Mama, it's okay. If it ever starts bothering you—consigning me to hell, I mean—just remember I loved you and kept on loving you.... I know more about betrayal than you'll ever know.... If I can forgive myself, which I'm doing or trying to do, well then, by God, I can forgive you too, can't I?" By attempting to reconcile with his mother over the phone—while reconciling the conflicting aspects of himself—Bo also is redeeming the gift of life that he is about to lose. The notion of "healing" that has seemed implicitly waiting for Bo, first in the unicorns' horns and then in the Sun Dance ceremony, turns out to be spiritual rather than physical. His life lasts long enough for him to do as much as he can for his surviving family. He also witnesses Sam and Paisley's reconciliation and Sam and Libby's discovery that they can become lovers. That is a much healing as this novel, this world, permits.

Essentially, as characters see that apparent opposites can be reunited, they can stop relying on words and the limits that words represent. Instead, they act. As Paisley reflects during the Sun Dance, "[s]he knew that to talk too much was considered folly. It cut one off from the trance state triggered by the heat, the drumming, the chanting, the pistoning of legs, the prayerful flailing of arms." This trance leads to power, for it moves the dancer into an intensely physical awareness that leads to a vision of the true, essential unity of all things. This silence is not the negative, dead absence of communication noted above and discussed by W.A. Senior in his essay "Silence and Disaster in the Novels of Michael Bishop"; on the contrary, it serves what Senior calls the "Jungian function" of silence as it does for a character in Bishop's *Brittle Innings* whose "pattern of engagement/disengagement from the world, as he retreats and then reenters it, recalls the figure of the shaman or sage pondering numinous truths." Thus it is fitting that, after reconciling with her father, Paisley accepts the name her mother gave her, Alma, and goes off to accept her role as spiritual-leader-in-training of her tribe.

Some connections between extremes appear random and absurd when we attempt to verbalize them. How can words, for example, explain the monstrous erection Sam gets whenever he confronts D'lo's angry ghost, at moments when he should be terrified rather than tumescent? Perhaps this unreasoning physical response is a sign of instinctive desire for an encounter with mystery, the uncanny, even if it involves mortal danger. Being human, we cannot long escape words and the kinds of understanding they permit. However, even early in the novel, characters recognize the importance of paying attention to nonverbal experience; when Sam is alone on the ranch, waiting for Libby to arrive with their AIDS-infected guest, for example, he lets go of his urgent worries for a moment, as "[b]eyond the barn, a magpie cawed, and Sam Coldpony knew that he was the only person in the entire world who had heard it." Later, the characters learn to share moments beyond the limitation of words:

> Suddenly, Libby felt Sam's arm around her shoulders. With his other hand, he was dabbing her eyes with a handkerchief that he probably had used to blow his nose in, twist the tops off dirty cans of axle grease, and wipe down dusty saddles. Well, so what? All that mattered was that he was beside her, trying, none too successfully, to dry her eyes, and letting the warmth of his body and the warmth of his concern do what they could to make the hurt go away. It was a lot, surprisingly—it was really a lot.

Bo's death, the climax of *UM*, is a characteristic jangle of discordant tones that somehow manage to harmonize. When his brother Ned drives up to Libby's house and sees it surrounded by friends and neighbors, he is deeply offended: "It looked as if the people of Snowy Falls had turned Bo's dying day into a public carnival." On the other hand, several of Bo's parting remarks, including his instructions to Ned to look after their mother—resemble Jesus' last words on the cross, connecting with an image from one of Paisley's dreams earlier in the book: a crucified Bo, asking his father why he has been forsaken. So should Bo's death be viewed as a sickeningly debased tragedy? Or is it a joyous demonstration of the spirit's triumph over death? Bishop refuses to give a simple answer. The important thing, Bo insists, is that he not be shoved aside but instead allowed to leave life surrounded by a disorderly crowd, "in the midst of life," so that others are reminded of the need to *feel* something.

An especially striking image juxtaposed with Bo's death involves "the god sheet," the Ute sacred relic that supposedly bears the footprints of Jesus, the Walking Man. When Bo collapses while watching Paisley at the Sun Dance, she insists that he be wrapped in the sheet, not because of its magical powers but because he physically needs warmth. After all, the sheet is handy, and it's not doing anyone any good while it's safely locked away in a trunk. The effect of jamming sacred and profane together is, typically in this novel, humorous: "Lord, thought Liddy, he looks like a burrito, a burrito grande from the Prairie Schooner Café." The sheet gets dirty on the way back to Libby's ranch, so Libby and Paisley do the practical thing by throwing it into the washing machine and hanging it out to dry, where, in the gusting wind, "the sheet whipped back and forth so that the Walking Man's footprints seemed to be doing a spastic boogaloo in the mountain-ringed dance hall of Remuda Creek Meadow." Just because Jesus is the Christ doesn't mean that He never feels like kicking up His heels—or that mere humans shouldn't be amused and delighted at the sight. As Libby imagines Bo looking out his window, "seeing the Master dance, seeing the dawn-colored footprints of the Walking Man jitterbug the mountain air ... well, could any leavetaking be better?"

Not that "leavetaking" is synonymous with "escape." Not in this novel. After his death, Bo is surprised to discover that he has new responsibilities. Led by a restored D'lo and mounted on the back of the abomination, which was created for this purpose, his resurrection body must cross from this reality to the unicorns' home to inform the immortal dead residents there how to do their part in saving the animals. He also finds a chance to reconcile with his dead lover Keith.

So, at the end of *UM*, at least some broken relationships have been mended and some new ones discovered. Clichés have been revitalized, insults have been redeemed, and some people have learned from experience. Not oblivious louts such as Gary, who appears in the last pages with a proposal to make the surviving unicorns trapped in this reality the center of a tourist attraction: "Unicorn Mountain." Sam agrees with Libby's rejection of the scheme because his own business dealings with insensitive outsiders were "'a disaster, m'lady. A disaster.'" She catches the redeemed honorific: "'M'lady.' Libby echoed Sam. 'You said "m'lady."' That's who you are," Sam said, rolling her into his arms. "It took your asshole ex's first cousin to show us, though, didn't it?"

Practically speaking, Libby and Sam are not much better off than they were at the novel's opening. In fact, they now are targets for swarms of predators like Gary who will try to disrupt their contentment in order to exploit the unicorns. That's how it goes. It's the same old world, with the same old people.

Nothing has changed.

## 4. Family Reunions

But everything has changed.

Taking stock at the end, Sam sums up what some of Bishop's characters have learned by what they've seen and done:

> All hell would soon be breaking loose up here—reporters, scientists, entrepreneurs, human scavengers of every kind—but for now if not forever, the Tipsy Q was the god home of Inu'sakats [unicorns].
>
> How have I come to be so blessed? Sam wondered. Even if it all ends tomorrow, I'll die happy.

This is a striking statement, considering how often the novel has demonstrated the uncertainty of human life and the limits of human understanding. Somehow, though, this conclusion feels right. Somehow, by natural though unknowable forces, people are drawn past their limitations into the presence of love. Reinvigorating our enfeebled wonder and demonstrating how that restores our fragmented mundane experience, *Unicorn Mountain* leaves its readers, like some of its characters, in a blessed state of comfortable awe. It was Bishop's best novel so far.

*Count Geiger's Blues* (1992) is subtitled "(A Comedy)," and John Kessel's introduction to the 2012 revised edition explains that Bishop began writing the novel during breaks from struggling with the dark AIDS-haunted material of *Unicorn Mountain*. Imagine an up-tight cultural snob suddenly finding himself living the role of a masked comic-book superhero! Possibilities for hilarious confusion and embarrassment will abound! Certainly that fun is part of what the novel offers readers, but Bishop is too smart and honest to stop there. A bite from a radioactive spider may bestow super powers in a comic book, but real-world exposure to radiation can lead to an agonizing death. That happens several times in *Count Geiger*, as the novel stretches the possibilities of "comedy."

At first glance, comedy should be easy to recognize; it's what makes us laugh. In the same way, distinguishing between comedy and tragedy seems simple at first. Unexpected things happen in both, but in comedy the people we feel positively about emerge safe or changed for the better, while unappealing characters get their comeuppance; tragedy dumps suffering on sympathetic people. By that simple-minded dichotomy, we should find it easy to recognize characters who deserve happiness or catastrophe. However, *Count Geiger* subverts this distinction from the beginning. Xavier Thaxton's odd-sounding name sets him apart from the common herd, as does the smug, aloof attitude that he exercises as Fine Arts editor of the *Salonika Urbanite*, major daily newspaper in the alternative/satirical Southern state of Oconee. The novel's first chapter "A Superior Man" shows Xavier energetically at work, revealing that his brain is stuffed with quotations from Oscar Wilde, James

Russell Lowell, and—always, always—Frederik Nietzsche, prophet for the *Ubermensch*, the superman. Xavier recognizes that with his great power as a newspaper critic comes great responsibility, and he is determined to raise the aesthetic awareness of the people around him. He is, in short, exactly the kind of pompous prig who deserves to be taken down a notch or two.... Except that he already respects the feelings of his less-obnoxiously-snooty staff when he makes review assignments—except that he realizes that the people at the paper see him as "their tight-assed editor"—except that he can laugh at himself, even while the novel is setting up situations that will make him even more laughable. When, later in the action, Xavier encounters people with radically different viewpoints, he can listen to them, even learn to love them. He is never *merely* a flat, "comic" character, blithely strutting along from one pratfall to the next.

Consider a serious comedy by another writer. George Bernard Shaw's play *Arms and the Man* (1894) is often performed as a farce, easy laughs directed at man who initially is spoken of as a glorious hero, the extravagantly Byronic Major Sergius Saranoff. I remember watching, for example, a production in which Sergius performed pushups on stage with his sabre clinched in his teeth. But Shaw explains Sergius' outrageous posturing in a stage direction:

> *By his brooding on the perpetual failure, not only of others but of himself, to live up to his ideals; by his consequent cynical scorn for humanity; by his jejune credulity as to the absolute validity of his concepts and the unworthiness of the world in disregarding them; by his wincings and mockeries under the sting of the petty disillusions which every hour spent among men brings to his sensitive observation, he has acquired the half tragic, half ironic air, the mysterious moodiness ... that has left nothing but undying remorse, by which Childe Harold fascinated the grandmothers of his English contemporaries.*

It is not so much that Sergius is a failure at playing the part of a headstrong, dauntless hero as that this brand of heroism doesn't fit the modern world. An audience should recognize that he is sad as well as silly. My wife pointed this out while we were watching that performance of *Arms and the Man*; moreover, as Shaw comments in his 1898 Preface to the *Plays Pleasant*: "Any fool can make an audience laugh. I want to see how many of them, laughing or grave, have tears in their eyes." Xavier Thaxton is not nearly as far gone in moody isolation as Sergius. He seldom broods, is not (quite) cynical, and is too personally engaged in his struggle to uphold artistic standards to feel (altogether) ironic about his position. Still, like Sergius, Xavier is sincerely but glaringly out of place, and thus he deserves tears as much as laughter. As Louis Crompton remarks in an introduction to the play, "Shaw's satire

## 4. Family Reunions

... not only presents a challenge to our critical intellects but also to our sensibilities."

*Count Geiger* shows how Xavier Thaxton responds to challenges to *his* sensibilities. After he goes skinny-dipping one night in a stream where radioactive canisters have illegally been dumped, he acquires typical comic-bookish superpowers such as extra strength, super speed, bodily invulnerability, etc. Before that happens, unfortunately, the accidental dose of radiation upsets his aesthetic balance. All the artifacts of high culture that he adored now produce uncomfortable or disgusting physical reactions, so he must restore his health with junk like supermarket tabloids, rock music, and comic books. He is lucky to have support from two somewhat bothersome companions. Thaxton admires the artistry of his lover Bari Carlisle's fashion designs, but he is deeply uneasy that she can let her unique creations be mass-produced. Even more disturbing is his nephew Mikhail Geoffrey Menaker, aka The Mick. This originally unwelcome guest is not only a high-culture-hating teenage punk who paints his room black but also is a fan of blaring rock bands like Smite Them Hip & Thigh and of tacky superhero comic books. That Thaxton at least accepts the presence of these diverse, disturbing individuals shows that he was somewhat—barely—tolerant of different viewpoints even before his good taste goes into reverse and he is forced to embrace pop culture. In any event, he is able to write a sincere, glowing review of the Smite Them concert that he attends with The Mick, and thus he informs his editor proudly that "[t]he spectrum of what [he'd] been able to appreciate has been expanded." Consequently, he is prepared, however reluctantly at first, to don the shiny metallic costume of comic-book hero Count Geiger when his radiation-induced physical superpowers emerge.

In a sense, like characters in Bishop's other novels of this period, Xavier is shifting "planes," moving from one reality to another, as his spectrum of appreciation expands. But how far does that succeed in *Count Geiger*? Xavier's own spectrum of appreciation may have expanded generously, but that doesn't mean that being Count Geiger will help him guide others into a similar healthy transition. Readers pay attention to Xavier's newspaper reviews for entertainment, not enlightenment. His pontificating in the role of Count Geiger is not much more effective. The general public's attitude toward superheroes is ambivalent, somewhere between those of worshipful Jimmy Olsen and indignant J. Jonah Jameson. Most adults wouldn't want to get too close to a superhero for very long—too childish and too messy. How, for example can a superhero avoid becoming infatuated with the glory of his own superiority? Count Geiger, Xavier is most successful at meeting short-term physical challenges. Rushing to the rescue of a woman being mugged by four hoodlums, he subdues all the attackers and leaves them trussed up and dangling from a light fixture. Though this takes care of the immediate problem, Bari notes that he should wrap up future exploits with less display of his super ego. As Bishop observes, "He was trying, with intermittent success, to guard against becoming the sort of monster he was now equipped to battle."

Beyond physically subduing evildoers, moreover, Count Geiger is less effective. His efforts to use his power and prestige to improve the cultural and moral tone of Salonika, Xavier's obsession, produce some of the novel's richest comedy. Early in the novel, when The Mick temporarily goes AWOL, Xavier and a companion go looking for him in the sleaziest part of town; in P.S. Annie's, which may be the sleaziest bar in that neighborhood, they witness scantily clad girls being drenched with jets of beer from water pistols wielded by cheering, leering patrons: "The Cutie Shoot." Later, Count Geiger returns to P.S. Annie's to end the degrading show. He tries to encourage empathy by interviewing the men in the crowd about their little daughters, questioning the young women on stage about their hopes and dreams, and announcing to the owner that "'next Thursday, Friday, and Saturday nights ... , P.S. Annie's will offer three introductory seminars, all free, on topics of lasting importance to our male citizenry: Ennobling Images of Women in Modern Southern Lit; Later-Day Etiquette and Sensitivity Training for Male Chauvinist Pigs; and Essential Points of Feminist Concern for the Twenty-first Century." If that *doesn't* happen, Count Geiger will be back .... He tells the stunned boss not to worry, that "we'll find ways to better our city and to keep P.S. Annie's solvent"—to which the stunned man replies, "Who wants to better our city?"

That is, remember, one of the major questions *Count Geiger's Blues* struggles to answer: Who else can share such an elevated goal? Who else wants to help build a better, more humane world? What do any human efforts—however "super" or at least sincere—matter? Xavier Thaxton certainly wants to better the city he shares with the barflies, and becoming Count Geiger certainly seems to give him more power to enforce his agenda. But that doesn't mean that he can force others to share his values. It's doubtful that the men in the bar will pay attention to those consciousness-raising seminars, even if they let themselves be coerced into attending. Still, the novel's description of The Cutie Shoot is genuinely disgusting, convincing readers that *something* should be done to stop it and maybe even to correct the conditions that created such a spectacle. This is just one of many places in the novel where honest concerns collide, struggling to reach a convincing synthesis.

The novel also admits the unlikelihood of radiation-based heroics changing the world for the better by mixing chapters describing Xavier's attempts to live up to his augmented best impulses as Count Geiger with chapters showing the real-life effects of radiation on a family that comes into possession of a discarded cylinder of radioactive waste. Breaking open the container, the dim but loving father gives the contents to his little daughter as a birthday present; she smears the glowing "Blue Fairy dust" on her face and goes to sleep with a lump of it under her pillow. Readers unhappily realize that the little girl and the rest of her family are now doomed, and succeeding chapters describe their terrible death by radiation poisoning. Fantasizing about magical benefits of exposure to radiation is fun, but the novel reminds us that what happens to real human bodies isn't amusing. What if, in fact, Xavier/Count Geiger's larger efforts are futile because his real enemy is not some individual supervillain but simple, slovenly human nature? At the novel's end, politics seems to be going along as usual. So is show biz; one of the women Count Geiger rescued from the Cutie Shoot winds up as a radio talk-show host who promises her audience a torrent of distraction: "an exciting hour of issues, arguments, and laughter." Even the dying redneck father wishes he could stay alive so he could see the inevitable movie about his family's fate.

This brings us to the novel's other main concern: our struggle to create art. A Count Geiger flick, a nimble orchestration of rabid phone callers, a teenager's punk costume—all those are deliberate creations that may display something personal to an audience and elicit some kind of response. The question is how much attention they do deserve, how "good" is it possible for them to be. At the novel's beginning, Xavier Thaxton seems to confuse quality with genre, assuming that performances of ballets are naturally superior to rock concerts, for example, so that the latter should be ignored while the former can be savored and evaluated. He learns better, eventually realizing that "art" can be any creation that expands the possibilities of human feeling and understanding. Such a generous working definition will let us focus on the *effect* of art rather than the means of delivery, so that almost any artistic performance can be critically evaluated. In his farewell newspaper column, Xavier maintains his dissatisfaction with the actual works of art around him but writes in a tolerant and hopeful tone: "I thank the would-be artists striving to show us the rainbow, and the beholders seeking to see as rainbows the jury-rigged arches winched into view by their hopeful makers. Sometimes the noise is bearable. Sometimes the guy-ropes are harder to see than threads. Sometimes the sky is afire with color and light and passion. Sometimes…"

People need to extend themselves in creating and appreciating art, but most of them don't bother to distinguish between different levels of challenge/satisfaction in the art they absorb. They remain willfully confused about what they want and what they're getting. Xavier himself attends religious ceremonies largely because he finds them aesthetically satisfying, but he is offended during a PR ceremony in which Tim Bowman, creative genius of Uncommon Comics, describes UC's new super characters to an audience (including The Mick) composed of "zealots, True Believers, hallowing the origin and exploits of Saint Torque, and every other UC 'stalwart' [super hero] like hagiographers hallowing the lives of the great Catholic saints." To comic fans, in other words, these trite adventures embody the Holy, reminding the novel's readers that the most apparently banal creations can feel like great art. Apparently, everyone wants to experience *being* more than normal—as long as that's not too personally demanding. Unfortunately, lazy or limited creators stop short of what Xavier demands: "'high art, the kind that stretches our God-given capabilities to the limit.'" Ideally, such art should enrich our human sympathy, but absorbing inferior art just leaves us stuck in our shallow presuppositions. Bowman himself claims to be trying to fulfill a Nietszchean program of encouraging readers to use whatever powers they have for good. Nevertheless, his creative imagination fails in real life when he shoots F. Deane Finesse, the tycoon responsible for the illegal dumping of radioactive waste, to save the elderly villain from a long prison sentence; the well-intentioned assassin is disappointed "that the look on Finesse's contorted face betrayed not a shadow of gratitude."

But though high art is rare it's not quite impossible. The same is true of genuine empathy. Xavier himself demonstrates as much by taking off the Count Geiger costume that somehow has been managing his dangerous level of radioactivity and giving it to the radiation-poisoned slob who dumped those deadly canisters in his swimming hole. It's true that Xavier does so in hopes that the man will recover enough to testify against F. Deane Finesse, and it's also true that he doesn't realize how fast his own body will deteriorate once he's not wearing the suit. Still, he demonstrates how a superior person can perform a generous act for someone who doesn't deserve it, in this case a man who's not only a criminal but has only inferior aesthetic sensitivity.

Perhaps Xavier's most heroic action is his choosing to give away the suit and let go of the role of Count Geiger.

As the chapter "A Feeble Cheer for Altruism" explains, recognizing the ultimate hopelessness of human efforts doesn't mean that we should be doing nothing. Xavier's sister Lydia dumped The Mick on Xavier in the first place so she could jet off to accomplish great humanitarian projects, but she later "conceded that making a humanitarian mind set last longer than five minutes is hard even for relief workers at the scene of misery and devastation.... In many ways, ... it's easier to be here doing something, even if it's semifutile, than watching it on TV. Being here reduces the guilt. It brings home the situation's unmanageability, too, but I'd rather be work-ridden than paralyzed by guilt."

So, if Xavier's death is one consequence of his action, why does the novel feel more like a comedy than a tragedy? How can readers smile while experiencing an example of what Shaw calls "perpetual failure"? In *Arms and the Man*, the audience finally is permitted to be comfortable with Sergius' absurd diminution because he accepts that he has been superseded by a new kind of "hero," a drab but efficient commercial manager. Bishop certainly doesn't glorify Xavier's abrupt physical decline. At the point of death, however, he specifies that although he wants his funeral service to be "dignified.... Tasteful. Aesthetically topnotch," he wants the casket itself to be "flamboyant and borderline tacky" and his own vestments to be "gaudy, maybe even vulgar.... Wildly out of Thaxtonian character." As Bishop explains, "Nothing about Xavier's ordeal ... had been fun. With this goofy last request, though, he clearly wanted to reverse that state of affairs."

Moreover, Xavier has successors who will not only criticize but create. His example vindicates Bari's imaginative but commercially savvy efforts. She will go on using her gift to expand the possibilities of fashion and encouraging better taste in a mass audience. The Mick, meanwhile, has expanded his spectrum of appreciation to embrace Swift and Faulkner along with rock lyrics. On *Count Geiger*'s last page, he is tearing his comic collection to bits by way of rejecting the "lies" it contains, then adds, "But it's better to make something." In the novel's very last sentence, he and Bari simply hug each other "until the angry music ended." They are examples of real life, genuine stalwarts.

Looking at this inconclusive but hopeful conclusion, remembering Xavier Thaxton's career, and also considering this work of art by Michael Bishop, perhaps we need to consider not only the example of George Bernard Shaw but also of Robert Browning's poem "Andrea del Sarto," which muses that "a man's reach should exceed his grasp,/ Or what's a heaven for?" John Kessel's introduction to *Count Geiger* ends with the reflection that "life can be so painful; it's hard to be an adult. I guess that laughing helps." That's fair enough too. Even if readers may leave the novel with the uneasy feeling that Bishop was trying to juggle too many chainsaws at once, it's easy to understand how *Locus* reviewer Faren Miller could judge that "in unleashing a startling talent for comedy and a wide-ranging knowledge of pop culture in both its absurdity and its splendor, Michael Bishop has written his best book yet."

Almost unquestionably, however, Bishop's very best book is *Brittle Innings* (1994), which won the Locus Award for Best Science Fiction Novel in 1995, and was nominated for the Hugo, World Fantasy, and Campbell Awards in the same year.

*Brittle Innings* is a breathtakingly successful novel, although its basic premise—Frankenstein's monster playing minor-league baseball during World War II—seems at least as outlandish as *Count Geiger*'s. Such intrusion of the fantastic into mundane life makes some people uncomfortable. Perhaps for that reason, *Brittle Innings*' original publisher labeled it simply "A Novel," and the first edition's dust jacket only hints at the identity of the identity of "the erudite seven-foot giant by the name of Jumbo Hank Clerval," coyly adding that main narrator Danny Boles eventually "realizes that Hank is not an ordinary man but something more complex ... more mysterious than he'd imagined." The New York *Times* reviewer liked the baseball part of the book but wished that the fantastic element had been segregated into a separate novel. And so it goes. Some readers can accept "magical realism" more easily than others. Actually, Bishop creates a solid everyday context for Henry/Jumbo to inhabit before his identity as the "creature," the "fiend," etc., can be recognized. The novel's setting in the early 1940s American South is convincingly layered without ostentations lumps of research, and it is almost half over before the first clear hint of the outré. As far as readers know, Jumbo is just a very large, very ugly man. If 17-year-old Danny suffers a panic attack when he is shoved together with Jumbo as a roommate, it's not so much because readers have reason to suspect that the big man might be an inhuman monster but because we appreciate how disturbed the young man was already. Danny, after all, is the novel's primary concern. Because his disturbed state of mind has built up convincingly, the looming presence of Jumbo/Henry becomes acceptable as part of the unfamiliar but not necessarily threatening surroundings. Bishop has done all he could to join the levels of his story together smoothly, without the sometimes disruptive satire of *Count Geiger*.

Bishop uses a variety of prose styles to ease readers into the story. At the very beginning and end, we hear from sportswriter Gabriel Stewart, who has sought out the elderly Danny Boles to write a book about the man's long career as a scout for a major league baseball team; Boles is willing to do help with the journalist's project but only if they first can transcribe the story *he* has to tell, from his time in the minor leagues. This establishes a supposedly-objective frame for the fantastic elements in Danny's narrative. But most of the novel is told by Danny, in a voice

## 4. Family Reunions

that naturally is more conversational than Stewart's prose, with a more colloquial, flavorful vocabulary as it moves into less familiar, everyday territory. When Danny discovers Jumbo's journal, continuing the real story of what happened to Frankenstein's creation, the style of that fantastic narrative is appropriately/incongruously self-conscious and elevated as it strains to match the height of 18th-century eloquence. But it's possible to play riffs on those different viewpoints. Here, for example, is a speech by Mister JayMac, owner of Danny's minor league team, the Highbridge [Georgia] Hellbenders, which mixes elaborate diction and downhome dialect as he rebukes members of the team for getting into a brawl that may disrupt the Hellbenders' race for the championship:

> "But this is no time to suppose that jes because we've got our percherons harnessed and our wagon on track, we're going to roll over everybody else like they were dust chickens. Uh-uh. So I am deeply perturbed that Mr. Curriden and Mr. Musselwhite, team *heroes*, elected by their off-the-field performance last night to sit out Wednesday's contest against the Boll Weevils [a rival team]. Their absence from the lineup—nor do I mean to disparage or demoralize their replacements—could well cost us that game and deny us the psychological momentum to make the entire road trip a success. The rest of yall will just have to gird up your loins in resolute and selfless compensation."

Feeling the flow of words, listening to different people talk in their distinctive voices is one of the book's pleasures.

Besides deftly working fantastic elements into a realistic setting and displaying an impressive variety of prose styles, *Brittle Innings* has a strong, resonant story to tell. As usual, Bishop doesn't wave the point in the reader's face, but it emerges clearly as the novel develops. The theme is suggested most directly while Danny is recuperating from the injury that ends his dream of playing baseball professionally; he spends part of that period brooding, but also devotes time to "reading a long downbeat novel about a young British doctor with a clubfoot." This description of W. Somerset Maugham's *Of Human Bondage* is as simplistic as calling *Brittle Innings* just a long magically-realistic novel about a young minor-league ballplayer whose roommate is Frankenstein's monster. In fact, Jumbo/Henry's description of his own journal fits both novels: "a tale whose theme remains occluded to its hero." The central characters of both novels have trouble grasping what is both real and personally important. Both novels show a young man seeking some system of values he can believe in, and both show him discovering that keeping faith with individual people is more important than maintaining abstract ideals. And so both novels, in somewhat different ways, present a similar and ultimately hopeful view of human possibility.

In both *Brittle Innings* and *Of Human Bondage*, the characters' efforts to understand themselves and their surroundings are complicated by their inability to come to terms with their parents. One necessary though painful stage of human development is deliberate separation from one's parents. After growing up dependent on them and echoing their values, one must end that childish role. Only then can a person decide which early relationships and behaviors are worth keeping. Then an individual is free to relate with others as a grownup. If, however, a child is unable to go through that process—if, for example, a parent is somehow absent when the child needs to declare independence—the result may be a stalled, frustrated condition in which the child is obsessed with finding a way to escape by recovering the parent directly or by constructing and demolishing some equivalent relationship. Mature independence will remain out of reach until that separation can occur, however much time it takes and however old the child grows in calendar years.

Philip Carey, Maugham's hero, is orphaned in early childhood. He has no memories of his father and few of his fragile, foolish mother. He is merely a temporary intrusion in the life of his elderly uncle, and his well-meaning aunt has no idea how to fill the role of a mother. As he grows up, therefore, Philip lacks any emotional haven. His position as an outsider is not altogether unfortunate, for it teaches him to think for himself rather than falling into some fashionable lifestyle. But having to try out many possibilities does use up a lot of time before Philip settles into his father's profession, medicine. And even then his inability to declare independence directly from his own parents means, that before he can truly strike out on his own, he must create and break a relationship corresponding to that between parent and child.

When Philip falls obsessively in love with Mildred, the most striking thing to readers—and to the uncomprehending Philip himself—is how thoroughly it infantilizes him. He gives up all control of the affair to her; he recognizes that he is behaving unreasonably, but having a relationship with her is more important than practical adult concerns such as his awareness of how unhealthy Mildred looks and how inferior her mind is. Though Philip naturally cannot make this connection, Mildred actually resembles his own mother as she appeared briefly in the novel's first chapter and as she has been described to him ever since. If at a preconscious level, Mildred represents Philip's mother, he finds a father substitute in his fellow student Griffith, who takes care of Philip when he is ill and gives him "motherly" attention. Soon, Philip is desperately trying to couple the two, against his conscious interests: "he had a fiendish desire to break down their scruples, he wanted to know how abominably they would behave toward him; if he tempted them a bit more they would yield, and he took a fierce joy at the thought of their dishonor. Though every word he spoke tortured him, he found in the torture a horrible delight." The fact that the two do betray Philip helps him distance himself from them. Once that separation occurs, he feels able to act more responsibly—i.e., like an independent adult. As the process continues, Philip's letter permitting Mildred to live in the same apartment with him but denying her sexual access provokes her to destroy all his possessions, mementos of his immature youth, just as he later tears up a freshly discovered letter in which his mother expressed inappropriate hopes for his life.

Philip Carey's struggle toward maturity is painfully messy. His behavior frequently is pathological, as he works toward a healthy resolution that he cannot imagine directly. Throughout his erratic wanderings, however, he shows that unconsciously he knows what he needs: connection to but then freedom from paternal authority so that he can determine his own goals.

Danny Boles, with similar needs, is certain that he already has found something to believe in: baseball.

Danny is not the only character in *Brittle Innings* whose life is centered on baseball, but the game is especially important to him because he connects in with his father. Richard Oconostota Boles deserted his family in Tenkiller, Oklahoma, when Danny was young. He had been unable to do his share of supporting the family—maybe because he was a happy-go-lucky drunk, maybe because he was discriminated against for being part Indian: Danny can't sort out the contradictory clues. What he does know for sure is that "[u]ntil I was eleven or twelve, Dick Boles'd been a sockdalager daddy, good as a boy could want." They played ball together for hours on end, in "The Boles & Son Jes-for-Fun Oklahoma World See-ries," and when his father abandoned him Danny practiced even harder by himself, "until my arms felt like window-sash weights. An outlet, you know. Therapy, a shrink today'd call it."

In *Brittle Innings*, Danny has been going through a gradual, fairly painless separation from his hard-working, practical mother by leaving his hometown to play class-C minor-league baseball during World War II. His father, however, is absent when Danny leaves. More seriously, years earlier, Danny wandered into a vicious quarrel between his parents during which each used him as a weapon against the other. First, his father accused his mother of infidelity, saying, "'My son ain't my son.'" Then, after Danny echoed his mother's insult "Lousy redskin scum," his father struck the boy in the throat, rendering him physically and later psychologically unable to speak: "Except for the mark on my throat, I must've looked more or less okay. When I started breathing again, I was okay. But I didn't talk again for two years. And when I did, I st-st-stammered." Not having an identity as his father's son means that Danny becomes nobody, unable to speak for himself. On his way to join his new baseball team, having regained some ability to express himself haltingly, Danny encounters a soldier who claims to know his father, then robs and sodomizes him at knifepoint, while simultaneously questioning Danny's legitimacy. When the young man arrives at his destination, he again has become totally mute.

Not that being a "dummy" will keep him from playing baseball. The Highridge Hellbenders of the Chattahoochee Valley League are an assortment of discards and misfits, of whom the towering, scarred, and spectacularly ugly first baseman "Jumbo" Clerval is not the oddest. It doesn't matter whether Danny can talk or not as long as he can hit and field.

Bishop's novel is startling in the characters' extreme devotion to what Danny later semi-ironically calls "a frivolous schoolboys' game." But baseball actually *was* allowed to continue during America's World War II mobilizations, and minor league clubs actually *did* flourish where people lived far from big-city stadiums. Besides being Danny's private obsession, the game offered special comfort and inspiration to many other Americans. Baseball's appeal lay, for one thing, in the fact that it is played by rules; players follow the rules so that all members of both teams get an equal chance to participate, limited only by their skill. And this in turn means that the players must accept or at least tolerate each other, even their opponents. In all, the game didn't offer a bad ideal for a country like the United States, struggling to justify its existence against the totalitarian Axis in a war without rules. It also offers an attractive model of voluntary cooperation for a young person who needs to be accepted as a distinct individual, independent of parental control. Danny is one of several characters in *Brittle Innings* with this need.

But it's not that simple. Unfortunately, neither baseball nor life always is played by such straightforward rules. Even on the field, the Hellbenders barely stay inside the rules as they struggle to outdo each other. Off the field, the players are as intolerant and selfish as any of the crowd in the stands. Even if Danny plays well, he becomes a focus of his teammates' resentment of any intruder. His inability to defend himself verbally makes him a safe target for cruel tricks. (While rescuing Danny from one especially nasty prank, Jumbo proclaims that his name is *Henry*; therefore, that is what he will be called in the rest of this discussion.) In particular, Buck Hoey becomes Danny's nemesis when the young man replaces him as shortstop. Although Henry has chosen to room by himself, partly to avoid physical scrutiny and partly to avoid direct personal rejection, he is forced to take in Danny because the "normal" players lump them together as freaks—"Jumbo and Dumbo."

Nevertheless, despite how far the sport falls short of its ideal, *Brittle Innings*' characters cannot walk away from it. In the almost mid-century American South, baseball is literally and figuratively the only game in town. In *Of Human Bondage*, Philip Carey has some freedom to move to different cities, professions, and lifestyles. Bishop's characters have less room to maneuver and must first try to liberate themselves and achieve independent maturity within their immediate context.

The person most obviously in need of liberation is Darius, the Hellbenders' African American bus driver/assistant manager. He is a superior athlete who never will be allowed to compete directly against white ballplayers. Even though Darius is given unusual leeway by Mister JayMac, the team's owner, he will never have a chance to earn his own adult dignity. For, as Mister JayMac's unacknowledged but tacitly accepted illegitimate son, Darius always will be treated as a child, under his father's control. Sometimes that control appears relatively benign, as when Mister JayMac pleads with Darius to take some pleasure in what is offered by "this world, not some pie-in-the-sky pipedream"; sometimes it is clear that Mister JayMac sees himself in godlike command of what the world can offer; and such unquestionable authority always can be abused, as when Mister JayMac grabs his son's shirt and exclaims, "'This club belongs to me—you pitch because I say you do, nigger!'" There is no possibility of real negotiation with a father who believes that his children are property.

The situation seems different for Phoebe Pharram, the outspoken teenaged girl who unexpectedly comes to care for Danny as a person. Phoebe's mother has abandoned her parental role and is acting like a hormone-crazed adolescent. With her husband away in the service, Mrs. Pharram is having a nonstop series of sexual affairs with the most glamorous men available, the Highbridge Hellbenders. This has forced Phoebe to take the position of the thoughtful, responsible adult in the family—but without the authority to correct her immature mother. Until she can restore a normal balance, Phoebe cannot begin to think of establishing her independence, and in the meantime she becomes increasingly desperate about her mother's behavior.

However, the character with the deepest need to establish a healthy relationship with a parent for the sake of achieving independence—and the one with the deepest obsession with baseball—is Henry. His presence dominates *Brittle Innings* from the first time Danny sees him, and he literally takes over long sections of the book through Danny's transcription of the journal he has kept for centuries, since the events described in *Frankenstein*, Mary Shelley's novelization of historical documents. After deciding not to die, as he had intended at the end of *Frankenstein*, Henry retrieved Victor Frankenstein's corpse from the explorer's ship that had been crushed in the Arctic ice and began a trek back toward humanity. He wanted to atone for the violence he had committed and to be accepted as a valuable member of some community; he titles this section of his journal "From Remorse to Self-Respect: My Second Life." But with him, always, he carries the desiccated corpse of the man who created and then rejected him, "both as a macabre talisman and a relic of loathsome veneration." He literally can't let go of his father.

Like Danny, Henry has been denied by his parent. Also, like Danny, he yearns for parental approval. Frankenstein had never given his creation a name, calling him "fiend," "wretch," "demon," etc. Bishop remarked during a phone interview that, by calling himself Henry Clerval, the name of Frankenstein's best friend, Jumbo is attempting to feel his dead father's affection at second hand. Though he understands that it is too late to soften Frankenstein's dying rejection, Henry does everything he can to grow up the way he imagines his father would have wanted. He tries to hide the monstrous appearance that initially repulsed Frankenstein by refusing to shower with the other Hellbenders. Before joining the team, to reduce his unusual height, he went so far as to saws sections out of his legs. Besides disguising himself physically, Henry is doing everything he can to remake himself spiritually: he practices vegetarianism so that he will not be responsible for any creature's death; in the middle of World War II, he is a dedicated pacifist; and he voraciously reads self-help books such as Harry Emerson Fosdick's *On Being a Real Person*.

But all these solitary actions seem rather futile. Because of his much longer experience, Henry has a better understanding than the other orphaned youngsters of what he needs, but he has as much difficulty as the others in finding a way to get it—until he and Danny begin interacting. Maugham's Philip Carey also stumbles upon his salvation by drifting into friendship with the Athelny family, during which young Sally Athelny begins to fix her attention on him. In much the same way, at the heart of *Brittle Innings* is the discovery by several characters that they don't need to solve problems all by themselves. Danny is the first to demonstrate this. After a Presidential visit to a Hellbenders game, Danny is taken aside by FDR and told that his father has died honorably in combat in the Aleutian Islands. The President encourages the young man to overcome his "estrangement" and "recall [his] father with a measure of fondness." With that encouragement, Danny recovers some ability to express himself vocally. The first word he speaks shows that he is no longer alone: "Phoebe."

At this point, Danny bounces between extremes of hate and love when thinking about his father. On the one hand, the man deserves eternal damnation for deserting his wife and hurting his son; on the other, Danny remembers their baseball games. Consequently, "the sump of my bitterness started to evaporate. Did Satan grant pardons? Reprieves? Weekend furloughs?" Having drawn slightly closer to his father—and safe in Phoebe's love and Henry's friendship—Danny becomes confident enough to stand up for himself when he again encounters the soldier who robbed and raped him. He doesn't stammer during his verbal and physical assault on the man; the only time he has trouble speaking is when he approaches the real core of his outrage: "If you don't have my money ... take back what you said about my f-father."

Danny is not so much demanding revenge for his own injury now as defending his father's reputation. It is only after doing this that he can weep for the dead man, a tentative beginning of the grieving process. And at this point it becomes even more obvious that declaring independence from one's parents does not mean choosing isolation. Much of *Brittle Innings* is about the characters' discovery of how deeply, imperceptibly they have become involved with other people. As they struggle to gain their freedom, they discover that maturity can mean not so much rejection but acceptance of other people and their emotional claims. Some of Bishop's characters even discover that they can depend on others as members of a different kind of team. As Danny says, "Thank God Phoebe cared for me. Thank God I had Henry for a protector."

One character who is too desperate to recognize this option is Darius. Because compromise with his father seems impossible, Darius runs away. He explains his plight to Danny and Jumbo, in the vocabulary of baseball:

> "My life's done crept into its brittlest part, like unto them innings when the whole thing could go either way—depending on jes when the critical bonecrack happen, and to whom. I awmost waited past the snappin point. Maybe I did. But if I beat it now, mebee I'll get past my brittle innings and play on through to a stretch that'll heal me, that won't jes shake me down to splinters and shards."

Danny recognizes Darius much later, playing exhibition ball with the American-Afrique Zanies, still a fine athlete but disguised under a green and purple wig and garish clown makeup. It is not clear whether he has successfully healed or still is running away. He rejects Danny's suggestion that his troubled father needs him. Danny comments that Darius disappeared after that: "So far as I know, he never played integrated pro ball, and I sometimes think he died overseas after enlisting ... under a phony name." However necessary flight may feel at the moment, it may not lead to genuine freedom if the parent-child relationship is still unresolved.

Another kind of freedom is found in voluntarily accepting responsibility for others. Bishop shows his characters learning to accept others—including their own parents and their own at least potentially parental roles. In Maugham's novel, Philip Carey concludes by giving up his dream of exploring the world, sampling the best life has to offer anywhere, because he realizes that what he really wants is to settle down with a loving wife and a child, as a doctor in a small neighborhood. To be sure, having freed himself from his parents, Philip now is free to select as much of their lifestyle as suits him. Readers may feel, however, that Philip is uncommonly blessed (by a *deus ex machina*) to find a glowingly healthy girl, Sally Athelny, who adores him at exactly the moment he has been offered an opportunity to share a practice with an older physician. The book's conclusion is less Philip's achievement than an avalanche of happy accidents.

*Brittle Innings* shows a less contrived conclusion because throughout the book readers have watched a variety of characters attempting different solutions. Phoebe, for example, worries about her mother so much that she becomes "unhinged" and lures Danny into one of the funniest, saddest, least erotic sex scenes in literature. At its embarrassing climax, she sends Danny away with orders to tell everyone, especially all the Hellbenders, what she has done. Her clear though unspoken purposes are first of all to hurt her mother ("I'm just following her example; look what she's teaching me") but also draw her mother back home ("Look what's happening to me; see how much I need you to intervene"). When she doesn't get attention that way because Danny cares too much for her to ruin her reputation, she makes a public spectacle by confronting the whole team and shaming them for their behavior with her mother.

Danny, still working out his relationship with his father, has put all his efforts into developing his baseball skills, so that's the context in which he receives the announcement that he and Jumbo are being moved up to a major league team:

"He's have t-to admit I could p-play," I said.
"Who?" Then Henry understood and laid his hand on my head like a priest giving a blessing.

In the last game of the season, however, jealous former teammate Buck Hoey deliberately slides hard into Danny, injuring him so severely that he never will be able to play ball again. In the hospital, Danny is forced to realize that playing the game was something he *did*, not who he *is*, as the doctor advises him to "redefine [himself] in quite different terms." He has had enough experience and is secure enough in his personal relationships to be able to start doing that. When Phoebe visits him in the hospital, she exclaims that his stutter is gone.

Danny has no choice about making this next step toward maturity. Henry does have a choice, and the choice he makes shows something important about what humans are and what we really need. Earlier, under the pretext of joining a human community, Henry had become obsessed with baseball as "an end in itself," so that he stopped caring about "tiresome social intercourse: Once I had wanted a spiritual sharer, but now.... I wanted only faceless teammates and unending occasions to exercise my intellectual and animal facilities playing baseball." Even so, he could not resist identifying with people at the fringes of society, calling himself "an honorary nigger." And eventually he encourages Danny to read his journal because, "like nearly everyone else, Daniel, I yearn for a kindred spirit. A friend."

After Danny's injury, Henry could simply move on to take a shot at playing in major league baseball. He does not. For one thing, his equanimity has been shaken by the fiery suicide of Miss Giselle, Mister Jay-Mac's wife, who had convinced herself that her affair with Henry would save her from dreadful isolation. For another, Henry simply cannot accept that Buck Hoey faces no consequences for spiking Danny in the thigh and groin. Despite his earlier, devoutly pacifistic behavior that might have pleased his father, Frankenstein, Henry can't let the matter rest. His visit to Hoey one night ends with the man broken and dying, which sounds like something the "fiend" in *Frankenstein* might have done. However, the fugitive Henry protests to Danny that he did not go to Hoey's house with murder in mind; he was driven not so much by a desire for vengeance as by a need to find *justice* for someone he loves. As he asks Danny in a letter, "*'Does this not prove that I have undergone an evolution worthy of your regard? Am I not your friend?'*" Readers actually may observe that Henry begins by asking Hoey to say publicly say he was sorry, to acknowledge his kinship with Danny. A simple apology might have been enough to avert Henry's rage at the man's selfish cruelty. But readers also should remember how much conflict the novel has shown: alienation between husband and wife and between parent and child, class and racial tension, and combat between whole nations in World War II. Despite his efforts toward moral perfection, Henry behaves the way people actually do; we all are mixtures of idealist and brute. Whether his personality is as it was created or whether it has accumulated into its present shape over time, Henry truly is one of us.

Confronting his personal "evolution," Henry is no longer dependent on his parent's approval. When he takes Danny to see Frankenstein's corpse—encased in a leather shroud made from old baseball covers—it is to let Danny mourn his own father through this surrogate. This makes Danny not simply his friend but his adopted brother, although at this time the young man can't transfer his feelings to the substitute father.

While Henry searches for some way to help his friend "let go of the whole sad jam-up inside" himself, Danny is back in Oklahoma, trying to make the most of what he has left of body and soul. Phoebe still writes to him, and they appear to have a future together. In addition, he begins to attend local baseball games and to analyze the players, preparing for his later career as a scout. Meanwhile, however, Henry travels to the far north (along the way finally interring Frankenstein's corpse in a cave with Aleut mummies) to locate the grave of Danny's own father. At least he finds what *could* be the correct burial site. As he and Danny stand there, reading the tribute written to "brave solider heroes" by the Japanese soldiers who had killed them, Henry insists that "his [father's] enemy's common integrity"-reveals a basic human impulse that deserves respect; consequently, Danny shows that he has at last become mature enough to accept his father and then say goodbye:

> Henry reached into his pack and rummaged out a brand-new National League baseball. He flipped it to me. I caught it in both hands like an amateur. I stood there for a minute turning that ivory ball in my gloves before it occurred to me to wedge it into the natural cup of the stone cairn supposedly marking my daddy's grave. In that cup, the ball glinted like a lighthouse beacon and focused the whole of Attu Island around it, a pivot for the world to turn on.

This is the climax of Bishop's novel, and the book ends soon after. The story does not end, however. The journalistic frame story reveals that Danny Boles was silenced again later in life by cancer; consequently, he was forced to learn to talk through a mechanical amplifier "that he still was able to infuse with personality." He and Phoebe had no children of their own, but he became a mentor to young ballplayers. There always seems to be some new difficulty that people must work through. Still, with determination, support from present companions, and memories of those who aren't present, people can discover what feels real and right for themselves. Danny's last comment on Henry is that—rather than simply "*being* human," as his self-help books promised—his friend was truly "becoming a real person."

This lingering uncertainty about details but firm emphasis on *becoming* is characteristic of Bishop's work. At the end of Maugham's *Of*

*Human Bondage*, the hero's struggle has come to a conclusion. He has recognized what he wants, and he has it. He is safe. Like security, knowledge is harder to come by in *Brittle Innings*, as shown by Danny's failure to catch how relevant Maugham's novel is to his own experience. Still, Philip Carey, Danny, Phoebe, and Henry do learn enough to free themselves from bondage to their pasts and to dreams that no longer matter. In fact, the hero of Maugham's novel responds to El Greco's art with a description that could fit Bishop's novel: "it was virile; it accepted life in all its vivacity, ugliness and beauty, squalor and heroism; it was realism still, but it was realism transformed by the more vivid light in which they were seen." By the way they learn to see life's vivid extremes and still struggle to see more, the characters in *Brittle Innings* successfully demonstrate that love sometimes can lead not to bondage but to freedom. To say this vividly and clearly, without slipping into clichéd moralizing, is a splendid achievement.

Part III
---
# Settling In

Following *Brittle Innings*, Bishop stopped writing fantastic novels for a time. The reasons aren't altogether clear. For one thing, he always has considered himself simply a *writer*. His 1990 collection, *Emphatically Not SF, Almost* contains stories from non-genre magazines such as *Alfred Hitchcock's Mystery Magazine* and *Playboy*. Several of them are impressive, and one, "Taccati's Tomorrow," is discussed in this book. Also, the previously unpublished novella "Blue Kansas Sky," in the 2000 collection of the same title, describes a boy's coming to manhood in the American heartland with only a perhaps-illusory touch of the fantastic. In a 2004 *Locus* interview, Bishop explains that he always had felt as much like a writer of mainstream fiction as of fantastic fiction; also, the cash from movie options on *Brittle Innings* removed the pressure to write another novel immediately, so that "I haven't published a solo novel since, it's ten years later, and who knows how the time got by?" Evidently, as with his decision not to stay in the commercially attractive groove of *No Enemy but Time* earlier in his career, Bishop wanted to explore new territory. Also, *Brittle Innings* evidently succeeded in saying something that Bishop needed to express about the relationship between fathers and sons. Following that, he turned to writing shorter fiction that could explore troubling concerns.

# 5

# Later Fiction
*Darkness, Wonder and Grace*

In previous chapters, I've discussed short fiction first, as prologue, then moved on to Bishop's novels from the time period. This time, it's the shorter fiction that makes up the bulk—and the most impressive part—of Bishop's writing.

Bishop's fiction frequently includes characters who are reaching for something *more*, even if they are unable to conceptualize—let alone verbalize—what that could be. That's certainly true of the slyly humorous "Tithes of Mint and Rue" (*World Horror Convention Program*, March 1999), which also offers a peek at religious Mysteries, more specifically a reverently disturbing meditation on the range of opportunities open to us for Christian ministry.

To do all that in one short story that requires a daring, jarring mixture of attitudes. The story must set up and then shatter readers' expectations—and then do it over again. The first sentence of "Tithe" introduces the central character, sweaty and grossly obese Callula Ward Carnahan, who is "marveling at how reliably her bulk made her invisible to men…, as if the larger she loomed in her flesh the lower she sank in their eyes." It turns out that "reliably" is the right word, for Lula explains to "her oldest friend, Sue Rose Foyt" that she deliberately buried her good looks under fat because that was the only way to keep men from trying to grab her beautiful body without regard for *herself* as a person. Readers also should note that Sue Rose is Lula's "oldest" but not "best" friend, since she doesn't appear to be close to anyone in her home town. Unfortunately, the repulsive success of her plan has left her alienated and bitter. And apparently trapped. We appear to be in Flannery O'Connor territory, where complacent Southerners deserve to be simultaneously disdained, pitied, and smirked at. And so the story's opening sets one mood.

## 4. Later Fiction 153

But that doesn't last long. Lula only appears to be hopelessly rooted in Abnegation, Alabama. "Abnegation," i.e., self-denial, is a word that suggests how the people around Lula have chosen to settle into dull, unthinking hopelessness. Meanwhile, countering this routine stasis, clothing in the local dry cleaner's store hangs "like the husks of the Raptured." Actually, Lula is about to leave Abnegation on a Greyhound bus because she has been having a recurring dream about a carnival set up outside the town of Festivity, Iowa. There, in a sideshow tent, she dreams that "'a man in a tuxedo tells everyone who comes in what they've got to do to find everlasting love.'" What *that* message turns out to be is essentially a paraphrase of Jesus' advice to a sincerely questioning young man: "'Sell what they have. Give to the poor. Forsake their birth place for the carnival midway.'" The first two commands repeat Jesus' words; the last is directed specifically at Lula. The tuxedoed carnie's next instructions seem even more applicable to Lula, as he advises people who want everlasting love to "'devote themselves to a lost soul who walks that midway looking not for answers or mysteries, but just for ... a true experience.'" In any event, before she leaves town Lula heeds her dream's directives as far as her limited background lets her imagine—giving her clothing to Baptist Thrift and spare cash to Talladega Mission—and sets off on a bus whose description mingles gritty and elevated moods. It moves "like a panting behemoth, its skirts tarred with road grime, its innards as mysterious behind its tinted windows as the holy of holies in a Hebrew tabernacle."

Her journey maintains the uneasy mixture of moods. Her bulk makes the trip uncomfortable, but after some initial hostility between Lula and Walter Cheatam, the skinhead who finally sits next to her, the two appear to become friendly. He admires the silver broach that she'd had made from a baby spoon after suffering a miscarriage. In Memphis, after he's carried her suitcase inside the station, Lula realizes that while he was doing her that kindness he must also have stolen the broach.

The next section of the story, after Lula arrives at Festivity and agonizingly hikes out to the Carnaval Milagosa, switches to first person to let Lula report what happens while Evelyn Stynchcomb, "Ten Performers in One," entertains a tent full of locals who've come for tacky amusement. Evelyn is described as "an immense human figure ..., a sort of Sumo wrestler in soft silver slippers, pearl-gray pantaloons, and tunic"; she is even grosser than Lula. As "Performer Number One," she displays herself as "The Strongest Woman in the World" by bending over, grabbing her feet, and lifting herself into the air. For Lula, this feat demonstrates that the impossible can be true, so "how could anyone at the Carvaval Milagrosa let the petty trials of our workaday lives oppress us?

Meanwhile, her labored breathing told us that *staying* aloft had a heavy price.... Although I ached for the pain of her energy expenditure, I felt lighter too—as if in escaping gravity like this, she had lifted a burden from my spirit." As Evelyn moves from one Performance to another, she is sometimes just freaky looking—revealing herself to be "The Bearded Lady"—sometimes marvelous—as when she burns her beard off as part of her fire-eating act, after which "her cheeks ... shone as smooth and rosy as a child's."

As Lula watches, she herself becomes the center of the action. She is especially fascinated by "The Human Chyclorama," in which she watches a host of tattoos move as Evelyn flexes her naked back. Everyone in the crowd can see something different, but Lula focuses "on a reenactment of that part of Plato's Symposium in which the god-split halves of primordial human beings seek to reunite." After that, in the next part of Evelyn's performance, her mind-reading act, she calls on Lula and announces that "'you have come a thousand miles to escape the contempt of sex-obsessed men and the cancer of your own self-hatred,'" following that accurate reading with the statement that "'your fondest wish—undiscovered until you entered this tent—is to assume my powers and trade places with me.'"

When a horrified Lula denies this reading, Evelyn turns her attention to the other people there. She says she won't reveal what really *is* Lula's very fondest wish—nor will she identify the smug audience members who "'*deserve* our scorn or punishment because they've borne false witness, committed adultery'"—in short, violated each of the Ten Commandments without being caught. The crowd reacts with defensive anger, especially one woman who accuses Evelyn of "'gluttony and immodesty,'" and encourages her neighbors to join in a chant that the whole carnival should be shut down. This rouses Evelyn's wrath, and she declares, "'*Alas for you Pharisees! You pay tributes of mint and rue and every garden herb, but still neglect justice and the love of God!*'" These are Jesus' words, from the book of Matthew, Chapter 23, verses 25–6. They prompt the following exchange, in which Evelyn quotes Jesus from Luke 11:42:

> Then the woman said, "'*The love of God*"? How can a person of your ilk, a lackey of Mammon, utter such words?
>
> "Because the love of God surrounds us too," Stynchcomb said. Then she roared, "*Alas for Pharisees! You clean the outside of cup and plate, but inside seethe with greed and wickedness, judgment and injustice!*"

Although the woman from the crowd objects that even the devil can quote scripture, Evelyn ends the argument by magically spelling everyone out of the tent and back to their homes with no memory of what they've seen at the carnival. Only Lula is left to help Evelyn off the stage, "smelling faintly of sweat and a mild eau de cologne." One part of the show is left, "The Discrete Epicene," which Evelyn defines as "a hermaphrodite ... a manwoman sex." When Lula asks what Evelyn would have shown the audience if they hadn't taken affront at her remarks, she replies, "'Only the imperfect temple of my body, which God made as it is. Would you care to see it? You, Callula, I can give a private audience.'"

Back in the third person, the story describes the two walking to Evelyn's trailer, where Lula "beheld in private what audiences of the Discreet Epicene beheld in public in groups segregated by sex and a curtain. She also ministered to Evelyn in ways that, only a few hours ago, she would not have imagined possible, much less acceptable to her as a woman of Christian upbringing. Evelyn, in turn, ministered to and accommodated her." Despite Lula's belated trepidation, the second sentence just quoted uses the obvious religious connotations of "ministered" to suggest that what Evelyn and Lula are doing is somehow holy, despite what doctrinaire churchgoers—such as the people Evelyn expelled from the carnival tent—might say.

Both of the story's moods are genuine: uneasy doubt and startling joy.

Lula wakes up alone the next morning, to find herself in possession of the carnie's trailer, "hanging file folders" and all. Evelyn has left a note explaining that she has left the carnival but that the rest of the show is already on its way to Blue Earth, Minnesota, and telling Lula, "*Continue to pay tithes of mint and rue, but do not neglect justice and the love of God. Last night, you showed me both. Thank you.*" When Lula looks outside the trailer, she sees only mundane debris: "tent stake divots, tire treads, animal dung, ticket stubs, cigarette butts, and blowing trash." The carnival's magic is gone, or at least relocated. But magic *was* present; next to Evelyn's note, Lula finds the silver broach that Cheatam stole from her back in Memphis.

Evidently, for readers who remember the partial but tantalizing results of Evelyn's mind reading, Lula has been given one of her true desires: She can take Evelyn's place if she wishes. An even deeper desire, however, appears to be that she should have a free choice. At the story's end, she isn't certain what she wants to do: "How long would it take to drive to Blue Earth, Minnesota? How long to return to Abnegation, Alabama? What other destinations might beckon if she let them?" Those questions are left open at the story's end, but the last paragraph seems to validate the wholesomeness of her new situation, especially in contrast to her earlier bus trip: "The key turned obligingly in the ignition. The engine rumbled in its mounts like a wind freshening over water."

The story never mentions Jesus by name, supposedly a precondition of salvation. However, it does show Lula reaching out to share the love of God with others; at least that's what Evelyn's note says. Instead of being trapped in Abnegation (capitalized or lower cased) like a beached whale, Lula has been set free to discover "a true experience," whatever that disturbance might lead to in her future. Jesus does say that anyone who wants to take Him seriously should appreciate and minister to the most unexpected needy in the most unlikely situations, "the least of these" (Matthew 25: 40), so perhaps a specific religious faith is something for Lula to discover later. At least, however bizarre and quirky that may look at first, it still can be *true*.

"Help Me, Rondo" (*J. K. Potter's Embrace the Mutation*, April 2002) continued Bishop's experimentation with form. Appropriately, since its subject is the memorably ugly film actor Rondo Hatton (1894–1946), the story is presented as a screen play. Most of it is a monologue in which Hatton's middle-aged widow explains Hatton's career and personality to a stranger, an 18-year-old boy who imagines that he is the man's illegitimate son. The title is a riff on "Help Me, Rhonda," The Beach Boys' 1965 hit, but that's the last lighthearted thing about the story. Hatton was afflicted with pituitary adenomas, the cause of his grotesque deformity, and this story lets Bishop consider serious questions of personal responsibility/impersonal circumstance.

The first thing readers see is "a life-sized ceramic statue of a lop-eared Alsatian puppy." Then a woman's voiceover narration explains that while people think that a puppy's oddly proportioned body is cute, a grownup human being with abnormally large head and hands would be unsettling: "we stare or look away depending on our upbringing, our allotment of gall, our degree of fascination with the grotesque. Even when we look away, we may *want* to look back, to obsess on the disfigurement that *we* have escaped (if only outwardly), and to take comfort in our own normality." Whereupon "two brutish hands" throw the puppy's statue away, and we hear it shatter. The hands are those of Rondo Hatton, a handsome and athletic young man until his appearance began changing monstrously while he was serving in the U.S. Army during World War I. His alarmingly distinctive appearance led him to small roles in films, eventually to B-movie celebrity as THE CREEPER. However, as his widow Helen, the drama's narrator, describes Rondo's decline, "the thickening of his tissues, as the acromegaly cruelly progressed, trapped his nerves, especially in his hands, rendering them weak as a baby's." So the looming on-screen menace actually was a feeble shell.

In fact, the story offers readers little certainty and less comfort. The young man hearing all this may or may not exhibit early-stage acromegaly; Helen Hatton can't tell by looking at him, though she does advise him to see a doctor for a real diagnosis. Of course, even if he does have the same disease that Rondo did, that wouldn't prove that he is Rondo's son—and even if he were, *that* wouldn't earn him a secure place in a family any more than Rondo's minor movie stardom made him real friends with the Hollywood elite. And anyway there's no cure for acromegaly.

Rondo himself, as the story's opening suggests, hated his condition. He tried to explain its cause by imagining that exposure to mustard gas in Europe might have sent something awry in his body. Or perhaps he was being punished for having too much sex as a wild youth. Or perhaps, an even more daring explanation, he was *destined* to endure exceptional physical and emotional suffering. Helen articulates Rondo's "conviction that the God of the Universe wanted him to star in penny-pinching Universal horror flicks." Furthermore, she draws the young man into Rondo's Keepsake Room to open a well-thumbed Bible to the Book of Isaiah, where she reads a message concerning a savior who was destined to come into the world but who would not be welcomed by the people he came to save: "He is despised and rejected by men: a man of sorrows and acquainted with grief." Christians read this passage as a prophecy of the painful reception of Jesus, and Isaiah continues that "He was wounded for our transgressions, he was bruised for out iniquities: the chastisement of our peace was upon him; and with his stripes we are healed."

If Rondo Hatton truly had been chosen to reenact the role of Christ, that would have given him some spiritual compensation for the pain he endured. It also would have justified the story's title. But the story itself doesn't show that. Although Helen reports that some people who have seen that room filled with family memorabilia have accused her of "turning my den into an idolatrous shrine," her purpose in enticing the young man into her web is not to proselytize him but to seduce him. Readers who remember that she originally spoke of most physically normal people being fascinated by disfigurement "that *we* have escaped (if only outwardly)" cannot be sanguine that Rondo's audience learned anything beneficial from witnessing his suffering. We are left with the memory of a scene in which Rondo's nerveless hands can't pick up a coin he's dropped on the floor, so that he goes berserk, throws bedroom furniture about, and "HOWLS" in frustrated anguish. The story's last scene, perhaps showing one of his dreams or perhaps set sometime after his soul has been freed by death, shows a naked Rondo climbing a beach on Easter Island and contemplating the sculptures of elongated, thick browed heads: "*Recognizing himself in every tall gaunt face, he offers a prayer of gratitude ... that the makers of these artifacts did not afflict them with feet or hands."* In other words, the less pain the better. By that token, if would have been better if he himself had not been born.

Unfortunately, not all suffering is redemptive.

"The Door Gunner" (*The Silver Gryphon*, May 2003) is one of Bishop's most challenging stories in both presentation and content.

Although the story's sequence of events is easier to follow than that of "Cats," the present tense keeps readers at least somewhat off balance here too. In addition, Bishop explains that fellow writer Andy Duncan reported that, after someone at a writers' workshop declared that a short story absolutely *can't* have more than one narrator, he immediately set out to write a short story with multiple narrators. Bishop also took up the challenge, to see what would happen if readers couldn't settle into one viewpoint. Thus the seven narrators of "The Door Gunner" form a chorus of observers grouped uneasily around the title character, the only important person who is *not* a narrator.

The background of "The Door Gunner" is also difficult to get into focus. The Vietnam War was a terribly divisive event in American public life, and it still ripples disturbingly through our mass consciousness. It was, for one thing, the first war that America simply lost—not just settled grudgingly for a stalemate as in Korea, but flat-out, turn-tail, abandon-your-allies *lost*. Accompanying this failure was a mind-numbing disconnect between official commentary and direct experience, between words and reality. In February of 1968, for example, one U.S. Army major defended the bombing and shelling of Viet Cong controlled civilian areas in the city of Ben Tre by declaring that "it became necessary to destroy the town to save it."

And so "The Door Gunner" presents readers with a group of people who must confront a situation that doesn't make sense but that is nonetheless unquestionably real: A dead soldier who won't just stop fighting and lie down.

Everyone in the story is uncomfortable in the presence of the undead man. Before a Viet Cong sniper shot him in the head, Joe Exley was door gunner on one of the helicopters that retrieve American soldiers from disastrous combat missions. He still does that task, and in fact since his death he seems to bring good luck for his rescue missions. However, none of the other soldiers around him wants to recognize him as a person. Everyone just refers to him as D. G., "as if saying any syllable of his name ... would hoodoo the whole company. As if reminding him of his past as a breathing, eating, eliminating, lovemaking human animal would revoke the miracle of his inhuman hanging on." His odd condition does create problems. For one thing, he is a rotting, albeit mobile, corpse; he is extremely disgusting to be around. Besides, people whose lives are organized according to neat categories have trouble fitting him in. Captain Dickman, company paymaster, complains about the paperwork he had to go through to switch D. G.'s status from KIA (Killed in Action) back to active duty. In the same finicky way, the company chaplain, Father Urbanec, objects that he "'can't give extreme unction to a dead man.... The Church reserves that sacrament for persons in imminent peril of dying.'"

Since D.G. doesn't address readers directly, we must rely on others' observations to figure out what's happening with him. Sergeant Pennington is the one who describes the way D.G. generally is shunned, and fellow Georgian Corporal Fearing makes that more immediate by saying that D. G.'s stench is so awful that it makes him "step into somebody's tent, cover my nose with a bandanna, and pray that he'll shuffle on by." When UPI correspondent Mike Lamonica interviewed Door Gunner Exley before his death, the only extraordinary thing he heard was Exley's matter-of-fact answer to the question how he could shoot women and children: "Easy—you just don't lead 'em so much" when aiming the machine gun. Lamonica used that quote in an article to sum up "the aimless barbarism of some of our operations." Now, he won't believe that D.G. really is dead until he is invited to stick his finger into the man's bullet wound; he manages to do so all the way to second knuckle before "reaching a psychic barrier that stops my probing." If this is reminiscent of Christ instructing Doubting Thomas to probe His wounds after *His* resurrection, D.G. promptly dispels the notion that he is any less callously barbaric than he was before. He has not seen the light, literally or figuratively. However, he is willing, when tentatively curious soldiers ask, to tell them who's among the living and who's not, including their comrades who officially are just missing in action—or Captain Dickman's wife back in the USA, who was just shot in the face by their little boy playing with a gun. Mainly, D.G. realizes that he doesn't fit in among the living. When he visits a Vietnamese bordello, it is only to quiz one of the prostitutes Miss Bu'o'um about a rumored island off the coast of Viet Nam where the U.S. government sends soldiers suffering from an incurable venereal disease, Black Syphilis, so that they can be disowned and vanish forever. Miss Bu'o'um insists that the island is a fantasy, a mind game that the soldiers play, but D.G. insists that he must find the place because "It sounds like a cross between Tahiti and Hell. The dead belong in hell.... I died with blasphemy on my lips and my M-60 rockin n rolllin. I *belong* in hell, hopefully one with a beach."

The climax of the story is a helicopter ride that may actually be intended to transport D.G. to the island of Black Syphilis but officially is authorized to take Captain Dickman on compassionate leave, and on which Lamonica tags along because he smells a juicy story. That trip out over the open water in the airship named *Hue Home* becomes increasingly, wonderfully and dreadfully hallucinatory. Although the reporter attempts to compose his report like an objective news story, with the heading "South China Sea, approx. 14.00 N, 110.25 E," their location becomes more and more approximate and unreal. The helicopter flies into a gigantic cave opening: "Astronauts approaching the funnel of a black hole might experience a like sense of exhilaration and terror, but who else would understand." A swarm of moths surrounds the *Hue Home*, supplanted by spectral images of self-immolating Buddhist monks that extend to infinity, then they fly over a vast lagoon where "float thousands of flat-topped vessels with the design of ancient barges but the dimensions of aircraft carriers." There, Captain Dickman closes himself inside an iron coffin containing an autopsy photo of his wife's corpse, literally sealing his fate. Shortly thereafter, Exley (as the story now uses his given name) demands that Lamonica push him out into "the deep purple maw of the Dragon." And thus the expedition ends.

The helicopter journey feels like a mixture of H.P. Lovecraft, Edgar Allan Poe, and Stanley Kubrick's *2001*. For Lovecraft, the root of "horror" was the recognition that human understanding could never stretch to grasp the play of vast, dark cosmic forces. Poe's *The Narrative of Arthur Gordon Pym* (1837) shows the title character cut from the support of social consensus and repeatedly imagining that he's figured out a situation but then being terribly surprised; Pym's story breaks off just as it apparently is on the verge of a huge revelation. And *2001* ends with a psychedelic trip through alien landscapes as the central character reaches toward an inexpressible truth. In Bishop's story, even if the helicopter's name *Hue Home* is not pronounced "Way Home," the journey appears to be simultaneously a return to the terrible, formless chaos of creation and a recognition of the endless profusion of possibilities that exist in our universe. Dangling plot threads abound. The helicopter pilot, for example, reassures Lamonica that "'I've done this before.'" He never explains how that took place, and he doesn't make it back from this trip. Essentially, the more readers are shown, the less we are able to understand. At the very end, only Lamonica returns, now confined to a psych ward and typing "addle-brained fairytales" about flying "to a secret well of hell, east of Vietnam, as if Vietnam itself doesn't qualify as a smoky annex of that everlasting rubbish heap."

The story's last speaker, however, has a somewhat more vital though definitely more challenging message to offer readers. When D.G. came to her brothel earlier in the story, Miss Bu'o'um did not reject him because he was a disgusting zombie. She tolerated his dead-man stench and tried to treat him like a human being. She is businesslike, but she also is kind. In the last scene, after her regular client Sergeant Pennington has had sex with her, he shows her an enigmatic photograph, a double exposure of a helicopter crew that shows only two recognizable faces, those of D.G. and two other men who died on patrol. When she asks him what that means, his reply is indecisive: "'I don't know.... Maybe that it's a bad idea to have your picture taken before going out on a mission.'" That lame advice is the best thing that the authorities, the people supposedly in charge of how the war is fought, can come up with. But the Vietnamese whore has an alternative answer that she heard in Catholic school: "*'Don't wait for the Last Judgment.... It takes place every day.'*" What the story shows is that humans can't predict the ultimate effects of their actions, just as Dickman couldn't imagine that the gun he gave his wife for her protection would be used to kill her. If humans thus are limited by mortality, we should consider our actions carefully and humbly. And so it becomes necessary not to destroy but to respect, even cherish, other people. Being placed in a position of natural emphasis as it is, this message counters the chaotic lack of meaning the story displays elsewhere. Exley/D. G. was too naïve/dead to discover this notion on his own, and Sergeant Pennington is mired too deep in the official mindset to listen carefully to what Miss Bu'o'um says. But readers can pay attention.

Bishop explains that "The Road Leads Back" (*After O'Connor: Stories from Contemporary Georgia*, September 2003) was intended as homage to Flannery O'Connor, but that the editors of the *Georgia Review*, where he first submitted the story, rejected it because they read it as a parody. That's an interesting mistake. It's worth noting that in the introduction to *Parodies: An Anthology from Chaucer to Beerbohm—and After* (1960), editor Dwight Macdonald opined that a good parody "usually is not achieved without sympathy, or at least empathy" with its subject. In other words, to do more than a superficial satire, a parodist should be sympathetically involved with the literary target, even though such affection may be mixed with uneasiness and exasperation. Whatever it's labeled, Bishop's story illustrates the uneasiness and exasperation with which human beings express their love for each other. The story also can be read as a study of missed connections, how grasping the truth about another person may be theoretically possible but practically unlikely. Bishop's story sometimes offers a tantalizing glimpse of what it *would* feel like to make personal contact. Unfortunately, however, humans are only mortal, not omniscient. So if we can't be sure what other people are like, what can we know about a supernatural presence—i.e., God? So perhaps the story also is about what we humans can accomplish in the frustrating condition of being alive. Perhaps in practice homage and parody can amount to the same thing.

If this sounds confusing, note how difficult it is to put a simple label on Flannery O'Connor's attitude toward her characters. They may be likeable theoretically, but their actual presence often is maddening. They can be genuinely laughable, but they more frequently elicit a painful grimace. And those conflicting emotions are provoked simultaneously.

"The Road Leads Back" manages to reproduce O'Connor's concerns and voice. The central character Flora Marie is, in fact, a stand-in for O'Connor herself. She is a talented and dedicated but as yet underappreciated Southern writer who is suffering from systemic lupus erythematosus, a crippling disease that killed her father and eventually will kill her too. As the story begins, she is about to set out on a "plaguesome" summertime visit to the Benedictine monastery in Alabama to pray for healing. Besides dreading the physical ordeal, she has mixed feelings about the several-day-long trip: (1) She hates the thought of interrupting her work, because she knows that her physical decline is likely to limit the time remaining to her for writing; (2) she needs to please Hetty Bestwick, her "unflagging encourager" from Atlanta, a cherished and intelligent fan of her writing; (3) she *wants* to spend time with Hetty, her only real friend; and (4) she hates being crippled and doomed, so that dubiously but devoutly she yearns for a miraculous cure.

Perhaps because of the tension arising from her mixed motives, Flora Marie doesn't notice connections that readers can, although the story quickly establishes her as a harsh but accurate observer of herself and her surroundings. Glumly inspecting her dowdy appearance, she admits that "she did not look like a woman to whom miracles happen." But even in these opening pages, readers note that she does not catch all the relevant details of what's happening. She can't—or won't—notice how Bestwick's greeting kiss on her forehead "tarried ... as if distilling nectar from the other woman's sweat." Thus she appears to be startled when, in their motel cabin near the monastery, Bestwick kisses her "on the mouth. Flora Marie stared at her in frank perplexity." Norbert Grimes, the woman-hating volunteer assistant of the monk who is constructing a miniature landscape at the monastery, is quicker on the uptake; after a few moments with the women, he is able to label Bestwick "'a high-horse lezbo.'"

Perhaps life simply offers too many details, flashing by too fast, for anyone to be able to connect all important details accurately or rapidly—let alone recognize what's important. During their car trip, Bestwick and Flora Marie pick up two hitchhikers, an Alabama State

Trooper and his hostile pre-teen son. The trooper explains that his car and gun were stolen by a man who was pretending to need help by the roadside; Flora Marie registers the detail that the boy is wearing "a tee shirt with a zigzag across it, like Charlie Brown's in the *Atlanta Constitution* funnies" but takes less notice of his rude comment that the hijacker "'didn't hoodwink *me*! That red-checkered rag over his face told me straight off he was a sneaky sumbitch!'" This kind of incidental detail appears unimportant until, at the monastery, Norbert Grimes "pulled a red-checkered rag from his pocket, and wiped his ferret face," though a moment later Flora Marie also notes "the hate in his eyes" and notes "his handkerchief with a tingle akin to recognition."

All this may appear incidental to the main focus of the story, Flora Marie's pilgrimage. It indicates, however, the difficulty Flora Marie and Bestwick experience in agreeing on the purpose of that journey, how they are able to conceive of this demonstration of faith. The two women, in their "avid" correspondence, have discussed "the probability of miracles in a secular age." However, Bestwick cannot imagine loving a male god "in his guise as Cosmic Bully"; "I have more faith in you than in God," she tells her friend. As Flora Marie sees it, despite Bestwick's "skeptical adult conversion to the Catholic Church, she had an ineradicable streak of guilty Calvinism in her makeup. That streak sometimes mixed with a severe blue nihilist tendency that caused her to pale about the dewlaps." Flora Marie's faith is harder to put into words. As she tells her friend, "'I ain't a good prayer …. My type of spirituality is almost completely shut-mouth.'"

At the monastery, Bestwick manages to trick their way into the grounds, by lying that Flora Marie's mother is completing a series of prayers at a specific time that day; her fib is aided by the strange coincidence that the monk guarding the gate had read and admired one of Flora Marie's stories in an obscure journal. Inside, they find that Brother Joseph Zoettl, the monk they are seeking, is hard at work building a "one-of-a-kind garden of miniature basilicas, churches and statues, 'The Scenic Shrine of the South.'" The schlocky-sounding project doesn't repel Flora Marie, although its "asymmetry, along with a childlike disregard for scale, blessed the whole garden with the waking unreality of a fever dream. Except for the sincerity, it all hinted at something akin to satire." There, under the malevolent glare of Norbert Grimes, Bestwick insists that Brother Joseph pray for Flora Marie's health; she also sternly demands that Flora Marie submit (to her and to the Virgin Mary) and accept the prayer and its accompanying miracle.

The prayer does work—but not as anyone could have expected. Flora Marie feels "a change in her blood, a fresh elasticity in her joints….

She half believed that she could walk unassisted back around the Ave Maria Grotto to the garden gate and Bestwick's car. She resolved to try." But this momentarily hopeful mood is overshadowed by a miraculous transformation of Flora Marie's aluminum crutches, which "stepped out onto the path *by themselves*. They scissors-hiked in mechanical cahoots along the route that she had just contemplated." Flora Marie collapses to the ground. She tells the distraught Bestwick not to fret: "'I'm fine—no different than before.'" But the commotion aggravates an already borderline-unhinged Grimes, who starts blasting the miniature, distorted buildings apart with the gun he'd stolen from the State Trooper. The gun misfires when he tries to kill Bestwick, so he dashes away, followed by the miraculously animated crutches.

The aftermath of this farrago shows the different ways in which humans react to a miracle. The monks are calmly concerned about Grimes' spiritual condition. They are comfortably certain that the man will come back; he keeps reaching for peace but fleeing when it gets too close, so they'll have more chances to save his soul. More focused on the immediate situation, Bestwick is disgusted by the undignified mess. She grabs Brother Joseph by his habit and rages, "'Can't you even do a simple miracle right?'" A month later, having reflected on the experience, she phones Flora Marie to tell her "that she had decided to leave the church. The events at the abbey had forced her to an irrefutable conclusion that the patriarchal God who had effected the 'miracle' of the crutches would rather play the fool than the physician." She attributes Grimes' failure to shoot her to simple "shoddy firearm manufacture." Though she and Flora Marie remain friends, Bestwick can't share Flora Marie's delight at being part of the experience, regardless of the results: "It wasn't every day you witnessed a miracle, even a splendidly bungled one." Evidently Bestwick never realizes that her mistake may have been to demand too much *in detail* from God: one specific miracle delivered exactly on schedule. Shortly after the phone call, Flora Marie sends "her apostate friend" a letter, using words from O'Connor, that opines, *"Faith is a gift but the will has a great deal to do with it.... Subtlety is the curse of man. It is not found in the deity."* And there the debate must end—except for one enigmatic image, as a cloud of red butterflies rises into the sky after Flora Marie's death years later, echoing the red rash that had appeared on her face before the pilgrimage began.

According to Bishop, "The Angst, I Kid You Not, of God" (*F&SF*, Oct/Nov, 2004) strives to deploy George Alec Effinger's lighthearted but fundamentally serious affect, as in Effinger's "The Aliens Who Knew, I Mean, Everything." In the case of "Angst," humans help the ztun, a race of interstellar do-gooder vegetables, to realize that easing God's unhappiness would hasten the end of the universe; therefore, the "best" thing mortals can do is to enjoy as much ungodly violence as possible.

Bishop makes this disquieting notion palatable in several ways. The story's first sentence, "The ztun stunned us," indicates that this will be a first person, personal narrative. Readers are informed that the self-righteous ztun have doped Earth's atmosphere to render people unconscious for a period "depending on the innate bellicosity of those incapacitated." Peaceable humans will thus be freed from domination by the violence-minded. But it is several paragraphs before readers discover that the narrator is one the most bellicose humans, one of those taken away for psychoanalysis on the ztun starship's homeward voyage. He is Myron "Pit Bull" Draper, Commander in Chief of the Global Interdiction and Liberation Force of the Half Vast Rocky Mountain Hegemon. Even if one doesn't imagine how "Half Vast" would sound aloud, this pompous self-advertisement signals that he's not to be taken seriously. Moreover, the story doesn't show Draper's direct responsibility for any atrocities—not against humans, anyway; as technical advisor to mass entertainment producers for the formerly peaceful ztun, he does proudly comment, "I had so many pods, flowers, and stems flying around the set that you would have thought we were using a Salad Shooter." He comes across as more amusingly quirky than evil.

The story also is notable for the other malefactors whom the ztun have picked up in their missionary trip. Bishop has fun creating the look and smell of *alien* aliens. Like Draper, they have earned their place among the most heinous beings in the galaxy, the ones in most need of therapy. There's the lizardy Al, "chief decapitationist of an inner planet of 61 Cygni A"; Seyj, "an energy creature from Epsilon Eridani IV," who shut off the energy fields of two million of her fellow entities; Kaa Lotcharre, a seven-armed caterpillar who "boasted of his expertise as a materials engineer and genocidal assassin"; a jellyfish named Gilneta; and a sentient granite slab named Bacmudsorak.

Somehow members of the group do bond and share their guilt and (literally) their dreams. It is Bacmudsorak who introduces the subject of its greatest fear, extinction as the universe itself eventually comes to an end. To reassure them, the ztun Counselor Ztang explains to them that their

> death fears were foolish.... Ztun science had discovered that our expanding universe was closed rather than open, and this fact meant that the universe would not diffuse into "a tenuous blanket of matter and antimatter debris," via the deterministic engine of the heat-death hypothesis, but would "cease its outward motion and contract." This action, in turn, would one day lead to a new Big Bang and the prospect of a fresh cycle of star making and civilization building.

To the reasonable objection that the universe does not contain enough matter to generate sufficient gravity, Counselor Ztang replies that ztun scientists have not only determined that God exists but that the deity's sadness creates hitherto undetected energy "that would keep the cosmos from slipping into ceaseless entropic decrepitude." He further explains that the source of God's angst is the "unrelieved, inventive brutality of intelligent creatures against their own kind," the very thing the ztun have been trying to eradicate. Evidently, however, the ztuns' moral elevation has kept them from following this train of thought to its conclusion: By easing God's angst, they are hastening the death of the cosmos. When Bacmudsorak points this out, the ztun change their goals. As the story ends, General Draper has been returned to Earth, where he has been appointed to direct the Western Hemisphere's Self-Defense Legions. He is happy that "tomorrow an all-out war will likely begin. Still, but for the unfortunate angst of God, I would aver, 'Life is good, my compatriots.'" He is talking to *us*, the readers. *We* are his compatriots, contentedly waiting for the atrocities of all-out war to begin. If we have been lulled by Draper's confident persona, smiling at the story's wry inventiveness, perhaps we should think again. And perhaps that was Bishop's intent.

"Bears Discover Smut" (*Sci Fiction*, October 26, 2005) was inspired by Terry Bisson's classic story "Bears Discover Fire," which begins with the narrator's noticing how it is helpful bears with torches who are providing the light by which he's been changing a flat tire at night. In Bishop's story, the narrator's perusal of pornographic magazines is interrupted by "one of the gene-tweaked black bears that our Bureau of Wildlife Labor Management had franchised to do menial jobs after our last sweeping deportation of illegal immigrants." That contrast in content and attitude continues through the stories, as Bishop gloomily considers our personal and social relationships.

The narrator of Bisson's story somewhat bemusedly accepts this new development as part of a natural process: It certainly is *unusual* that bears are now using fire, but it's not necessarily alarming. He's willing to fit this unexpected fact into his laid-back routine. Bishop's narrator is a pastor in the small town First Full-Gospel Testifying Church, married, with small children. He also is a pornography addict, who sneaks off into porn shops and strip clubs in Atlanta while telling his wife Sandi that he's doing marriage counseling in the big city. This is typical of his behavior. When Sandi discovered his stash of porn, he loudly apologized to her and repented—and moved the stuff to a storage locker she doesn't know about. He feels uneasy around bears, but while cruising the city streets at night he is attracted to a hooker who is "an especially tall woman in bearskin boots." And so it goes. In short, the narrator's hypocrisy, which he readily admits to the reader, is so outrageous that it becomes almost laughable—as long as readers can ignore the plight of his wife and children. Less amusing, however, is the story's social context. As the sentence quoted just above indicates, the government has gotten rid of sometimes restive foreign workers and replaced them with more submissive gene-altered bears. The narrator supplies more information about American society, explaining that "black bears got special treatment under the Disunioning Act owing to a clause championed by President Shallowford," who recently won a third term in office and shortly afterwards had his opponent exiled "to the barrens of the Arctic National Petroleum Dig." Evidently an even more outrageously hypocritical America is following the narrator's pattern of behavior: deny, conceal, and exploit.

Bishop's story's conclusion certainly doesn't give the narrator a happy ending, when his double life is exposed by his angry wife so that he is thrown out of his church and reduced to living in half of a doublewide trailer, sharing space with the bear/PI who was doing surveillance on him at the story's opening. He also is forced to share his half of the trailer with his soon-to-be-ex-wife's brother Angus, "a vet who'd lost an arm in our ongoing foreign war." This arrangement displays one further difference between what Bisson and Bishop do with the idea of people living together with perhaps-almost-human bears. In "Bears Discover Fire," the narrator's nephew has an adolescent whim to go out and shoot at the bears gathered around a fire in the highway median, but the older man explains to him why this would be immoral, impractical, and illegal:

> "I explained why that would be wrong. 'Besides,' I said, 'a twenty-two wouldn't do much more to a bear than make it mad.'
> "'Besides,' I added, 'it's illegal to hunt in the medians.'"

In "Bears Discover Smut," on the other hand, Angus bitterly resents the bear that took his job and also the bear that ended his sister's marriage. The narrator himself is rather puzzled by why *he* is not the main focus of the man's anger rather than the bears who essentially are innocent bystanders. In any event, though, Angus is practicing shooting with a 30.06 rifle: "Hunting season's coming up again, he notes, and licenses are readily available from the Bureau of Wildlife Labor Management." The narrator drops the subject immediately, leaving the implication that If Angus pays the government for a license, he'll be able to express his resentment with hot lead. It appears that Americans have gotten themselves so deep in a confused mess that the only solution they can imagine is more concealment and violence.

"Miriam" was first published under the pen name of Noni Tyent. Bishop wrote the story to fill a hole in an anthology he was editing, *A Cross of Centuries: Twenty-Five Imaginative Tales about the Christ* (Thunder's Mouth Press, April 2007), using a pen name because he already had selected another of his own stories, "Sequel on Skorpios" (*Interzone*, August 1988). That story, although provocative in being narrated by a disciple who has faithfully looked after a fugitive Jesus since his faked death and resurrection, ends with a genuine Resurrection that validates the essence of His ministry. "Miriam" is shorter but much more subversive. Bishop is assuming that, whatever their religious faith or lack of faith, readers know the outline of Jesus' career and that they can recognize "Miriam" as an alternate version of "Mary," Mother of our Savior. So here is the story's first paragraph:

> On the night of the blessed infant's coming, things got complicated. Miriam felt her fetus lodged athwart her birth canal: prelude to a disaster of which the archangel had given no warning. *Don't be afraid*, he had told her, *for you've found favor with God*. She had no certainty of that favor now.

Here is its last:

> But One was resurrected; and Dorcas, in lifelong atonement for her betrayal, traveled and preached and healed and wrote, so that, several generations on, Miriamism overcame the entire world, and much in the world that was stupid, arbitrary, and cruel inevitably, albeit gradually, lost its foothold.

In the few pages connecting these visions of catastrophe and triumph, Bishop offers an alternate story of a Savior's life and death.

As the story begins, Miriam's forebodings prove accurate. First, the divine child is stillborn. Then her husband dies of a heart attack. After all this, when the angel Gabriel returns to tell her that she should rejoice because she is "'*among women ... most favored and blessed*,'" Miriam angrily denies God's right to put her through another useless pregnancy. Then she is told that there is a different plan now.... Much of the story is a summary of Miriam's career as weaver and messiah, showing her at a distance and leaving it uncertain whether she simply *obeys* God (as if she had a choice) or whether she *submits* to Him. That is one of the story's many unresolved issues. Readers recognize that much of the action parallels the Gospels' account of Jesus' life, and Miriam also has "a suspicion that she was not only shadowing her stillborn Son but also extending His lost ministry." As part of this extension, she calls both male and female disciples. She has as little patience with demons and human failings as Jesus did, but her overall approach may be milder. Rather than the dramatic act of turning water into wine, for example, she makes "bad wine sweet," while "the arrogant, avaricious, and cruel she rebuked with authority but also with tenderness." Despite using an apparently gentler tone than Jesus, Miriam still frightens and angers the people she tries to correct. Like Jesus, her calls for repentance and justice are too disturbing to be endured. Like Jesus, she is condemned, crucified, and discarded. The story never has shown her receiving an official endorsement from God, along the lines of "This is my beloved daughter, in whom I am well pleased," and her last words on the cross are "'Father-Mother,' rasped Miriam lowly, 'why have You forsaken us?'" She never moderates that despair by finally exclaiming "Father, into your hands I commend my spirit." Apparently, then, all Miriam's efforts have been futile.

The story's last paragraph, quoted earlier, reverses this impression. Rather than evading responsibility for her betrayal (as Judas did by committing suicide), Miriam's traitorous disciple Dorcas uses her guilt as motivation. She takes on the role of Paul in the New Testament, spreading Miriam's message throughout the world. The statement "One was resurrected" is never developed. It is Miriam's message, rather than the promise of exemption from death or protection from terrifying end times, that draws believers, so that "much in the world that was stupid, arbitrary, and cruel inevitably ... lost its foothold." The fact that "much" rather than *all* the negative aspects of humanity faded suggests that some remained; on the other hand, the fact that they had only a "foothold" in the world suggests that they were invaders rather than native traits. And the fact that this happened "inevitably" suggests that it was what God had intended all along. So, remembering Miriam's final moments, readers still may wonder: Why couldn't this result have been achieved more simply, with less pain?

Perhaps the most basic question about "Miriam" is *how* the story's world winds up so much better than the one that readers inhabit, where so much remains "stupid, arbitrary, and cruel." How is Miriam's suffering so much more effective than ours?

On April 16, 2007, Michael and Jeri Bishop's son Jamie was among the people murdered at Virginia Tech by a deranged student. Jamie was a German teacher who also was a gifted artist and an aspiring writer; he left notes on his computer for future stories, and to honor his memory Bishop wrote several of those stories. One of them is "The Pile" (*Subterranean Online*, Winter 2008), which won the 2008 Shirley Jackson Award for best short story.

At first glance, "The Pile" looks simply like an updated version of W.W. Jacobs' 1902 classic story "The Monkey's Paw," in which a happy, close-knit family is ruined by the disastrous consequences of three requests that the mother and father make of the titular magic-saturated object. The point seems to be that we should be careful what we wish for—or perhaps shouldn't even wish for things beyond normal human reach.

But "The Pile" extends this idea, laying blame for most catastrophes on normal human impulses. Most allusions to supernatural forces are verbal and irrelevant. A neighbor of Roger Maharis, the main viewpoint character, considers a beat-up coffee table to be "as haunted as a cumquat"; when a salvaged steam iron seems to leap off a shelf and he jokes that it is "'Haunted,'" she retorts that it's simply "'Defective.'" There's little spookiness in the action either. Rather than a remote house on a dark and stormy night, "The Pile" is set in Fidelity Plaza, a shabby townhouse development populated by members of the underemployed quasi-lumpenproletariat: "retirees on Social Security, language tutors, rookie cops, or administrative assistants with live-ins who tended bar, stocked shelves, or schlepped out to the corner every morning to wait with the Hispanics, druggies, and dropouts for pickup day jobs." Roger Maharis lives there with his sister Renata; she is finishing her Ph.D. in marsh ecology, while he just "worked part-time at the college in IT." And the people in "Bishop's story don't encounter the repulsive shriveled paw of a dead monkey, just a stupid-looking 20-inch gorilla doll that can dance jerkily to its own recording of 'The Macarena.'" Roger finds the thing on The Pile, an ever-changing conglomeration of not-quite discards at the outskirts of Fidelity Plaza: "stuff too good to feed to the Dumpsters' maws, jettisoned junk with potential adaptability to other people' uses."

It's not magic that brings the dancing gorilla, which Renata names Q.T., to life, just Roger's tinkering. "The Pile provided the ever-coming-and-going folks of Fidelity Plaza with a *resource*—Roger's apt term—for losing what they no longer wanted or needed, and for acquiring what they hoped they could put to life-brightening use"; in other words, the mishmash of Stuff reveals the discarded interests or intermittent enthusiasms of transient people, and it can spark interest and enthusiasm in similar folks. Roger himself is dissatisfied with his routine, dead-end job and so begins haunting The Pile to discover "not only items with which to furnish or decorate their place, but also a source of stuff that he could repair, remake, or put to good aesthetic use in imaginative artifacts of his own creation." In his desire to brighten his life and show off his own creativity, Roger evidently is not unique among the residents of Fidelity Plaza, where something as inherently worthless as Q.T. can become an object of desire that eventually leads to a murderous brawl.

Three things in the story may suggest that supernatural forces are at work. First of all, once Roger has fixed Q.T. by inserting fresh batteries, he and Renata joke about the ugly thing, but Roger can't stop imitating its routine. She objects that he's gone bazooka—"a silly Maharis family term for berserk"—but he is truly unable to leave Q.T. switched off. His compulsion goes from irritating to thoroughly maddening. The second thing that stretches readers' assumption that "natural" causation controls everything that happens is that, when Renata and Roger try to return Q.T. to Mrs. Hartsock, the neighbor who put it in on The Pile in the first place, they learn that the doll was a hate-gift from the woman's ex, "as a gag, if not a torment." Mrs. Hartsock's 14-year-old son Brad, meanwhile, looks like 40 because progeria is aging his body toward a premature death. The Hartsocks have such a load of personal troubles that they refuse to take Q.T. back. So it is returned to The Pile, passing from resident to resident of Fidelity Plaza despite, in the story's own words, "the punishments, deliberate or accidental, that possessing the thing often inflicted." And thirdly, there's the shockingly insensitive way Roger reacts to Brad Hartsock's deteriorating physical condition. Before the disease's name is announced, Roger notices that the boy looks older than his years, and "An evil imp made Roger say, 'You seem a tad mature to be toting around an ape doll'"; readers must decide how literally or figuratively "evil imp" should be read. But finally, after one Q.T.-obsessed man has drowned another in the Fidelity Plaza pool, when Roger catches sight of shrunken, used-up Brad in a wheel chair, he reacts with unprovoked, outrageous cruelty: "Despite Brad's screaming fit earlier in the week, he felt that he should give it [Q.T.] to the kid as a pool-party favor charm against early oblivion." Brad stops breathing the instant Q.T. is dropped on his lap.

But the "spooky bullshit" isn't over. Sometime later, after Mrs. Hartsock has moved away, Plaza residents gather around The Pile to gaze at the latest offering: Brad's La-Z-Boy, containing a stylishly dressed mannequin resembling Brad and holding Q.T. It is wearing a sign that reads "TAKE ME HOME" and "CHAIR AND ITS OCCUPANTS NOT TO BE SEPARATED." Most of the onlookers are simply stunned, but after Roger contemplates the scene for a while he tells his sister that he "'could make something with this Laz-E-Boy and this creepy Brad-thing.... a sort of found-art installation, maybe.'" The story adds, "No moon shone. The pool lights cut off. A wind rose. Roger could feel the night, the month, and the year all going dreadfully *bazooka*."

Unlike "The Monkey's Paw," Roger never verbalizes a "wish." He doesn't simply want more Stuff. He just wants to have the satisfaction of being a special, unique individual, and all he's doing is expressing himself aesthetically, innocently unconcerned with the consequences. He's simply being human. He can't help it. Readers might be more comfortable if they could blame what happens on a good, old-fashioned intrusion of supernatural malevolence, but that's not clearly present here. Somehow, the situation has just gone bazooka. Something is terribly wrong, and it is beyond human power—or desire—to fix.

Actually, although "The Pile" was published earlier, the surrealistic "Vinegar Peace; Or the Wrong-Way, Used-Adult Orphanage" was actually the first story Bishop wrote after his son's murder. "Vinegar" was published in *Asimov's* (July 2008) and was short-listed for the Nebula Award as a novelette.

"Vinegar" is extremely, deliberately painful to read. It confronts readers with accepting something that should be unacceptable, unthinkable. The story is a wail of grief by a parent whose child has died violently and pointlessly; it also is a howl of rage at a culture that endorses violence as a solution to human problems.

Told in the present tense, second person, the story begins as "you," Mrs. K_____ (names of the living usually are redacted), are unwillingly transported to "a used-adult orphanage," which turns out to be a government-sponsored warehouse/therapy center for elderly people who have no family to look after them. The rationale for this remains unclear. When you beg one of the attendants to tell you why you are here, "she stops, stares you in the eye, and says: Oldsters who've lost children in the war often make trouble. Hush. It isn't personal. We're sheltering all orphaned adults in places like this, for everyone's benefit." As you reflect later in the story about what is being done to you, "none of these rules makes much sense, but little about Vinegar Peace ever does, even if it sometimes seems to have a coherent underlying principle of organization that you can't fathom owing to an innate personal failing." Portions of the institution appear to be designed with individual compassion, to help people come to terms with the death of their loved ones; however, everyone is herded together into a noisy, stinking dormitory to sleep. There's no objective standard by which to measure or judge what goes on here, and there's no escape. You certainly don't want to be considered an "oldster" troublemaker. The safest thing is simply to accept what happens, to admit that you can't act on your own and need to be "sheltered," to blame your lack of understanding on you own "personal failing."

What you eventually do realize is that you are responsible—to blame—for your daughter Elise joining the military. She did it to bond with you. After her brother Brice was killed in action, Elise realized that you had felt closer to *him*. Consequently, as her last letter tells you, she felt that she "*had to change myself into the one you claimed.*" Now she's dead too, another casualty in "the interminable War on Worldwide

Wickedness." You think about her in the crematorium at Vinegar Peace, where a chorus of soldiers sings updated lyrics to an old hymn: "*Out for patriot glory,/ Brave maid and gallant stud,/ We all revere Bold Gory—/ Its **Red**, its **Wine**, its **Blood**!*" In Bold Glory, this new version of Old Glory, the "stars and stripes are mutedly visible as different shades of red." When one of the soldiers tries to drape a flag over you as a gift from the dead, you politely refuse: "No, I can't. I'm partial to the old version, even at its foulest."

That's about as far as you can express your discontent. Instead, at the story's end, you confide to another resident that you're hoping for "adoption," to be taken out of Vinegar Peace by a war veteran, whom you picture as "a compassionate Brice or Elise, a soldier who has survived six tours, [and] wants nothing more than to rescue a poor wrong-way orphan from terminal warehousing." When your friend scoffs at this notion as "a fat load of bunkum," you don't contradict her; still

> that night, huddled on your cot amid the hubbub in the Sleep Bay, you envision a woman very like Elise perched with you on a porch in late autumn or early winter. You sit shivering under scarlet lap robes, while this person spins a soothing tale and tirelessly rubs your age-freckled hands.

And so, finally, you choose to be soothed, to accept that you're helpless and that all you're fit for is sheltered impotence, passively draped in the red banner. You tell yourself that this is the most you could hope for, that fading away like this would be a satisfying happy ending.

Readers who are appalled by what they see in Vinegar Peace—the story and the place—will disagree.

The last story in *The Door Gunner* is "The City Quiet as Death" (*Tor.com*, July 9, 2009), based on a fragmentary opening and a sketchy conclusion that were supplied by fellow writer Steven Utley. In an author's note, Bishop indicates that the story was influenced by Poe's "The Fall of the House of Usher" and by the work of South American magical realist writer Gabriel Garcia Marquez, and the story itself refers to "Lovecraftian horror." Other literary comparisons could be made to Mathew Arnold's "Dover Beach," with its description of being stranded between two world views, or to W.B. Yeats' "The Second Coming," with its hint of something dreadful looming at the threshold of perception. In any event, this is perhaps Bishop's grimmest short story.

The story's protagonist believes that there are no worthwhile possibilities open to him in this life, and he proves to be correct. Elderly Don Horacio Gorrion is the last of his family, confined by agoraphobia to the first floor of his mansion on a Caribbean island. All his experience, in particular his immersion in literature, has convinced him that life is futile. He debates killing himself with a shotgun (too messy), or persuading his housemaid Adelaida to poison him (forbidden by her religious scruples), but eventually runs down to the dock and throws himself into the sea. In the meantime, he is oppressed by constant echoes of the Big Bang and "the unbearable nightly clamor of the stars."

His misery is interrupted by two visitors whom the fearful Adelaida summons to persuade her master to go on living: his doctor and his priest. Readers may assume that what Don Horacio hears next represents the most encouraging prospects that this world can offer. His doctor reassures Don Horacio that he is healthy enough to live many more years, extremely uncomforting news, and mentions a pair of proposals for investments: One is immediately practical, exploration for oil under the ocean; the other is more theoretical, support for a researcher who aims "'to create baby universes. These will inflate as ours once did, but then cut their ties to ours via the closing of microscopic black holes and then float away on other-dimensional tangents. Then we will lack any vantage from which to see or understand how these baby universes grow.'" Don Horacio finds the first idea meaningless but the latter even more unappealing. Even if he could play God by creating a universe in which "'the laws … could be different from those governing ours,'" Don Horacio would be unable to enter and enjoy that universe in his role as a god. When he confers with his priest, on the other hand, the only religious consolation he receives is that perhaps God is not omnipotent but instead is a struggling artist who sometimes, "'briefly loses his focus, with forces so grand that even the slightest misstep leads to catastrophe for the creation that he brought into being with painstaking love.'" This image of a well-meaning but maladroit God may be very slightly more comforting than the image of a God who can't interact with His creation at all, but Don Horacio can't really focus on either notion. The stars are too loud.

As he rushes toward his death in the sea, uppermost on his mind is the thought of returning to the water the locket that Adelaida gave to him as a focus for hope. She insisted that the little container held a giant squid; he suddenly, somehow believes that "the largest known invertebrate on the planet, with eyes the size of basketballs—wanted out. It would boil in the sea water in its diminutive amniotic sac, that is, *the locket*, until it burst from its prison." He may be correct. At the end of his run, "patience itself, the sea waited to accept the cargo-laden locket and the hollow Horacio Gorrion." This concluding sentence could be written from Don Horacio's point of view, indicating that the locket really is "laden" with something amazing because Don Horacio was living in a universe with different physical laws. Or perhaps not. In any event, there is no livable, quiet place for him in this universe.

## 4. Later Fiction    175

To conclude this discussion of Michael Bishop's shorter fiction, we'll briefly consider three longer stories that have appeared/been revised since the publication of *The Door Gunner*. *The Sacerdotal Owl* contains two revised stories, "To the Land of Snow" (*Going Interstellar*, ed. Les Johnson and Jack McDevitt, June 2012) and "The Gospel According to Gamaliel Crucis; or The Astrogator's Testimony" (*Asimov's*, November 1983); "Of Rattlesnakes and Men" first appeared in *Asimov's*, February 2015, and was included in the collection *Other Arms Reach Out to Me: Georgia Stories* (2017).

To consider the most recent story first, "Rattlesnakes" offers a savage indictment of America's self-destructive fascination with firearms, when the narrator and her family move to the hamlet of Wriggly, Georgia, and are greeted with the news that they need to keep a rattlesnake in their home. The locals blandly insist that all inhabitants conform; they insist it's for everyone's protection. There are hints, later in the story, that the snake dispensers are profiting by promoting ownership of multiple snakes, but the risky custom appears to be based primarily on the snake owners' fear, on a craving for safety that's gone berserk. Consider, for example, this parody of a favorite NRA slogan: "'The best defense against a crook with a carry-snake ... is a household with a certified and imprinted TBQC rattler.'" Bishop develops this outrageous situation strikingly but stops short of suggesting how it could be corrected. After escaping to Tennessee, the narrator reflects that "one day we would return to Nokuse County ... to atone for our failures there—not with its BioQuirked rattlers, but with the men whom those snakes had so easily and thoroughly beguiled." But there the story stops. Perhaps the only effective way to stop what ought to be obviously dangerous behavior is for people to come to their senses, and perhaps "Rattlesnakes" can help show readers that they have been tolerating sheer lunacy. As part of a story, though, this conclusion is vaguely disappointing.

The magazine publication of "Gospel" provoked so much controversy that Isaac Asimov was impelled to write an editorial in the magazine that bears his name (June 1984), later used as the foreword to Bishop's collection *Close Encounters with the Deity* (1986) under the title "Religion and Science Fiction." To one magazine reader's angry reaction that the story was "'a burlesque of the scriptures,'" Asimov argued that, whether one held one particular faith or not, religion was a legitimate subject for speculative fiction. Bishop's story doesn't so much speculate about the truth of Christianity as test the ability of faithful Christians to open their minds to new possibilities. He wants people to think, not just believe. First of all, "Gospel" mimics the Bible's form by being divided into numbered chapters and verses form and (usually) written in a somewhat archaic, elevated prose style. Readers whose perceptions are constrained by to the worldly limits of the familiar Bible, however, will be shocked by the story's content, for *this* is the gospel, "good news," shared by a crewman on one of the exploring starships sent out from a desperate, ruined Earth, which has returned with an alien Savior. She looks like a giant, inevitably threatening praying mantis, "a female mantid of untoward delicacy and strength, easily as large as the largest Russian wolfhound, in hue a lovely avocado, in movement a clockwork ballerina, gracefully strange, strangely graceful, and ever glittering at the eye"—who proclaims herself to be the local representative of The One, which makes her literally our Savior. That is the crux of Bishop's story: How can human beings stretch their imagination to accept Salvation from a non-human source? And what does "salvation" mean anyway?

Careful readers will notice how thoroughly humans need to be saved from what they have done and are preparing to do. As Mantikhoras, the mantid Savior, flies over the American continent (in an episode corresponding to Christ's 40-day sojourn in the wilderness, just as many parts of Bishop's story are skewed echoes of the New Testament), she "registered radioactive hot spots, and always was struck by the numbers of malformed people and animals dwelling in the blasted continent." One nuclear war evidently has been fought, and the survivors do not seem to have learned how to avoid preparing to fight the next/final one. Perhaps, then, "salvation" might be based on respect for the unique significance, the potential holiness, of any living creature. By her example of reaching out to dolphins and apes—and, of course, simply by being who she insists she is—the mantid Savior challenges bystanders to accept kinship with all the precious forms of life around them, rather than competing with and preparing to destroy them. After Mantikhoras is physically obliterated by a Bible-quoting war lord, her disciples wait uncertainly and vainly for her resurrection. They should have learned to expect the unexpected: At the story's end, another of the last-gasp starships returns with a hitchhiker, an "energy being, a plasmoidal intelligence scooped from the skin of a gas giant in the Alphard solar system ... [that] was insistently proclaiming itself a visible fragment of the 'soul' of The One." At this heartening display of how much effort The One is willing to expend in broadening the community of worshipers, the mantid's disciples shout "Hallelujah," apes dance in the jungles, and orcas and porpoises leap in the water. Fundamentalist, intolerant readers probably have stopped reading in horror by now, but Bishop hopes to leave more tolerant people somewhat unsettled but more productively thoughtful about who we really are and what we really need.

Like "Cri De Coeur" (*Asimov's*, September 1994), "To the Land of Snow" is set on a huge sub-light-speed, interstellar ark carrying emigrants from Earth to a fresh start on a new planet. SF readers are used to seeing the failure of such a voyage, either on the way as in Robert A. Heinlein's *Orphans of the Sky* (1963, fixup of the 1941 novellas "Universe" and "Common Sense") or after the landing as in Roger Zelazny's *Lord of Light* (1967); the whole grandiose enterprise seems a perfect opportunity to display the hubris of crew and passengers. Bishop's stories, on the other hand, stress how decent humans can be to each other.

The more recent story, "Snow," begins with the seven-year-old narrator being awakened from the dormant state in which, like most of the other people on board the UNS *Kalachakra*, she endures long stretches of the voyage, with the news that she has been identified as the new Dalai Lama. The rest of the story consists of selected computer logs that show Gretta Bryn's maturing into that role until, at age 31, she is ready to lead the shipload of Tibetan refugees down to their new home on a free but marginally habitable world. Along the way, Bishop dodges many tempting opportunities for melodrama. The rumor that someone killed the previous Dalai Lama, for example, appears to set up a locked-starship murder mystery, and Gretta plays amateur sleuth for some time before learning that the old man willingly stopped living when he realized how tired he was and saw that her youth and fresh energy would make her the better guide his followers needed. This revelation does not make him less worthy of veneration. In the same way, although the starship's captain overlooks an almost-catastrophic error in mid-flight, he still is honored for his years of wearisome concern, self-destructive though that turned out to be. Though major problems do arise aboard the *Kalachakra*, Gretta and the crew deal with them calmly. This is not to say that the story is about a shipful of serene, simpering little Tibetan Buddhists, but Bishop insists on seeing humanity's potential for healthy decision making. The prevailing mood is not suspicious dread but empathetic curiosity.

During his vacation from writing longer pieces of fantastic fiction, Bishop collaborated with Paul Di Filippo, under the joint pen name "Philip Lawson," on two mystery novels. The first, *Would It Kill You to Smile?*, was published by Longstreet Press of Marietta GA in 1998. It is an amiable enough yarn of a young man's efforts to come to terms with the memory of his father—a familiar Bishop theme, except that in this case the father turns out to be more malevolent than his son supposed. Details from the protagonist's job as an empathetic elementary-school guidance counselor probably are drawn from the experience of Bishop's wife Jeri. Otherwise, it's a competent but unmemorable book. A sequel, *Muskrat Courage*, was published in 2000.

Much more impressive is a mainstream novel that has yet to find a publisher. In his *Locus* interview, while the manuscript of "An Owl at the Crucifixion" was on the market, Bishop describes it as "wholly mainstream, about a young man in a small town who discovers that his Sunday school teacher (who is also his drama teacher in high school) is gay." Beyond that core of events, the story is about the difficulty of settling into a role—on or off stage. It's a distinctly odd novel, sometimes lurching into polemic, sometimes painfully sympathetic in depicting family tensions, but it's always vividly alive. It deserves to be published.

After a long wait since *Brittle Innings*, the first new novel to appear under Michael Bishop's name appeared in 2016, *Joel-Brock the Brave and the Valorous Smalls*, intended as "A Novel for Young People, Whatever Their Age." The story centers on the quest by little Joel-Brock Lollis to rescue his sister and parents, who've been kidnapped by the fungoid minions of Pither M. Borsmutch, evil genius behind the chain of Big Box Bonanza stores that are smothering local mom and pop commerce. Actually, although J-B's mother in particular has taken part in protest demonstrations outside the local BBB, her family sometimes shops there—hey, those prices are *super-low*; nevertheless, Borsmutch has decided that the whole family should be brought to his underground lair in Sporangium and brainwashed. But the inept not-quite-human kidnappers arrive at the Lollis house while J-B is away at a Little League Baseball game. The almost-ten-years-old boy is left to fend for himself. Eventually, hungry and dirty, he's forced to trek over to the BBB to ask his favorite clerk for shelter. While helping her around the store, he and another employee watch snatches of TV broadcasts from an alternate reality, in which a grownup J-B is a star for the Atlanta Braves. And then, accompanied by diminutive store detective Vaughnathan Valona and by slightly-older-but-still-short Alelaide-Bridget Coe, J-B sets off to save his parents. It's an odd odyssey, though the caverns where mushroom people are trained to work as uncomplaining drudges for BBB. When the Valorous Smalls reach the subterranean command center, Condor's Cote, J-B saves Borsmutch's life by administering CPR, leaving the old miscreant weakened and vulnerable to justice. Eventually, a young-adult J-B receives a cellphone call from his older self, who reports that his own story didn't work out as happily as the novel's protagonist; since he couldn't bring himself to save old Borsmutch, he never was reunited with his family. Now, though, he's out of professional baseball but content to be a master cabinet maker. At the very end, J-B himself is content to be a Little League coach where he can nurture smaller players. He has been a Valorous Small himself, and he wants to help young people appreciate how literally wonderful their world can be regardless of their physical size:

> And at every practice.... I break from teaching baseball fundamentals and get my team to go out and roll in the unwired world. I show them rocks, sand grains, mouse skins, garden slugs. I urge them to sniff—on the wind I mean—rain, chicken trucks, cow manure, auto exhausts, hickory smoke, their own skinned knees, potting soil, pine cones, dog poop, deer hair, dandelion puffs, human sweat, and lightning strikes. Nothing is too big or too small for us to delve into, and although I am not sure where the ghostly J.-B. Lollis has gone, I have an idea, and I am content—at least for the time being, that time being now.

Eloquent as it is, this conclusion isn't supported very well by *Joel-Brock*, which is more of a laidback, episodic tall tale than a novel. Lacking a picture of how rewarding J-B's family was like before the action starts—or what fate the evil Borsmutch is planning for them now, readers don't have much sense of urgency as they watch one interesting event follow another in the narrative. J-B has his goal, true, but events tumble along without a lot of emotional weight. Perhaps this is due to the book having been written for two "big-hearted Smalls who inspired and helped with it," Annabel English Loftin and Joel Bridges Loftin; it was the latter, for example, who wanted the cast of characters "to feature a shelf stocker, a private eye, and a baseball player." A writer who feels this close to characters—who is, in fact composing a tale to entertain the real-life originals of those characters—is unlikely to let the action get uncomfortably intense or menacing.

The novel has, nevertheless, some features of continuing interest. For one, the mushroom people turn out to be potentially human. One of them, Father Meece, not only protects the Valorous Smalls from a mob of fungoids but reveals that while working aboveground at a BBB he loved and married a woman, with whom he had a child: He is Addi's father! *Joel-Brock*'s end leaves open the possibility of integrating BBB slaves and surface-dwelling humans. And J-B's conclusion does perhaps make sense of one of the book's more annoying aspects, the way characters simply shrug blankly at each new development: "Beats me," "I can't say for sure," "I don't know," "Who knew?," "I have no idea," etc. In fact, these people frequently *don't* have any idea of what's going on. Not really. Time and again, they just have to adapt to strange events without fully understanding the overall situation. That's what the Valorous Smalls must do as they trek through Sporangium, what J-B must do as he contemplates the almost-dead Borsmutch, and what the young-adult

J-B must do at the very end: He's not become what he hoped for himself in the novel's first sentence, "Home Run Hitter of the Future," but he has become someone who can help little kids grow up healthily. So perhaps the novel is insisting that people do have meaningful choices to make, even in vague and confusing situations. And with that, like J-B, readers should learn to be content.

# Other Works

Michael Bishop is responsible for several anthologies.

In 1983, Bishop co-edited the Ace paperback (*Stories of Metamorphosis: An Anthology of Speculative Fiction About Startling Metamorphoses, Both Psychological and Physical*), a combination of reprinted and original stories. The introduction is by co-editor Ian Watson.

In 1989, he published *Nebula Awards 23* and continued annually through number 25. These represented the Science Fiction Writers of America's choices for each year's outstanding fiction; each volume contained the winning novella, novelette, and short story, along with Bishop's selection of stories from the finalists in each category. Although he could choose from the list of nominees, the choices were limited; each volume is subtitled "SFWA's Choices for the Best Science Fiction and Fantasy" of that year. The books are products of a public duty, honorably performed.

Much more interesting are four anthologies Bishop produced using more of his own taste.

Bishop's first solo anthology was the trade paperback *Light Years and Dark: Science Fiction and Fantasy of and for Our Time* (Berkley, 1984), contains 44 stories and poems from "a 'generation' of writers who came of literary age after the inauguration of John F. Kennedy." Rather than the term "science fiction," Bishop still prefers to consider that these people were writing "speculative fiction" that is "thoughtfully realistic, a function of our inevitable recognition that military might, popular democracy, advanced technology, and space travel do not—in and of themselves—provide long-term solutions to every human conflict and need." The book's mood is not uniformly downbeat, but contributors are aware that we need to ponder carefully the choices we make for humanity's future. It is a strong, thoughtful assembly, and it won a Locus Award.

Even stronger is *A Cross of Centuries: Twenty-five Imaginative Tales About the Christ* (Thunder's Mouth Press, 2007). The writers range from

Fyodor Dostoyevsky to Ray Bradbury, from Karen Joy Fowler to Barry Malzberg, and they show a stunning variety of attitudes toward the person and role of the person responsible for so much of the worship and turmoil in our world; Bishop intended to show "the documentable impact on our species of the figure of Jesus Christ." The book's own impact seldom is meekly comforting, with stories running "from belief to doubt, from dismissal to slapstick and folk humor, from philosophical inquiry to piquant nostalgia, from existential absurdity to the use of Jesus as a template for christs of the authors' own devising."

Bishop and Steven Utley produced the anthology *Passing for Human* in 2009, which focuses on what stories about aliens in disguise can show about the disguises humans wear.

Bishop is also a notable poet. His first collection of poetry was *Windows and Mirrors* (1977). His most recent is *Timepieces* (Edgewood, 1998), especially interesting for several autobiographical pieces and for the long "In the Lilliputian Asylum: A Story in Eight Poems and an Interrogation," a spinoff from Swift's *Gulliver's Travels*. The poem's narrator is a Lilliputian reduced in size twice over—by being Lilliputian and *also* being a dwarf—who is confined to a lunatic asylum because he can't deny that his country was visited by the Man-Mountain Gulliver; everyone else has decided that in order to avoid recognizing how small they are they must forget they were ever in the presence of a giant.

Finally, a selection of Bishop's thoughtful non-fiction writings was collected by Michael H. Hutchins in *A Reverie for Mister Ray : Reflections on Life, Death, and Speculative Fiction* (PS Publishing, 2005). The title honors Ray Bradbury, one of Bishop's original influences, and the seventy some odd pieces include book reviews, autobiographical fragments, and critical essays written throughout his career. Of special interest is "Light Years and Dark," a 1983 speech in which Bishop prepares the way for the discussion of contemporary sf writers that fills the introduction to his 1984 anthology of the same title. Essentially, Bishop chooses Damon Knight and James Blish as models of clear-headed, active writers who cared deeply about sf and hoped to encourage others to do better by paying close attention to their writing.

# A Final Q & A

Without commenting on the validity of the opinions in these analyses, Michael Bishop has been a supportive reader of the manuscript as it has accumulated. Here, to conclude this book, is a final Q&A from October 3, 2019.

*1. How did your rootless childhood prepare you for writing?*

My childhood wasn't so much rootless as peripatetic. Once my parents divorced, in about my fifth year, I lived with my mother but visited my dad, wherever he happened to be stationed, either abroad (Japan, Spain) or in the States (Cheyenne, Wyoming; East St. Louis, Missouri; Memphis, Tennessee; Denver, Colorado; Lincoln, Nebraska), for at least three months every summer. These places exposed me to different surrounds, terrains, weathers, and mindsets, and gave me material as well as lessons to write about.

*2. And how have those building blocks been remade/rearranged by your long residence in Pine Mountain?*

We still travel, or did until my two separate bouts with cancer exempted us from that option for about three years, 2015–2018, and resumed on a modest basis just this past year (summer of 2019). But my long residence in Pine Mountain, from fall of 1974 to the present, steeped me in Georgia history, politics, and culture, and turned me into a bona fide Southern writer as well as a committed science-fiction and fantasy writer.

*3. Do you think your career would have been different if you'd lived in one of the media centers, such as NYC or LA?*

Yes, of course, but I don't regret living here in the least and feel privileged to have resided so long, relatively comfortably, in Pine Mountain, here in Middle West Georgia, not really all that far from Atlanta and Columbus (both thriving cultural centers) or from Montgomery, Alabama, where we frequently drive (or drove) to take in plays at the Alabama Shakespeare Festival complex on the east side of that city.

Further, Emory Healthcare facilities in Atlanta proved crucial in helping me overcome both the rectal cancer and the malignant sarcoma in my right thigh in the three or four years prior to this one.

*4. Looking back over your career, are there any stories you'd like not only to leave unrevised but forget about?*

A couple of abortive novels, one for adults and one for children, that you've reminded me I should yank from the filing cabinet in my upstairs office and burn. Most of my stories have eventually wound up in collections. Those that haven't are, for the most part, ones that I'm not particularly proud of or attached to. Some are unpublished and probably deserve the fate of the unfinished novels I've just mentioned.

*5. How do you choose which piece of your writing to revise, and what kind of revising do you find yourself doing?*

If I value a published novel or story and still think relatively highly of it, I will revise it for a fresh appearance of that particular piece, as I am doing with all my published novels right now for Patrick Swenson's Fairwood Press and my own imprint there, Kudzu Planet Productions. To date, we've done almost all my novels but *Unicorn Mountain*, which I'm revising now, an early novel called *Stolen Faces*, and my Nebula Award winner from the early 1980s, *No Enemy but Time*, which I plan to revisit after finishing work on the new edition of *Unicorn Mountain*. While revising, I try to smooth out infelicities of both style and substance with a specific concentration on wasted words.

*6. What's next?*

I've long hoped and now plan to write a World War II era novel set in the South Pacific with an unusual fantasy element. The research for this project has occupied me far too long, I'll admit, but there's so much to encompass that I'm sometimes overwhelmed by it. However, I remember that I treated this same period in *Brittle Innings* with some success and would like to think I can bring the same energy and insight to a novel centered on the war. To that end, I keep waiting for the final volume of Ian Toll's Pacific War trilogy (of which I've read and taken notes on the first two titles) to come out, and Toll keeps delaying. So I, too, delay. Which is really a shameful way to drop the blame for my procrastination onto Toll and cravenly sidestep my own culpability. Nor am I getting any younger.

*7. Finally [a question you politely ducked some time ago], what responsibilities does a writer of faith have, to the faith and to the writing?*

The major responsibility is to tell the truth and not to make up untruths to support any specific agenda, political, religious, or cultural. I am a Christian, although not necessarily a totally orthodox one, but I do regard the Old and New Testaments' unequivocal elevation of love over loathing, of hospitality over hostility, and of fortitude over fear as sacrosanct and thus worthy of truthful dramatization, even if that dramatization sometimes requires fictional lies that subvert false piety, blind partisanship, and unhealthy institutionalized evils. And I believe humor, radical as well as gentle, a God-given human attribute for helping us all—not just fiction writers—discern and tell the truth.

# Works Cited

Bishop, Michael. *Ancient of Days*. (1985) Rev. ed. Bonney Lake, WA: Fairwood, 2013.

_____. *And Strange at Ecbatan the Trees*. New York: Harper & Row, 1976.

_____. *Apartheid, Superstrings, and Mordecai Thubana*. Eugene, OR: Axolotl, 1989.

_____. *At the City Limits of Fate*. Cambridge, MA: Edgewood, 1996.

_____. "The Blessing and the Curse" [interview]. *Locus*, November 2004.

_____. *Blooded on Arachne*. Sauk Center, WI: Arkham, 1982.

_____. *Blue Kansas Sky: Four Short Novels of Memory, Magic, Surmise & Estrangement*. Urbana, IL: Golden Gryphon, 2000.

_____. *Brighten to Incandescence*. Urbana, IL: Golden Gryphon, 2003.

_____. *Brittle Innings*. (1994) Rev. ed. Bonney Lake, WA: Fairwood, 2012.

_____. *Catacomb Years*. New York: Berkley Putnam, 1979.

_____. *The City and the Cygnets: An Alternative History of the Atlanta Urban Nucleus in the 21st Century*. Bonny Lake, WA: Kudzu Planet, 2018.

_____. *Close Encounters with the Deity*. Atlanta: Peachtree, 1986.

_____. *Count Geiger's Blues*. (1992) Rev. ed. Bonney Lake, WA: Kudzdu Planet, 2015.

_____. *The Door Gunner and Other Perilous Flights of Fancy: A Michael Bishop Retrospective*. Ed. Michael H. Hutchins. Burton, MI: Subterranean, 2011.

_____. *Emphatically Not SF, Almost*. Eugene, OR: Author's Choice Monthly [Author's Choice monthly Issue 15], 1990.

_____. *Eyes of Fire* [thorough revision of *A Funeral for the Eyes of Fire*]. New York: Pocket Books, 1980.

_____. *A Funeral for the Eyes of Fire*. New York: Ballantine, 1975.

_____. *A Funeral for the Eyes of Fire*. Rev. ed. of *Eyes of Fire*. Bonney Lake, WA: Kudzu Planet, 2015.

_____. *Joel-Brock the Brave and the Valorous Smalls*. Bonney Lake, WA: Kudzu, 2016.

_____. *A Little Knowledge*. New York: Berkley Putnam, 1977.

_____. *No Enemy but Time*. New York: Simon & Schuster, 1982.

_____. Note to author. December 28, 1998.

_____. *One Winter in Eden*. Sauk Center, WI: Arkham, 1984.

_____. *Other Arms Reach Out to Me: Georgia Stories*. Bonney Lake, WA: Kudzu, 2017.

_____. *Philip K. Dick Is Dead, Alas*. (1987) Rev. ed. Bonney Lake, WA: Kudzu Planet, 2015.

_____. Phone conversation. November 21, 1995.

_____. Phone conversation. August 13, 1998.

_____. *A Reverie for Mister Ray: Reflections on Life, Death, and Speculative Fiction*. Ed Michael H. Hutchins. Hornsea, UK: PS, 2005.

_____. *The Sacerdotal Owl and Three Other Long Tales*. Bonny Lake, WA: Kudzu Planet, 2018.

_____. *Stolen Faces*. New York: Harper & Row, 1977.

_____. *Time Pieces* [poems]. Cambridge, MA: Edgewood, 1998.

_____. *Transfigurations*. (1979) Rev. ed. Bonney Lake, WA: Fairwood, 2017.

# Works Cited

_____. *Unicorn Mountain.* New York: Arbor, 1988. Rev. ed., subtitled *A Novel of an Alternative 1985 in the History of the United States.* Bonny Lake, WA: Kudzu Planet, 2020.

_____. *Who Made Stevie Crye?* (1984) Rev. ed. Bonney Lake, WA: Kudzu Planet, 2014.

_____, and Ian Watson. *Under Heaven's Bridge.* New York: Ace, 1981.

_____, ed. *A Cross of Centuries: Twenty-Five Imaginative Tales about the Christ.* New York: Thunder's Mouth, 2007.

_____, ed. *Light Years and Dark: Science Fiction and Fantasy Of and For Our Time.* New York: Berkley, 1984.

_____, ed. *Nebula Awards 23: SFWA's Choices for the Best Science Fiction and Fantasy 1987.* New York: Harcourt Brace Jovanovich, 1989.

_____, ed. *Nebula Awards 24: SFWA's Choices for the Best Science Fiction and Fantasy 1988.* New York: Harcourt Brace Jovanovich, 1990.

_____, ed. *Nebula Awards 25: SFWA's Choices for the Best Science Fiction and Fantasy 1989.* New York: Harcourt Brace Jovanovich 1991.

_____, and Ian Watson, eds. *Changes: Stories of Metamorphosis: An Anthology of Speculative Fiction about Startling Metamorphoses, Both Psychological and Physical.* New York: Ace, 1983.

_____, and Paul Di Filippo [as Philip Lawson]. *Would It Kill You to Smile?* Atlanta, GA: Longstreet, 1998.

_____, and _____. *Muskrat Courage.* Atlanta, GA: Longstreet, 2000.

_____, and Steven Utley, eds. *Passing for Human.* 2009.

Bisson, Terry. "Bears Discover Fire." In *Bears Discover Fire.* New York: Orb, 1983.

Blake, William. "The Lamb" and "The Tiger." www.famousliteraryworks.com/blake.

Borges, Jorge Louis. "The Library of Babel," in *Labyrinths: Selected Stories & Other Writings.* New York: New Directions, 1964. 51–8.

Burgess, Anthony. *A Clockwork Orange.* London: Heineman, 1962.

Calder, Robert Lorin. *W. Somerset Maugham & the Quest for Freedom.* Garden City, NY: Doubleday, 1973.

Campbell. Joseph. *The Hero with a Thousand Faces.* New York: Bollingen, 1949.

Clute, John. "Michael Bishop." *The Encyclopedia of Science Fiction.* Ed. John Clute and Peter Nicholls. New York: St Martin's, 1993. 126–127.

_____. Review of *The Bloody Chamber and other Stories* (Angela Carter) and *Transfigurations* (Bishop). *Foundation* 19 (June 1980): 70–73.

Conrad, Joseph. *Heart of Darkness.* www.gutenberg.org/cache/epub/526/pg526-images.html.

Dick, Philip K. *UBIK.* Garden City, NY: Doubleday, 1969.

Frazier, Sir James George. *The Golden Bough: A Study in Magic and Religion.* New York: Macmillan. 1958.

Gilbert, W.S., and Sir Arthur Sullivan. *Patience* in *Martyn Green's Treasury of Gilbert & Sullivan.* Ed. Martyn Green. New York: Simon & Schuster, 1961. 217–73.

Golding, William. *Pincher Martin.* New York: Harcourt Brace, 1956.

Heinlein, Robert A. *Farnham's Freehold.* New York: G. P. Putnam's Sons, 1964.

_____. *Have Space Suit—Will Travel.* New York: Ballantine, 1977.

_____. *Orphans of the Sky.* New York: Putnam, 1963.

Hemingway, Earnest. "Big, Two-Hearted River." https://samkoenen.com/wp-content/uploads/2013/09/big_twoheart.pdf.

Jacobs, W. W. "The Monkey's Paw." https://americanliterature.com/w-w-jacobs/short-story/the/monkeys/paw.

Kelly, George. "Michael Bishop." *St. James Guide to Science Fiction Writers.* Ed. Jay P. Pederson. Detroit: St. James Press, 1966. 73–75.

Kessel, John. "Michael Bishop's Blues: An Introduction to *Count Geiger's Blues.*" In *Count Geiger's Blues*, 11–13.

Kubrick, Stanley. *2001: A Space Odyssey* [film]. MGM. 1968.

Lansdale, Joe R. "The Night they Missed the Horror Show." in *The Best of Joe R. Lansdale.* San Francisco: Tachyon, 2010. 355–69.

Le Guin, Ursula K. *The Left Hand of Darkness.* New York: Ace, 1969.

_____. "Is Gender Necessary? Redux." In *Dancing at the Edge of the World:*

*Thoughts on Words, Women, Places.* New York: Harper & Row, 1989.

Levy, Michael M., and Brian Stableford. "The New Wave, Cyberpunk, and Beyond: 1963–1994." Anatomy of Wonder. Ed. Neil Barron. 4th edition. New Providence, NJ: Bowker, 1995. 222–377.

Lovecraft, H. P. *Supernatural Horror in Literature*. New York: Ben Abramson, 1945.

Macdonald, Dwight. "Preface" to *Parodies: An Anthology from Chaucer to Beerbohm—and After*. London: Faber and Faber, 1960. Xi–xvi.

Maugham, W. Somerset. *Of Human Bondage*. New York: Penguin, 1963.

Michael Bishop (author). Wikipedia. https://en.wikipedia.org/wiki/Michael_Bishop_(author)

"Michael Bishop: The Blessing and the Curse" [interview]. *Locus* 526 (November 2004): 9, 76–78.

Miller, Faren. "Locus Looks at Books." *Locus*, April 1992: 17.

O'Connor, Flannery. "Good Country People." In *O'Connor: Collected Works*. New York: The Library of America, 1988. 263–84.

———. "A Good Man Is Hard to Find." In *O'Connor: Collected Works*. New York: The Library of America, 1988. 137–53.

———. *The Habit of Being: Letters Edited and with an Introduction by Sally Fitzgerald*. New York: Farrar, Straus, Giroux, 1979.

Poe, Edgar Allan. "The Fall of the House of Usher," in *The Short Fiction of Edgar Allan Poe*, ed. Stuart and Susan Levine. Indianapolis: Bobbs-Merrill, 1976. 88–98.

———. *The Narrative of Arthur Gordon Pym of Nantucket*. www.pinkmonkey.com/dl/library1/pym.pdf.

Pringle, David. "Michael Bishop: No Enemy but Time." In *Science Fiction: The 100 Best Novels*. New York: Carroll and Graf, 1985. 215–216.

———. *Modern Fantasy: The Hundred Best Novels: An English Language Selection, 1946-1987*. London: Grafton, 1988.

Senior, W. A. "Silence and Disaster in the Novels of Michael Bishop." *The New York Review of Science Fiction* 96 (August 1996): 12–15.

Shaw, George Bernard. *Arms and the Man*. Ed. Louis Crompton. Indianapolis: Bobbs-Merrill, 1969.

———. *Back to Methuselah: A Metabiological Pentateuch*. London: Constable, 1949.

———. *Major Barbara*. Ed. Elizabeth T. Forter. New York: Appleton-Century Crofts, 1971.

Shiner, Lewis. "What Has Gone Before" [Introduction]. *Apartheid, Superstrings, and Mordecai Thumbana* by Michael Bishop. Eugene, OR: Axolotol Press, 1989. N.p.

Silverberg, Robert. *The World Inside*. New York: Orb, 2010.

Sophocles. *Oedipus the King*. Johnstoniatexts.x10host.com/sophocles/oedipustheking.html.

Stableford, Brian. "The Modern Period: 1964–1968." *Anatomy of Wonder: A Critical Guide to Science Fiction*. Third Edition. Ed. Neil Barron. New York: R. R. Bowker, 1987.

Strugatsky, Arkady and Boris. *Roadside Picnic*. Trans. Oleana Bormaskenko. Chicago: Chicago Review, 2012.

Watson, Ian. "A Rhetoric of Recognition: The Science Fiction of Michael Bishop." *Foundation* 19 (June 1990): 5–14.

Weinbaum, Stanley G. "A Martian Odyssey." In *The Science Fiction Hall of Fame*. Ed. Robert Silverberg. New York: Avon, 1970. 13–39.

Wynne Jones, Diana. *The Tough Guide to Fantasyland*. London: Vista, 1996.

Yeats, William Butler. "The Second Coming" in *Selected Poems and Two Plays by William Butler Yeats*, ed. M. L. Rosenthal. New York: Macmillan, 1962.

Yolen, Jane. "Oh God, Here Come the Elves!" *State of the Fantastic: Studies in the Theory and Practice of Fantastic Literature and Film* [Selected essays from the Eleventh International Conference on the Fantastic in the Arts, 1990.] Ed. Nicholas Ruddick. Westport, CT: Greenwood Press, 1992. 3–11.

Zelazny, Roger. *Lord of Light*. Garden City, NY: Doubleday, 1967.

# Index

Alexander the Great  19
*Alfred Hitchcock's Mystery Magazine*  151
"Allegiances" [Bishop]  62, 65
"Alien Graffiti (A Personal History of Vagrant Intrusions)" [Bishop]  79–81
"The Aliens Who Knew, I Mean, Everything" [Effinger]  164
*Anatomy of Wonder*  87, 108
*Ancient of Days* [Bishop]  108–15, 117
*And Strange at Ecbatan the Trees* [Bishop]  6, 46–50, 55
"Andrea del Sarto" [Browning]  137
"The Angst, I Kid You Not, of God" [Bishop]  164–6
anthropology [including Anthropological, etc.]  9, 55–62, 7
"Apartheid, Superstrings, and Mordecai Thubana" [Bishop]  81–4
Argentina  116–7
Arkham House  103
*Arms and the Man* [Shaw]  132–3
Arnold, Matthew  173
Asimov, Isaac  175
"At the Dixie-Apple with the Shoofly-Pie Kid" [Bishop]  62
*Atlanta Constitution*  33, 163

*Back to Methuselah* [Shaw]  77
Ballantine, Betty  34
Ballantine Books  34
Ballard, J.G.  80
The Beach Boys  156
"Bears Discover Fire" [Bisson]  166–7
"Bears Discover Smut" [Bishop]  166–7
*Beauty and the Beast* [film]  107
*The Best American Short Stories 1985*  15
Bible  110, 157
Biblical books/authors  110, 113, 117, 154, 156, 169
*The Big Book of Science Fiction*  25
"Big Two-Hearted River" [Hemingway]  47
Bishop, Jamie  2, 169, 172
Bishop, Jeri  2, 169, 178
Bishop, Michael  1
Bishop, Stephanie  2

Bisson, Terry  166–7
Blake, William  69, 105
Bleiler, Richard  3
Blish, James  182
*Blooded on Arachne* [Bishop]  6
"Blooded on Arachne" [Bishop]  17–20, 50
*Blue Kansas Sky* [Bishop]  6, 151
Bogart, Humphrey  29
Borges, Jorge Louis  79
Bradbury, Ray  11, 182
*Brittle Innings* [Bishop]  2, 3, 128, 138–149, 151, 178, 184
Brown, Charlie  163
Browning, Robert  137
Bulwer-Lytton, Sir Edward  111
Byronic  132

Campbell, John W.  4
Campbell, Joseph  4, 87–9, 93–6
Campbell Award  138
Carr, Terry  72
*Catacomb Years* [Bishop]  5, 9
"Cathadonian Odyssey" [Bishop]  12–5, 20, 55
*Changes: Stories of Metamorphosis* [ed. Bishop & Watson]  181
*Childe Harold* [Byron]  132
Christ  7, 65, 98, 114, 117, 130, 182
Christian [including Christianity, etc.]  7, 69, 152, 155, 157, 175–6
*The City and the Cygnets* [Bishop]  3, 6, 68
"The City Quiet as Death" [Bishop]  173
Clareson, Thomas D.  5
*A Clockwork Orange* [Burgess]  59, 86
*Close Encounters with the Deity* [Bishop]  175
Clute, John  87, 103
Cold War  75
comedy  123, 131, 137
Compton, Louis  132–3
Conrad, Joseph  56
Cooper, Gary  30
*Count Geiger's Blues* [Bishop]  131–8
Crane, Stephen  16
"Cri De Coeur" [Bishop]  177
*A Cross of Centuries* [ed. Bishop]  168, 182

# 192  Index

D'Ammassa, Don 1
Daredevil 119
"Death and Designation among the Asadi" [Bishop] 56, 57
"The Death of Ivan Illych" [Tolstoy] 7
"Death Rehearsals" [Bishop] 62, 66
Deep South Con 77
De Mille, Cecil B. 29
de Tarde, Gabriel 63
Dick, Philip K. 105, 120, 124
Di Filippo, Paul 1–4, 179
Disney, Walt 107
"Dogs' Lives" [Bishop] 5, 15–7, 85
"The Door Gunner" [Bishop] 158–161
*The Door Gunner and Other Perilous Flights of Fancy* [Bishop] 5, 6, 28, 173, 175
Dostoyevsky, Fyodor 182
"Dover Beach" [Arnold] 173
Dylan, Bob 116

*Eden in My Dreams* 98
Effinger, George Alec 164
El Greco 149
Ellison, Harlan 5, 15
*Emphatically Not SF, Almost* [Bishop] 77, 151
*Encyclopedia of Science Fiction* 87, 108
*Eyes of Fire* [Bishop] 6, 9, 34–46

*F&SF* [The Magazine of Fantasy and Science Fiction] 1
Fairwood Press 184
"The Fall of the House of Usher" [Poe] 173
*Farnham's Freehold* [Heinlein] 75
Fonda, Jane 116
Forster, E.M. 63
Fosdick, Harry Emerson 144
Fowler, Karen Joy 182
*Frankenstein* [Shelley] 144, 147
Frazier, Sir James 102
*A Funeral for the Eyes of Fire* [Bishop] 6, 9, 34–46, 55

Galaxy 1, 11
Gaughan, Jack 1
*Georgia Review* 161
"A Gift from the Graylanders" [Bishop] 75–7
Gilbert, W.S. 31
Glaktik Komm 18–20, 50–5, 56–61
God 161, 163, 164–6, 174
Golding, William 30
"Good Country People" [O'Connor] 28
"The Gospel According to Gamaliel Crucis; or The Astrogator's Testimony" [Bishop] 175–7
*The Grasshopper Lies Heavy* 105
*Gulliver's Travels* [Swift] 5, 182

Haggard, H. Rider 111
*Hamlet* 36

Hartwell, David 7, 56
Hatton, Rondo 156
"Heart of Darkness" [Conrad] 56
*Hee Haw* [tv] 30
Heinlein, Robert A. 5, 75, 109, 177
"Help Me, Rhonda" [song] 15
"Help Me, Rondo" [Bishop] 156
Hemingway, Ernest 47
Henley, William Ernest 29
"Her Habiline Husband" [Bishop] 115
*The Heritage of Heinlein* [Clareson & Sanders] 5
*The Hero with a Thousand Faces* [Joseph Campbell] 87, 89, 93, 102
*High Noon* [film] 30
*Hiroshima mon amour* [film] 29
"The House of Compassionate Sharers" [Bishop] 21–5, 55
Hugo Award 56, 138
Hutchins, Michael H. 5, 182

"If a Flower Could Eclipse" [Bishop] 62
"In the Lilliputian Asylum: A Story in Eight Poems and an Interrogation" [Bishop] 182
incest 105–6
International Conference for the Fantastic in the Arts 7
"Invictus" [Henley] 29

Jacobs, W.W. 169
Jakobsson, Ejler 11
James, M.R. 3
Jameson, J. Jonah 133
Jesus 129, 153, 156, 157
*Joel-Brock the Brave and the Valorous Smalls* [Bishop] 178–80
Jones, Gwyneth 122
Jones, Indiana 60

Keats, Will 2
Kelly, George 122
Kessel, John 131, 137
King, Stephen 3, 103
Kipling, Rudyard 111
Knight, Damon 182
Kubrick, Stanley 86, 160
Kudzu Planet Productions 184

"The Lamb" [Blake] 105
Lansdale, Joe R. 28
"The Last Dangerous Visions" 5, 15
"Lawson, Philip" 177
*The Left Hand of Darkness* [Le Guin] 42
Le Guin, Ursula K. 42
"The Library of Babel" {Borges} 79
"Life Regarded as a Jigsaw Puzzle of Highly Lustrous Cats" [Bishop] 84–6
*Light Years and Dark* [ed. Bishop]
*A Little Knowledge* [Bishop] 5, 55, 62
Locus 137, 151, 178

# Index 193

Locus Award 138
*Lord of Light* [Zelazny] 177
*Love of Life* [TV] 30
Lovecraft, H.P. 26, 160, 173
Lowell, James Russell 131–2

Macdonald, Dwight 161
"The Machine Stops" [Forster] 63
*Major Barbara* [Shaw] 28
*The Making of a Counter Culture* [Roszak] 35
Malzberg, Barry 182
*The Man in the High Castle* [Dick] 105
Maroney, Kevin 7
Marquez, Gabriel Garcia 173
"A Martian Odyssey" [Weinbaum] 12–4
Marx, Chico 104
Marx Brothers 104
*The Masks of God* [Joseph Campbell] 87
Maugham, W. Somerset 3, 139–41, 144, 146, 149
Merton, Thomas 117
"Military Brat: A Memoir" [Bishop] 89
Miller, Faren 137
"Miriam" [Bishop] 7, 168–9
Mishima, Yukio 31, 32
*Modern Fantasy: The Hundred Best Novels, an English Language Selection, 1947–1987* 103
"The Monkey's Bride" 107
"The Monkey's Paw" [Jacobs] 169, 171
*Mythologies* [fanzine] 1

*The Narrative of Arthur Gordon Pym* [Poe] 160
Nebula Award 56, 87, 108
Nebula Award anthologies [ed. Bishop] 181
*Nebula Award Stories 20* 15
*New York Review of Science Fiction* 7
*New York Times* 138
Nietzsche, Frederik 132, 136
"The Night They Missed the Horror Show" [Lansdale] 28
Nixon, Richard 116–9
*No Enemy but Time* [Bishop] 71, 87–103, 108, 151

O'Connor, Flannery 28, 152, 161–2
*Oedipus Rex* [Sophocles] 53
*Of Human Bondage* [Maugham] 3, 139–41, 143, 146
"Of Rattlesnakes and Men" [Bishop] 175
"Old Folks at Home" [Bishop] 62, 64
Olsen, Jimmy 133
*On Becoming a Real Person* [Foskick] 144
*Orphans of the Sky* [Heinlein] 177
*Other Arms Reach Out to Me* [Bishop] 6
"An Owl at the Crucifixion" [Bishop] 178

Page, Gerald W. 25
*Parodies: An Anthology from Chaucer to Beerbohm—and After* 161

*Passing for Human* [ed. Bishop & Utley] 182
*Patience* [Gilbert & Sullivan] 31
*Philip K. Dick Is Dead, Alas* [Bishop] 115
"The Pile" [Bishop] 169–72
*Pincher Martin* [Golding] 30
Pine Mountain GA 2, 116, 183
"Pinon Fall" {Bishop] 11–2
*Playboy* 151
*Plays Pleasant* [Shaw] 132
Poe, Edgar Allan 160, 173
Pound, Ezra 17
Pringle, David 87, 93, 103
Proust, Marcel 31
Pulphouse Publishing 81

"The Quickening" [Bishop] 72

Readercon 2, 3–4
Reader's Digest Condensed Books 31
*The Return of Dr. X* [film] 29
*A Reverie for Mister Ray: Reflections on Life, Death and Speculative Fiction* [Bishop] 182
"The Road Leads Back" [Bishop] 161–4
*Roadside Picnic* [Strugatsky] 80
Rockwell, Norman 20, 21
Roszak, Theodore 35

*The Sacerdotal Owl* [Bishop] 6, 175
Saha, Arthur 72
The Samurai and the Willows" [Bishop] 20–1, 33, 62, 64
Sanders, Joe 1, 3–4
Sanders, Mary 8
*The Science Fiction Hall of Fame* 12
*Science Fiction: The 100 Best Novels* 87
Science Fiction Writers of America 12, 181
"The Second Coming" [Yeats] 173
Senior, W.A. 128
*Seppuku* 20, 32, 33
"Sequel on Skorpios" [Bishop] 168
Shakespeare, William 36
Shaw, George Bernard 28, 77, 132–3
Shelley, Mary 144
Shiner, Lewis 6, 81, 121, 122, 123
Shirley Jackson Award 169
*Shrek* [film] 107
"Silence and Disaster in the Novels of Michael Bishop" [Senior] 128
Silverberg, Robert 63, 75
"A Small Brown Dog" [Crane] 16
*Stolen Faces* [Bishop] 50–5, 109
"Storming the Bijou, Mon Amour" [Bishop] 28–30
Strugatsky, Arkady 80
Strugatsky, Boris 80
Sullivan, Sir Arthur 31
*Supernatural Fiction Writers* 3
*Supernatural Horror in Literature* [Lovecraft] 26
Swenson, Patrick 184
Swift, Jonathan 5, 15, 182

"Taccati's Tomorrow" [Bishop] 77–9, 151
"The Tiger" [Blake] 105
*Timepieces* [Bishop] 182
"Tithes of Mint and Rue" [Bishop] 152
"To the Land of Snow" [Bishop] 175, 177
Toll, Ian 184
Tolstoy, Leo 7
tragedy 50, 123, 137
*Transfigurations* [Bishop] 55–62, 71, 103
*Twilight Zone* [tv] 124
*2001* [film] 160

*UBIK* [Dick] 119
*Under Heaven's Bridge* [Bishop & Watson] 9, 68–70
*Underground Man* [de Tarde] 63
*Unicorn Mountain* [Bishop] 6, 120–31
United States Air Force Academy Preparatory School 11
UrNU [Urban Nucleus] 9, 44, 62–8
Utley, Steven 173, 182

Vandermeer, Ann 25
Vandermeer, Jeff 25
Van Gelder, Gordon 7
Vietnam War 54, 116, 158
"Vinegar Peace; Or the Wrong-Way, Used-Adult Orphanage" [Bishop] 172–3

Watson, Ian 9, 34, 68, 111, 181
Weinbaum, Stanley G. 12–14
Wells, H.G. 11, 63, 92
"The White Otters of Childhood" [Bishop] 49, 109
*Who Made Stevie Crye?* [Bishop] 103
Wikipedia 9
Wilde, Oscar 131
*Windows and Mirrors* [Bishop] 182
"The Windows in Dante's Hell" [Bishop] 62, 64
"Within the Walls of Tyre" [Bishop] 25–8, 72
World Fantasy Award 138
*The World Inside* [Silverberg] 63
World War II 25, 138, 142, 184
*Would It Kill You to Smile?* [Bishop and Di Filippo] 177
Wynne Jones, Diana 121

*The Year's Best Fantasy Stories* 72
*The Year's Best Horror Stories* 25
Yeats, W.B. 173
Yollen, Jane 121
"The Yukio Mishima Cultural Association of Kudzu Valley, Georgia" [Bishop] 30–3

Zalazny, Roger 177
Ziesing, Mark 2